THE ROAD TO MARTYRS' SQUARE

THE **ROAD** TO
MARTYRS' SQUARE

A JOURNEY INTO THE WORLD
OF THE SUICIDE BOMBER

■

ANNE MARIE OLIVER AND
PAUL F. STEINBERG

OXFORD
UNIVERSITY PRESS

2005

OXFORD

UNIVERSITY PRESS

Oxford   New York
Auckland   Bangkok   Buenos Aires   Cape Town
Chennai   Dar es Salaam   Delhi   Hong Kong   Istanbul   Karachi
Kolkata   Kuala Lumpur   Madrid   Melbourne   Mexico City   Mumbai   Nairobi
São Paulo   Shanghai   Taipei   Tokyo   Toronto

Copyright © 2005 by Anne Marie Oliver and Paul F. Steinberg

Published by Oxford University Press, Inc.
198 Madison Avenue, New York, New York 10016
www.oup.com

Oxford is a registered trademark of Oxford University Press

Library of Congress Cataloging-in-Publication Data
Oliver, Anne Marie
The road to martyrs' square : a journey into the world of the
suicide bomber / Anne Marie Oliver and Paul F. Steinberg.
p. cm.   Includes bibliographical references and index.
ISBN-10:   0-19-511600-3
ISBN-13: 978-0-19-511600-7
1. Suicide bombers—Gaza Strip.
2. Suicide bombers—West Bank.
3. Terrorism—Gaza Strip.
4. Terrorism—West Bank.
5. Harakat al-muqawama al-Islamiya.
I. Steinberg, Paul F.
II. Title.
HV6433.G39O55 2004
956.9405'4—dc22
2004008861

Illustrations are drawn from the authors' collection of
political ephemera and underground media of the intifada.

1 3 5 7 9 8 6 4 2
Printed in the United States of America
on acid-free paper

Contents

■

Acknowledgments

This book has long been something of a collaborative enterprise, and we are disappointed that at this time many people who helped us along the way must remain disguised or unnamed. We owe a special debt to "'Ali," friend and teacher, who helped us with transcriptions and translations and taught us a great deal about Palestinian political culture. We thank him and his entire extended family. We owe an equal debt to "Yusuf," who taught us about Arabic music and poetry and all kinds of things. He and his family have our profound gratitude. Ruth Debel, the late Etienne Debel, and Yoni Debel made their home our home and gave us countless balmy nights watching the lights come on in the village of 'Ein Kerem. Many others kept us out of harm's way, spurring us on with Arabic and Hebrew lessons, political debate, and culinary temptations.

Yaron Ezrahi, Sidra deKoven Ezrahi, Roberta Apfel, and Bennett Simon guided us, particularly in the early years. Hannah Amit-Kochavi, Louis Dupré, Geoffrey Hartman, Peter Hawkins, Mark Juergensmeyer, Herb and Rose Kelman, Dori Laub, Kanan Makiya, Tony Martin, Stephen O'Leary, Martin Peretz, Benjamin Pogrund, Eyad as-Sarraj, Anne Sassoon, Sherman Teichman, and Peter Waldman helped us at critical points. Karen Colvard at the H. F. Guggenheim Foundation showed faith in the project from the beginning, and it was through her help and goodwill that we first attained the resources necessary to engage in the fieldwork that eventually led to this book. We thank her and the Guggenheim Foundation. Cynthia Read of Oxford University Press was a probing editor and continually pressed us onward as did Theo Calderara, Helen Mules, Barbara Fillon, and Sara Leopold. Bob and Holly Doyle gave us welcome access to their august institute in Cambridge. At the Truman Research Institute of the Hebrew University of Jerusalem, we thank especially Edy Kaufman, Dan Biton, Naomi Chazan, and Dalia Shemer. The Center for Middle Eastern Studies at Harvard provided us with a home during some of the many years it took to write this book. We thank Susan Miller, Bill Graham, and Tom Mullins as well as Lenore Martin and Sara Roy.

Institutions that gave us a venue for our work, early and late, include the University of Chicago, Yale University, Princeton University, the Carter Center, the Hebrew University of Jerusalem, the Center for Policy Analysis on Palestine, Columbia University, Emory University, Harvard University, the Middle East Institute, the Palestinian Academic Association for the Study of International Affairs, the San Francisco Psychoanalytic Institute, Stanford University, Tufts University, UCLA, the University of Pennsylvania, the University of Southern California, and the University of Washington.

Part of chapter 21 of the book is based on an essay we wrote for *The Garland Encyclopedia of World Music* (Garland Publishing, Inc., 2001), vol. 6: The Middle East, edited by Virginia Danielson, Scott Marcus, and Dwight Reynolds. Some of the introduction is based on a talk given at the CMES workshop "Muslim Societies and Islams in the Age of Globalization and Postmodernity," in 1999, and will appear in 2004 in the collection *Globalization and the Muslim World: Culture, Religion and Modernity* (Syracuse University Press), edited by Birgit Schaebler and Leif Stenberg.

Last but foremost, we'd like to acknowledge Ann Fedoroff, Lew Oliver, Naomi Glenn Oliver, William L. Oliver, Mariana Steinberg, and Stanley A. Steinberg, and thank the many friends and family members who made the writing of this book a less lonely enterprise.

Needless to say, none of the people who appear here necessarily agrees with our presentation or analysis. Indeed, it might be difficult to find two people who agree completely about the Israeli-Palestinian conflict, and we thank those friends with whom we have argued, sometimes into the wee hours, and yet remained friends.

The vast majority of Israelis and Palestinians, we continue to believe, refuse to give in to voices from burning bushes. This book is dedicated to them . . . and to their unwritten future.

A Note on Translation

We have left as is many Arabic words and phrases that have entered the English vocabulary such as *jihad*, "holy struggle" or "holy war," and *Allahu akbar*, variously translated as "God is great," "God is greater," and "God is greatest." Although these terms are now part of the English language, they are not self-explanatory. *Jihad*, in particular, has been the subject of a great deal of controversy, with some arguing that the term refers solely to "the greater jihad," an interiorized or spiritual struggle, as opposed to "the lesser jihad," or holy war. When the word appears in this book, it refers to "fighting by the sword." Similarly, *Allahu akbar* appears herein primarily as a cry of victory, expression of empowerment, and assertion of God-given grace, as when an enemy is killed, or as an invocation and prayer of dedication upon the death of a martyr, while in everyday life, the phrase expresses a multitude of sentiments, often contradictory—faith, power, astonishment, envy, pride, humility, even mockery. Throughout, we have chosen to leave *Allah* as *Allah* rather than rendering it as the more universal "God," not only because the word is well known to English speakers, but also because it is the word intended by the authors of the discourse found in this book. Other Arabic terms that occur frequently include *mujahid*, or "holy warrior" *fi sabil Allah*, "on the path of Allah," and its plural, *mujahidun*. For the sake of simplicity, we have kept the plural of this and like terms in nominative form regardless of actual usage.

A term deserving special note is *suicide bomber*. Although it neglects the homicidal aspect inherent in suicide bombings, its meaning is widely understood, and we have used it. The word preferred by Palestinians is *shahid*, which appears here in translation as "martyr." The term is problematic, given that it can be used to signify approval of a person or action. In this work, we are merely replicating the usage of Palestinians during the intifada, as in the book's title, which makes reference to "Martyrs' Square," an actual place as well as a figure. Derived from the verb *shahada*, "to witness," *shahid* possesses rich cognates such as *ash-shahadatain*, "the double witness," the formula uttered by the worshipper with index finger raised toward the end of the second *rak'a* (prostration) of the Islamic prayer cycle, and *shahida*, a word that means both "tombstone" and "index finger," and in the media of Hamas, "trigger finger" as well. In addition, it is the name given to the "one-way sign," the fist with the index finger raised heavenward, used by Islamist activists to signify their allegiance to the ideology of the Islamic Movement.

Last, we would note that the declamatory style of writing that characterizes many intifada texts poses particular problems for the translator. Entire paragraphs are not infrequently composed of one long sentence, continuing for a page or longer. Typically, many clauses are strung together with little attention paid to continuity of tense or person. To reproduce exactly this kind of rhetoric would result in an unreadable text; to translate it into fluid English would be to lose much of the flavor of the genre. We have aimed for a middle course.

O madmen of Gaza
A thousand welcomes
to madmen
if they liberate us.
Truly, the age of political reason
slipped away long ago
so, then, teach us madness . . .

—Nizar Qabbani

The limits of my language mean the limits of my world.
—Wittgenstein

And he turned away from them, and said, O my sorrow for Yusuf!
And his eyes became white on account of the grief, then he repressed it.

—Qur'an 12:84, "Yusuf"

Introduction

For six months at the beginning of the intifada, we lived with a Palestinian family in the Gaza Strip. Having recently arrived in the region (separately and from opposite coasts), we knew Gaza and the West Bank largely through what we'd read. We were open to large numbers of often competing forces and ideas, and gladly talked to anyone who would talk with us—nationalists and Islamists, leaders and followers, stone throwers and spokesmen, militants and bystanders.

We later settled in the Armenian Quarter of the Old City of Jerusalem, whose massive stone walls were something of a cryptographic puzzle, covered as they were by layers of graffiti that would appear seemingly out of the blue, disappearing often as quickly. We soon began photographing and translating the messages, which proved far more interesting than we initially could have imagined, offering a new means for understanding the uprising and a way of bypassing the scripts usually reserved for journalists and researchers, scripts that by then we knew well. Although the beginnings were largely haphazard, by 1990, we had something of a project going; by 1996, we'd amassed a substantial collection of the political ephemera and underground media of the intifada—graffiti, posters, martyr cards, videotapes, and audiocassettes.

Graffiti comprised one of the very earliest media used during the intifada and came to cover not only the walls of the West Bank and Gaza Strip but almost every conceivable surface. The graffitists were mostly young men in their teens and twenties whom Palestinians referred to as *shabab* (singular, *shabb*), a word connoting testosteronic swagger and street machismo and perhaps best translated as "the guys." One of the major tasks of the shabab in the early days of the uprising, as they saw it, was informing and mobilizing the general public. With conventional modes of communication heavily censored by the Israeli military government, and Palestinian newspapers and other media remaining largely in the hands of an older and more cautious elite, graffiti quickly came to be used for this purpose. Palestinians referred to it, some with a wink, as "our newspaper." The Israelis, as quickly, recognized the power of the medium and declared the posting of graffiti illegal.[1] If the graffitist were wearing a mask, he could be shot and killed.

Graffiti frequently reproduced lines from the leaflets of the Unified National Leadership (UNL), a nationalist umbrella group, and those of Hamas and the Islamic Jihad, the two major Islamist organizations in the territories. While many messages were highly formulaic, consisting of elaborate greetings, calls for national unity, factional advertisements, and territorial markers, graffiti actually served a wide variety of functions. It was used, among other things, to announce strike days, call for boycotts, and warn accused collaborators. Regardless of content, messages were commonly erased or edited within days, sometimes hours, by passing Israel Defense Forces (IDF) patrols or, less often, by Israeli settlers and competing Palestinian factions. Only in the more isolated villages, where Israeli patrols rarely ventured, did messages avoid being whitewashed, sometimes staying up for months—a fact that often made it difficult to pinpoint when they had been posted.

Less ephemeral than graffiti were the posters and sometimes massive canvases that filled funeral tents, public squares, and mosques throughout the Bank and Strip. Although some were printed on underground presses, many posters were simply photocopied drawings, often taped together to form long banners. When more time was available, activists created elaborate canvases, making do with whatever materials could be had—bed sheets and house paint, newspaper clippings and fluorescent highlighters, poster board and crayon. Whatever their media, artists visualized elemental themes and long-standing obsessions—life and death, suffering and revenge, martyrdom and apocalypse, Paradise and Hell.

As the intifada evolved, the often predictable slogans of the early days gave way to more sophisticated media—audiocassettes of political music, videotapes of the interrogations of collaborators and the last words of suicide bombers, martyr books recalling hagiographies. The transformation was sudden and rather unexpected, beginning in the early 1990s, when Hamas produced its earliest video on the group's military wing, the Battalions of 'Izz ad-Din al-Qassam, named after one of the influential clerics and leaders of the Arab Revolt in Palestine against the Jews and the British. We collected these media as well, smuggling them out of Gaza under the suspicious gaze of IDF soldiers and, later, the Palestinian Authority (PA). In the end, we spent about six years off and on archiving the political ephemera and street media of the intifada in Jerusalem and 125 of the cities and villages of the West Bank and Gaza Strip, seeing it as our task to record or collect material before it disappeared; in many cases, our record is the only one that exists.

If collecting and translating were difficult, writing was especially so, due to the often macabre nature of much of the material as well as the many problems inherent in writing about political and religious issues that take the form of Manichaean dramas. Anyone who has tried to write about the Israeli-Palestinian conflict, tried to understand both sides of that conflict, will know what we mean when we compare it to walking through a minefield. Every term carries within itself a preemptive judgment—a burden evident not only in fateful dyads such as "Judea and Samaria" versus "the West Bank and Gaza Strip," "terrorist" versus "militant," "Palestinian" versus "Arab," "Jew" versus "Israeli," and so forth, but also in the overabundance of determiners, capital letters, and exclamation marks that pepper discourse on the conflict. Every choice is forced; there are no neutral terms. An ideological proclivity—indeed, often an entire worldview—is marked in the most minute of details—the choice, say, between "territories" and "Territories," "Occupied Territories" and "occupied territories," "the occupied territories" and "the Occupied Territories." For the writer who refuses to submit to this sort of determinism, the result is exhaustion and often paralysis.

Part memoir, part travelogue, part journey into the underground media of the intifada, part exploration of the links between martyrdom and "identity politics," this book is neither a political analysis nor a prescription for foreign policy. We do not attempt comparisons, whether with the Japanese kamikaze pilots of World War II or the suicide squadrons of the Tamil Tigers in Sri Lanka. We do not provide a history of the Israeli-Palestinian conflict, nor do we chronicle other forms of violence within that conflict—that of extremists in the Israeli settler movement, say, or Kach, the radical right-wing Israeli party headed by the late Rabbi Meir Kahane and barred from the Knesset in 1988 for its racist platform—subjects for other books. No doubt, these groups exert tremendous influence on Israeli society at large, driving the wider culture in dangerous, even catastrophic directions. During the time we lived in the region, Israeli Prime Minister Yitzhak Rabin was assassinated by Yigal Amir, and Baruch Goldstein, an American doctor and Kahane follower, mowed down twenty-nine Muslim worshippers in the Tomb of the Patriarchs in what soon became known as "the Hebron Massacre." These acts were widely regarded with revulsion by Israeli citizens and condemned as acts of lunacy and terror by Israeli politicians, right and left. Be that as it may, Goldstein's monument continues to be rebuilt in Kiryat Arba, no matter how many times the Israeli army knocks it down; and there are more than a few people among the more ardent champions of the settler movement who will mutter something about a higher purpose guiding the hand of Rabin's assassin. At this point, however, due largely to the heterogeneity of Israeli society and its strong secular tradition, people like Yigal Amir and Baruch Goldstein have failed to inspire admiration in the larger population, much less mass movements in the state of Israel.

And beyond. For here is a conflict that magnetizes not only Israelis and Palestinians, but also people around the globe—pilgrims, spiritual accountants, disaster groupies, conspiracy buffs, armchair revolutionaries, frustrated fascists, apocalypticists, spymasters, victimologists, and saviors manqué—as well as those who don't yet know they are true believers. Indeed, it would not be too far off the mark to say that the Israeli-Palestinian conflict has itself become the crux of a new religion, piggybacking the old, transmuting its power while denying its origins. Call it *religion*, call it *ideology*, but the flow of life and history is always being punctured here from above, transforming everything into parable, morality play, and prophecy. Indeed, the vertical, or grandiose, element is one of the most fundamental characteristics of the Israeli-Palestinian conflict. Even when, or perhaps especially when, the most banal events are related, the language inevitably references God, and even when scripture, that most vertical of languages, is not directly quoted, it lingers in the background, tenacious and determinative.

In a not dissimilar way, although the Israeli-Palestinian conflict is barely a hundred years old, it is treated by expert and layperson alike as "ancient" or even "timeless." This mythology should be questioned. Its basis is often simply ignorance. Many cannot seem to separate the present conflict from the biblical narratives they grew up hearing. Perniciously, reliance on the notion of "from time immemorial" signals a predestination and fatality, too often serving as a justification for whatever needs to be justified.

We do not pretend to have escaped the lures and pitfalls of writing about the Israeli-Palestinian conflict; we but note that we are aware of their existence and have tried to avoid them. We gave serious thought, for instance, to the question of whether to include the names of the suicide bombers that appear in Part III,[2] as well as their victims, in the end deeming it necessary. Indeed, almost every term in this book has been debated not only between ourselves but also with others. As with so much of the material in our collection, people tended to see what they wanted to see—some insisting on flowers where there was blood; others seeing blood where there were flowers.

In Part I, we tell the story of our introduction to Hamas and Sheikh Ahmad Yasin, the movement's late founder, spiritual leader, and symbol. It is also a recollection of our time in Gaza and the West Bank during the intifada, a personal account of bewilderment, betrayal, conversion, adolescent absolutism, witness, the limits of witness, and what could be called "the literalist quest."

In Part II, we offer a portfolio of some of the major scripts of the intifada through examples drawn from our archive. From the beginning, the uprising was presented as the fulfillment of long-cherished scripts of jihad, martyrdom, self-sacrifice, and victory. Youth, in particular, saw these scripts as programs to be actualized, their truth instantiated with each death occurring under their banner.

In Part III, we focus on the videotaped last words of one cell of Hamas suicide bombers, weaving scenes from the tape with interviews with their families, themselves last words of sorts. Our intent is not to provide insight into "the mind of the suicide bomber," an impossible task, but rather to explore the transformative power granted those who not only speak the old scripts but also carry them out.

Our focus throughout is Hamas ("zeal" in Arabic), a movement whose motto appears as "the eighth subject" of the group's covenant: "Allah is its goal, the Prophet its ideal, the Qur'an its constitution, jihad its way, and death in the service of Allah its aspiration." Not only did Hamas pay the most attention to the production and dissemination of media in the West Bank and Gaza Strip during the first intifada but it also shaped the uprising in a way unlike any of the other Palestinian factions that participated in the intifada, nationalist or Islamist. These factions included Fatah, the largest and most popular subgroup within the Palestine Liberation Organization (PLO), founded and led by Yasir Arafat; the Popular Front for the Liberation of Palestine (PFLP), a Marxist group that was the faction of choice for those who rejected what they saw as the conciliatory policies of Fatah, but who were not particularly religious; the Democratic Front for the Liberation of Palestine (DFLP), a left-wing faction that split off from the PFLP in 1969; the Communist Party (Hashaf), renamed in October 1991 "the Palestinian People's Party" (PPP), a faction that has long argued for moderation; and the Islamic Jihad, a militant Islamist group. Hamas initiated suicide bombings in 1994 and led them until the Aqsa Brigades of Fatah, Hamas' primary political and military rival, also began carrying them out during the second intifada. By then—indeed, by the end of the first intifada, we would argue—suicide bombings had gathered their own apocalyptic momentum.

Having the last word is, of course, the essence of all forms of power; and in suicide bombings, we see this truth exhibited in radical form. Hamas has long advocated suicide bombings, disregarding all conventions by which the acceptability of killing is calculated. "Glory does not build its lofty edifice except with skulls," wrote the famed Palestinian Islamist 'Abdullah Yusuf 'Azzam[3] in "Martyrs"; "honor and respect cannot be established except on a foundation of cripples and corpses."[4] Killed by a car bomb in Peshawar, Pakistan in 1989, 'Azzam is considered the quintessential mujahid and martyr by members of Hamas. He was the commander of the Palestinian "Afghans," the name given to Arabs who volunteered to fight in Afghanistan against the Soviets, many of whom saw the jihad in Afghanistan as the prelude to a greater jihad to be fought against Israel, holding as their slogan, "The road to Palestine leads through Afghanistan," reminiscent of the PFLP's erstwhile slogan, "The road to Palestine leads through Jordan."[5] 'Azzam is also believed to have been the mentor of 'Usama bin Laden, the two later together founding Maktab al-Khidamat, a recruiting office for young men aiming to become mujahidun—an office that, in many respects, can be seen as the precursor of al-Qa'ida, which bin Laden set up shortly after he and 'Azzam parted ways in the late 1980s.

One would be hard pressed to find a more unanswerable rhetoric than that of Hamas or a more unanswerable act than the murder-suicides, the "happy deaths," rehearsed and carried out by the young men of its suicide squads. Since Oslo, Hamas has increasingly found itself on the defensive; significantly, it was at this critical turning point that "hunters" and suicide bombers began to displace the stone throwers and demonstrators of the early years of the uprising. The visceral rhetoric of many of the texts examined in this book can be said to represent a final attempt to have the last word, to invest an increasingly threatened program with the aura of physical reality, as though the "tears and screaming and death" of the enemy—to quote one of the movement's documents—could compensate for the lack of a blueprint, as though the ultimate proof of the movement's effectiveness were the degree of fear it inspires in the enemy.

The rhetoric of Hamas has long been characterized by a peculiar blend of self-righteousness and the lurid, the visceral and the abstract, grandiosity and matter-of-factness. It is precisely through such rhetoric, one could say, that the organization has successfully relegated substantive issues to the shadows of irrelevance. Those who seek to understand Hamas and like movements but ignore the scripts they use to lend their agenda the force of prophecy and divine command neglect a major means by which they have chosen to distinguish themselves. "Indeed, our words remain dead until we die in their cause," wrote Said Qutb, the seminal Islamist thinker and Muslim Brother, whose writings continue to inspire mujahidun in Palestine and around the world, "so they remain alive amongst the living." The logic is circular. The more scripts are invested with the power to determine life and death, the more they are sacralized; the greater the number of people willing to die on their behalf, the more power they accrue. This is, of course, the literalist project, which initially promises to jumpstart change in overdetermined systems through the actualization of texts, but which almost inevitably results in a radical constriction of the world. Literalism, it should be clear, is more than "just" a philosophy of language. It is capable of creating and destroying worlds. It closes the door on confusion and uncertainty but also on what could be called the salvation of accident, the ways in which contingency facilitates freedom, allowing people to move in multifarious directions, a feeling as necessary for language as it is for life itself—for life, that is, to be felt as life.

Far from being an aberration, suicide bombings are the most complete realization of a particular rhetoric and ideology; for many years, they were a, if not the, primary means by which Hamas attempted to differentiate itself from the PLO. By the end of the first intifada, they had become thoroughly institutionalized. The families of bombers were given compensation packages by Hamas and Iraq, martyr videos featured advertisements for coming attractions, and bereaved families could purchase ready-made martyr plaques with appropriate Qur'anic scriptures and a blank space in which to paste a photo of their beloved dead. By the second intifada, dubbed "al-Aqsa intifada," lengthy indoctrination and training sessions for suicide bombers were no longer deemed necessary. Indeed, the script was so well known that someone who wanted to become a bomber, it was said, was simply given a bomb; he decided the coordinates for himself. More significantly, the practice jumped across the nationalist/ Islamist divide when in 2002, the Aqsa Brigades of Fatah also began carrying out suicide bombings. Soon enough, the group began doing something that Hamas had never done by sending out young women as well as young men on these missions. In the winter of 2004, Hamas followed suit and sent out its own female suicide bomber, a twenty-two-year-old woman from a wealthy family in the Gaza Strip and the mother of two young children, one of whom, reportedly, was not even yet weaned. Before her martyrdom, she posed with her three-year-old in coordinating outfits and headbands inscribed with sacred writing against an elaborate Islamist backdrop. She held an assault rifle in her hand; the child held a rocket-propelled grenade. After she blew herself up, Sheikh Ahmad Yasin hailed the act as "a new development in resistance against the enemy."[6]

Support for suicide bombings went far beyond the military wings of the nationalist and Islamist movements. Parents dressed their babies and toddlers as suicide bombers and had them photographed in local photography studios. Children marched with suicide belts around their chests. University exhibitions included one that recreated an actual suicide bombing carried out in the Sbarro restaurant in Jerusalem, replete with pizza slices and bloody body parts. The Palestinian Authority named popular soccer tournaments after martyrs belonging both to Fatah and the rival Hamas, with even the suicide bomber who blew himself up during an Israeli family's celebration of Passover, killing thirty of them, thus honored. On public TV, the Palestinian Broadcasting Corporation aired videos of men being lured away by the *hur*, the beautiful virgins of Paradise promised to martyrs, as if they were commercials or public service announcements. If the term *cult* did not suggest a fringe phenomenon, we might begin to speak of a cult of martyrdom; as it is, the devotees of death on all fronts have become too numerous and too diverse for us to do so any longer.

PART ONE

Saint Yasin

1. Welcome to Planet X

When we first moved to Gaza in 1988, not long after the intifada had broken out, Sheikh Ahmad Yasin of the Islamic Resistance Movement—better known by its acronym *Hamas*—was virtually unknown. By the time we left the area five years later, a series of suicide bombings had made him famous around the world, and ordinary people in the West Bank and Gaza Strip had begun to express some degree of sympathy with the man and the movement. Even good friends began to renounce the leftist ideology of their youth, gave up occasional drinking sprees, got married, and got religion. Getting religion obviously didn't mean you were necessarily a Hamasawi, a Hamas devotee, but in the highly politicized world of the Bank and Strip, the lines between the two were easily blurred.

The first casualty in our circle was Yusuf—poet, musician, luftmensch, and longtime member of the Popular Front for the Liberation of Palestine. Yusuf had enticed us down to Gaza to be teachers in a school that never seemed to materialize. He would lead us to a cinderblock shell of a room somewhere in the camps, and there, standing among small mountains of sand and glass and shreds of fiberglass roofing, announce, "And here we will have a blackboard . . . and here we will put a bookcase . . . and here . . ." In his mind, the place just needed a little spring cleaning.

Instead of starting a school, we spent most of our time talking about "the situation" and "our dear cousins," as Yusuf ironically referred to Jews, and going on "adventures," as he liked to call busting curfews and generally being reckless.

We mean the word in a benign, nonfrivolous way, a sort of openness to risk and life, for Yusuf lived every moment as though there might be no tomorrow, as though at any moment he might open his hands and give you everything he had and never look back. There are people in the world like that, their every word and gesture bespeaking a rare and true curiosity, an exuberance of spirit, a munificence directed toward the greatest and smallest of things.

Those were heady days on "Planet X"—a kooky, sci-fi-like phrase one of Yusuf's brothers had discovered in a BBC English course book and applied to Gaza, as in "Welcome to Planet X!" The phrase, invariably uttered in a mock-epic tone, aptly captured the isolation of Gaza, a thin strip of land sandwiched between Egypt, Israel, and the Mediterranean Sea, crammed with somewhere around a million Palestinians, the majority refugees. The words also served as a disdainful commentary on the massive McDonald's-style "Welcome to Gaza" arches that the Israeli civil administration had erected in Arabic, Hebrew, and English at the entrance to the major cities in the Strip after the 1967 war (a war in which Israel had defeated the armies of Egypt, Jordan, and Syria over the course of six days and had been left holding the Sinai peninsula, Gaza Strip, West Bank, and Golan Heights). It also symbolized the small and fragile universe the three of us had created around ourselves, the strangeness that descended whenever one of us did something that threatened that universe.

Yusuf's conversion was of this order. A year after we left the Strip and moved back to Jerusalem, his twinkling style suddenly turned serious and foreboding. He abandoned his romantic quests, got married, and began to frequent the mosque on a daily basis. An explanation of some sort was necessary, but Yusuf didn't have the words for it. "I grew tired, my friends," he said with a sigh and embarrassed smile, as we stood together before a pen containing a fattened white goat that would soon be sacrificed for an upcoming feast. Later, he would say that an angel had come to him in a vision and commanded him to change his ways. It didn't last.

Not long after, our friend 'Ali grew a beard, which by then had become the major corporeal marker of the Hamas disciple. We'd been friends with 'Ali since 1987, and had spent so much time together that his family had practically adopted us. Unlike Yusuf, his old college buddy, 'Ali was not big on adventures, and we mostly just hung out together in the small house rented by his family in a little town in the West Bank not far from the Green Line, the old ceasefire line of 1948 separating Israel from the West Bank and Gaza.

The flat held two large sofas, twin beds, a TV, and a refrigerator. There was no running water. Nine people slept in the two rooms that comprised the apartment, sometimes more. On any given day, there might be sixteen people scattered in and around the house, barely able to move. The refrigerator was the centerpiece of the house, its hinge, so to speak, for it was situated an inch or two from the front door in the three-by-three space that connected the two rooms of the house. If its door were open, you could neither enter nor exit the house nor could you go from the living room to the bedroom, and vice versa.

Outside, there was a garden, which contained an outhouse, a plum tree, and the tattered remnants of a yellow couch from which one had an unobstructed view of an Israeli settlement. Its white houses with their huge plate-glass windows and synthetic red pan-tile roofs glittered like Lego constructions; when hit by the sun in the right way, they would send blinding reflections across the wadi, like messages with no content.

Once a week on Saturday, 'Ali's mother, who in keeping with local tradition was called *Im-'Ali*, or "mother of 'Ali" after her eldest son, would set off in the morning to buy a couple of chickens, returning home hours later from the neighborhood oven with a huge moveable feast balanced neatly on her graying head. Before lunch, 'Ali's father would kneel and pray on the concrete path in front of the apartment, oblivious of the wild sounds emanating from the window directly above him—Ninja avengers, Egyptian belly dancers, Kung Fu kings, Indian lovers, Syrian partygoers, Israeli actors playing Arab terrorists in cheesy Globus-Golan movies, Hamas suicide bombers. A video was constantly playing. They were all pirated, of unknown generation, barely visible through the bootleg fuzz. You really got your money's worth out of the Indian ones, which could last for up to four hours. It was after watching a version of *Boyz N the Hood* that 'Ali started calling his little part of the West Bank a "'hood" without a trace of irony.

Once in a while, we'd talk 'Ali into going out with us. It wasn't his favorite thing to do. Sometimes, we'd be stoned. Sometimes, children would stop our rental car at the entrance to a village and demand to know our political affiliation. "What are you," they'd demand to know with kiddie bravado, "Fatah or Hamas?" Sometimes, they'd warn us not to enter the village, saying that if we did, we'd be killed.

'Ali's sister Nadia would often accompany us on these expeditions, and we'd stop here and there and visit friends of hers scattered across the Bank. Once, she took us to a very powerful "witch" who possessed a magic well and whose husband walked around with a pistol on his hip—a sure sign that he was an Israeli collaborator. The witch told us that the jinn that lived in her well—it was a red jinn, to be exact—could grant us any wish we desired, but that it would need to "borrow" a hundred-shekel note for its efforts. At the time, one-hundred shekels was a huge amount of money for us, so we hemmed and hawed a bit. "Come on, come on," said Nadia, elbowing us, her eyes becoming as wide as saucers, as though our hesitation were embarrassing her, "do you think you'll never see it again? Give it to her. Come on!" And with that, she handed the witch a crisp hundred-shekel note of her own, an act that made the prospect of seeing our money again a little brighter. So we handed a note to the witch, which she then appeared to slip in an envelope and burn with great ceremony, the flames licking preternaturally high in the air. We never saw the money again. Moreover, our wish was not granted.

Another time, Nadia took us to a village north of Nablus to meet a local PFLP artist who proudly showed us an idyllic scene he'd recently painted in his best friend's bedroom—a little man fishing beneath a setting sun. The artist had seemed quite charming till we learned that he ate his daily hummus out of an ancient Roman skull he'd disinterred from its final resting place in the hills above his home, and he had recently broken all the fingers, one by one, of a guy he'd accused of collaboration, a guy who but a couple of months before had hosted us for the night.

If you expressed a little shock at such things, 'Ali would cluck his tongue and shake his head and say that there were good people and bad people in the world. This was his most basic philosophy by which he explained the craziness around him. Goodness and badness, moreover, were fairly evenly distributed across the planet, in his mind, and had nothing to do with religion per se; otherwise, he wouldn't be hanging out with unbelievers like us. He was a guy of few words, but he would argue with any visitor who had succumbed to the Manichaeanism of the intifada. He spoke when it was his nature to be silent, and kept friends who made him not a little suspect. "Bring'em to Kalandia [Refugee Camp]," his neighbors down the road once told him, "and we'll show you what to do with them!"—"them," of course, being us.

When he called to say that he too had become religious, it was a sad day. When we saw him again, his nationalist mustache had been permanently supplemented with an Islamist-style beard (he had gone back and forth for awhile); he was reading Garaudy, the French convert to Islam and Holocaust denier, for pleasure; and he had finally given in to his mother's wish that he marry the sister of his brother's wife, a cousin from the camps of Gaza. He said that at long last he had acquired peace of mind.

By then, the once fuzzy line between being religious and being a Hamasawi was for most people virtually nonexistent. The very presence of a beard was a strong and unmistakable signifier of a radical political as well as religious affiliation, and the two could no longer be separated. What had happened? Sometimes we could almost blame ourselves. At our instigation, 'Ali had helped us translate masses of Hamas propaganda—leaflets and documents, videotapes and audiocassettes, stuff we'd collected over years of fieldwork in the Bank and Strip. Had the stuff been so potent it had managed to pull even him over?

'Ali had drawn his own green line. Thenceforth, we could only look across to a place beyond and remember. If we would remain friends to the end, it was because 'Ali's jump into Islamism felt less like betrayal, a transgression of the unwritten rules by which we lived, than it did suicide.

2. Look with Your Ears, My Friend

The induction ceremony had been held shortly after we first arrived in Gaza, which suddenly promised to live up to its reputation as the worst place on earth. Asked if we liked "adventure," Yusuf had led us into Beach Camp, then under siege by what seemed like hundreds of Israeli soldiers. The municipal workers had been on strike for weeks, and the tropical Gazan sun had fermented mountains of uncollected trash into a sweet stink you could almost feel. We stumbled over black dunes and through narrow alleys where absurdly fat and bold rats squealed at us as we passed. "Look with your ears, my friend," warned Yusuf.

The events of the evening proved to be even better than Yusuf had anticipated. Hundreds of people were eagerly awaiting a face-off with the soldiers. These mass confrontations between hundreds, even thousands, of Palestinians, and Israeli soldiers would later be replaced by battles between organized groups of shabab and soldiers; but for now the intifada was young, and the throngs on the street were ordinary people. Shadowy figures dashed in and out of the dense black night, illuminated briefly by the smoky orange flames of burning tires and smoldering barricades. Screams in Hebrew were answered by screams in Arabic. Yusuf soon became lost trying to avoid both the hyper-excited "sons of the camps" and their equally hyped-up Israeli adversaries. The gut-wrenching booms of tear-gas grenades competed with what Gazans called "sound bombs," lighting up the dunes in strident yellow-white flashes. At times, the alien crackle of field radios and the gunning of jeep engines signaled that we had strayed too close to an Israeli patrol, forcing us to scurry for cover behind the prickly-pear hedgerows that pepper the Strip. Looking back, our basic philosophy must have been to trust in the benevolent power that keeps young people alive despite their own stupidity. In reality, we were too young and stupid even to have such a philosophy.

We soon bumped into a young Palestinian on guard duty. Eminently capable of lending an air of plausibility and authority to the most insane of enterprises, Yusuf said to the guard, "Salamu alaikum, I am Yusuf al-Masri"—as if they'd just found themselves seated next to one another at a dinner party, as if his name alone were enough to explain our little stroll through a battle. "And these," he said, gesturing toward us, with impeccable magnificence, "are our friends from America. They are here to teach school."

Although it seemed amazing at the time, the young man was prepared to believe the truth—that we were just a couple of foreigners on a nighttime jaunt through the neighborhood. He led us to sanctuary, leaving us in the care of his mother, a worried-looking woman who mumbled entreaties to the deity whenever the skirmishing outside swept too closely. She made us tea despite the battle and despite the fact that we had never seen each other before and would no doubt never see each other again. We sat sipping the tea in a room that still bore the marks of the fragmentation grenade that had killed her eldest son some twenty years before during Gaza's heyday as a center for armed attacks against Israel. He had been a fighter affiliated with Fatah, also a body-builder. The dead son, framed and posed with rippling, tumescent black-and-white muscles, peered down at us from above.

At length, the battle died down, and we were able to navigate our way out of the camp and back to the relative safety of the streets of Deir al-Balah. Our eyes and throats stung from tear gas, burning trash, and rubber. Yusuf knocked at the iron door of one of the small shops that are found every block or two in the cities of the Strip. He bought banana-flavored ice-cream popsicles, which we licked quietly in the darkness.

3. Lunch with Hasan

The major road through the Strip paralleled the old Beirut-to-Cairo railway line. The railway was no more, and the road, like everything else in Gaza, was ugly and beautiful and dangerous. Dingy grey sand from the camps blew over it, mingling with the decaying garbage piled in heaps at every corner. Eucalyptus trees, bony and majestic, lined much of the road, providing cover for the shabab when they lobbed Molotovs at passing Israeli patrols. Scores of burned tires had left the street pocked with angry black posies.

Hasan, the older brother of Yusuf's best friend, Jamal, had found us standing in Maidan Filistin (Palestine Square), in Gaza City, the major city of the Strip. We'd been attempting for over an hour to muscle our way aboard one of the crowded taxis plying the main road of the Strip. He stopped to pick us up.

"How long have you been waiting?" he asked. "Two hours? Three? More? You are very lucky; usually I take the Beach Road, but today I am off work early. You are lucky."

And we were. On Fridays, the men who worked during the week in Tel Aviv and elsewhere in Israel flooded back to the Strip to be with their families. The Mercedes saloon cars that served as public transport were swamped by shoving and pushing workers even before they rolled to a stop. Unable to compete, we'd been reduced to sitting atop our bags under the suspicious stares of the Gazans and the Israeli soldiers manning the lookout post across the square.

It was good to be found by Hasan, to be whizzing along the road in his red "Bijo," as everyone called a Peugeot in Gaza, there being no "p" in Arabic. It was good to be spared the interrogation session that each taxi ride inevitably became, during which our fellow passengers played Munkar and Nakir, the fabled creatures whose job it is to interrogate the dead in their tombs, attempting through clever questioning and carefully planted Hebraicisms here and there to learn whether we were spies.

Hasan had his own questions. "You are writers," he said, "but will you tell the truth? The newspapers print only lies. And why? Because they are controlled by the Jewish." It was standard stuff in the Strip. We'd almost gotten used to it.

He insisted we come home with him and have lunch. He was an excellent "chief," he said. We would soon see for ourselves.

His family's house was situated at the major war zone between Bani Suhaila and Khan Yunis. Pointing out a charred mess of steel and rubber on the street, Hasan said that the day before, the Jews, by which he meant IDF soldiers, had kicked open the front gate and rolled a tire that the shabab had set on fire into the garden. Nobody had been home but his mother. "Only my mother, and she is a woman!" he exclaimed. "Haram! Forbidden!" Heavy green lufa pods hung over a blue steel gate at the entrance to the house. A sun-faded scrap of fake leopard skin was stretched across the iron bars, which guarded a small garden, about eight by eight, replete with mint and trees, and a deep tank of fish. During curfews, which could stretch on day after mind-numbing day, Jamal would often strip to his shorts and submerge himself in the pool, sharing his misery with the dumb little brown fish.

Inside, the house was cool, sparsely furnished, painted in blocks of chocolate and white. Colorful placards advertising Klorane shampoo decorated the walls. An almost American plastic eagle perched above the door.

After a cup of hot, sweet tea, Hasan led us into the back room of the house, where his friend Amjad was watching a brand-new color TV. Hasan pulled at his Cocaine brand jeans and casually picked up a remote control device lying on the couch. He switched the new set on and off, on and off, on and off.

He said he was angry, but, strangely, he smiled and pointed to a bottle on the table. "I am like this," he said, pouring its contents into a cup till it overflowed onto the table. "Anger is coming out of the top of my head." He marched off to the kitchen leaving us with the new TV and Amjad.

"I studied psychology in Alexandria," Amjad said, twiddling a keychain in the shape of "all of Palestine" between his fingers. "They do electroshock therapy in Bethlehem and give them pills, you know," he added. "But no lobotomies yet." Everyone laughed. The man had a sense of humor.

Back in the kitchen, Hasan handed us some kidney and showed us exactly how he wanted it cut up. He'd learned how to cook, he said, when he'd lived on his own in Cairo. Sometimes, he sheepishly confessed, a servant-woman had helped him out a little bit. Six days a week for six dollars a month—can you imagine?

"Do engineers make money in the States?" he asked, chopping up pieces of baby camel with great whacks of a thick knife. "I could make money there, do you think?"

Lunch was the kidney and the baby camel stewed in a viscous green leaf called *mulukhiya*, a spicy kind of meatball called *kufteh*, homemade bread, and *fuul*, an earthy paste of brown beans that constituted a major staple in Gaza and was eaten at breakfast, lunch, dinner, and in between.

"They call themselves a democracy," Hasan said of the Americans out of the blue over a cup of postprandial tea. "A democracy when man and woman are on the street doing things . . . like . . . you know. . . . Is that a democracy?"

"Well, that's not all there is to America," we replied feebly, uncertain as to what might be the best response.

Hasan smiled in an enigmatic way as if one of us had been caught in a lie.

"We want to die," he said suddenly, a strangeness about his mouth. "I want to die. From the Golan to Eilat, it's ours. They came and stole it from us. Do you know what is a kibbutz?" he asked. "There was one man there to every two or three hundred women, and you know . . ."

"O please, Hasan, really."

"It's true, I swear," he insisted.

"Now we understand the appeal of Zionism," we said, laughing, trying to lighten the mood.

"O.K.," said Amjad, "Maybe there were two or three men." He smiled at us, clearly embarrassed by what his friend was saying.

"If you had ten children, and they were taken away from you, and then four of them returned," we said, "would you say, No, kill them all?" In retrospect, it seemed a stupid thing to say.

"Yes, all of them. Kill them all! You've broken the whole," he answered, smiling. And he was still smiling when he told us that all Americans should be thrown out of the Middle East. He didn't mean it completely, we felt. It was just his way of making us feel that the problem was as much ours as his, or should be.

"Yes, we want to die," he said again and again, seeking an effect. "And perhaps it is already written," he added, scribbling on his palm with invisible ink from an invisible pen.

"Written?" we said. "Where?"

"In our eyes," he said, narrowing his.

4. A Complete Darkness

Stuck. Stuck again. Stuck, stuck, stuck. We were stuck. We'd experienced enough curfews to know that if you saw one coming, you'd better get the hell out of Dodge as fast as possible. The main thing one soon discovers about curfews is that they're boring. They're so boring you think you might die of boredom. Gaza was already a claustrophobe's worst nightmare, but during curfews, the world would close in so fast that even the illusion of space disappeared. A feeling of panic would descend upon you like a demon.

We'd managed to escape back to Jerusalem but once, and then narrowly. Yusuf had come home saying that a *man'a at-tajawwul*—literally, "forbidden to move"—was imminent, whereupon we'd rushed off to Gaza City and paid a taxi driver a small fortune to take us to the border. We soon found ourselves sitting on the edge of the city in a traffic jam of like-minded people, mostly Palestinian workers trying to get back into Israel, but also directly before us, an

Israeli settler, who at the time we were sure would be lynched before our very eyes. We watched with horror as a crowd gathered and began stoning the man's car from every direction with small boulders, some hurled from a distance of only a few meters. The stones fell like rain, making sick metallic thuds on the car, which suddenly seemed alive in the way that inanimate things can seem animate when in the process of being destroyed. We stared ahead, instinctively sinking in our seats, becoming smaller and smaller but for our eyes, which, conversely, grew larger and larger. We wondered if we might be next when, suddenly, the line of cars before us lurched forward, and we were off again and breathing.

There would be no escaping this time around, and no one had any idea as to how long it might last. Still holding high hopes for a school, Yusuf suggested that we spend the coming days recording educational tapes for children in radio English. And so with the last rays of the sun—the IDF had cut off the electricity—we read sentences into an antiquarian recorder so slowly and with such ar-ti-cu-la-tion that they began to sound like minimalist poems. The author of the text from which we were reading had, disastrously, applied to English the Arabic practice of attaching the definite article to the noun it modifies; and as the sun sank lower and lower in the Gazan sky, it seemed both horrifying and funny to realize that an entire week might pass with nothing to do but render couplets like "This is not anapple. This is anorange," and that, far worse, we might even be grateful for such a diversion.

In the early days of the intifada, there were lots of curfews. The plug would be pulled, and everything would suddenly and without warning be immersed in complete darkness. People accustomed to an unlimited supply of electricity cannot fully imagine how black a black night can be. The stars above seemed preternaturally bright and, strangely, very close to earth, as though you might reach up and grab one, as in a child's book. Sounds were at once louder and more nuanced, as though your ears had grown larger by necessity. A pin dropping could be heard half a mile away. There would be long periods of silence, and then the white owl of the neighborhood would make its nightly swoop across the garden under the white moon, a baby would cry, a donkey would bray; and then you might hear the gut-wrenching boom of tear-gas grenades, the roar of tanks and gravel throwers, amid shouts and screams of "Allahu akbar!" of guys rushing into battle with rocks in one hand and onions (the local antidote for teargas) in the other. People had heard the pops and whizzes of IDF bullets so often they could frequently distinguish the kind of gun that had fired them. "Ah," they would say, "did you hear that one? That, my friend, is an Uzi." Flares would light up the sky like Fourth of July fireworks.

When things quieted down, we would settle around a lone candle in the middle of the innermost room of the house and listen to Radio Monte Carlo, or Um-Kulthum, or odes to Molotovs sung by local bands turned up loud enough to drown out the continuous invocations of "O Lord! O Lord!" of

Yusuf's grandmother, who reigned over the house from a perch of pillows and old blankets. Sitti, the grandmother, had been married at the age of twelve and shortly thereafter, had become blind in both eyes. She was a midwife. Once, she was proud to say, even a Jewish woman had traveled from afar to see her— a fact she presented as the greatest proof of her powers and in need of no elaboration. Hamas, even in its glory days, would never be able to put an end to such exchanges, which witnessed to a parallel history and anti-epic force, and drew their strength from the old folk religions of the region and the bonds of women for whom the desire for a child completely overpassed creed.

Like his grandmother, Yusuf was also blind, having lost all vision in his right eye and most in his left at the hands of a local doctor, and he would often request that we read aloud to him from whatever was on hand—T. S. Eliot, Rilke, entries from Cowie and Mackin's *Oxford Dictionary of Current Idiomatic English* (such as "scratch out," as in, "Be careful, Harry, she'll scratch your eyes out if you so much as glance at another woman"), Meyer's turn-of-the-century *History of the City of Gaza.*[1] Gaza, we soon discovered, had a long reputation for stone throwing. Alexander the Great was almost killed in Gaza by an anonymous stone. The Christian Fabri, who visited the Holy Land in 1483, records in his diary that the pilgrims always made sure that they arrived at Gaza around nightfall so as to avoid being stoned by "the little Muslim boys." A British railway official, according to an eyewitness of 1937, was killed by a stone in the Arab Rebellion of the 1930s when he "foolishly went out in his car to see the fun." In contrast, one British doctor escaped death four times by showing his "passport." He had "the presence of mind to remove some of his clothing and conclusively prove that he did not bear the mark of Abraham's flesh."

Sometimes, we'd work on improving our Arabic. Or Yusuf would give us a lesson in braille, and we'd close our eyes and pretend to be blind like him and with our fingers try to memorize the bumps and hollows of the strange, three-dimensional language. Or Im-'Abdullah, Yusuf's mother, would instruct us on how to crack and pickle olives or how to do cupping, a treatment she performed on the neighborhood women who flocked to her for help. Or we'd sit with the family, drinking freshly squeezed guava juice and watching reruns of *Knots Landing*, which were constantly interrupted by Egyptian public service announcements on the proper way to wash one's hands and the proper size limit for the modern Egyptian family. On such occasions, Yusuf's middle brother would provide additional entertainment by repeating with great delight and at every conceivable opportunity a phrase he'd found along with "Planet X" in the BBC course book—"the emancipation of women," the "c" of which he always purposefully mispronounced as "sh," as in "emanshipation." Other times, we'd lie beneath the swinging blue light bulb in the back room of the house, and watch the light play off the pea-green walls and the cream-yellow door, listening to the fan whirl round and round, or perch ourselves in an open window and watch the humongous rats, which everyone said the Israelis had brought in on trucks one night and released en masse across the Green Line. The rats, many the size of small dogs, would scurry around under the light of the moon, darting furtively from bush to bush in search of another victim that would have made a tasty *maqluba* (a dish of chicken, rice, and cauliflower).

With a crate of freshly picked Gaza oranges by our side, we could stay up half the night. "I will tell you a story about my childhood," Yusuf's older brother, whom we called "the Lion," would announce with great ceremony, "and then you must tell me a story about your childhood," and the night would begin. Yusuf, above all, loved telling stories—about Gaza, about the short time he'd studied music abroad, happy at last to have found a world as big as himself. When the Israelis had invaded the Strip in 1967, he had been only a child, but he still had vivid memories. Once, he said, he had wandered out to the street, where he saw small, round things rolling around in the dust. When he looked closer, he realized they were human eyes, staring up in unblinking witness.

Another time, we might be taught a lesson in subjugation. One of Yusuf's younger brothers had long been keen on showing us what it felt like to be handcuffed the way the Israelis did it, and so one hot afternoon up on the roof, after we'd all listened to Yusuf play the accordion in his pajamas for awhile, he took a cigarette wrapper and fashioned a band from it, crossed our hands under the knee, pulling the forefingers up at the top of the knee and wrapping them with the plastic Moebius Loop he'd just constructed. It was hard to believe what somebody could do with a Craven A wrapper. "The more you struggle," he warned, "the tighter it will get." Indeed, the device was remarkably efficient. "Sometimes," he said, as we vainly tried to escape, "they leave people like this for a whole day, sometimes a week, sometimes a month. Sometimes, they tie you up like this behind the back or even behind the head." And with that, he just walked away, leaving us there like doofuses. He seemed to derive great satisfaction from this little demo.

Long expanses of time could go by like this, and then Something would happen. There was no pattern to these events—revelation constituted their sole aim. Yusuf was fond of calling them "adventures," but they often seemed more like midnight ambushes. Sleepy-eyed and dazed, we might be taken across the street and set down on an old sofa to watch a video. We might be served birthday cake with preternaturally green icing. The video might feature ominous-looking men brandishing knives and guns, preparing for an operation, apparently murder, and then we would look around and suddenly notice that the guys sitting next to us on the sofa looked an awful lot like the ones on the television screen—in fact, by God, they *were* the same guys.

We might be requested to donate some books to a friend's library, and absentmindedly throw some old books we had in Jerusalem in some boxes and cart them down to Gaza—a primer on cryogenics, collections of Talmudic laws on perforated flowerpots, the folktales of southern Georgia, Kahane's *Never Again*, whatever, we didn't really think about it much at the time—and several

years down the road, after collaborators had begun to be killed in large numbers, we might discover *A History of Torture* in the home of someone whose
business, it turned out, was taking care of "the fallen ones," a category that by
then included not only gun-toting Palestinian traitors who collaborated with
the IDF, but also political nonconformists, backsliders in the faith, drug dealers, heretics, women of questionable repute, and social misfits of all colors,
who were killed so often that by the end of the intifada, their number equaled
that of Palestinians killed by the IDF. They were often tortured beforehand,
their bodies displayed on the streets, chained to poles or just dumped there.

Or we might be photographed, and then years later find our picture in a
book along with masked men and intifada Rambos. We might be whisked away
to a house, where we would sit for hours drinking cups of hot tea with mint and
then a man would enter the room, and the story would begin. The man would
begin to talk, as if revealing a secret, or making a confession; a crowd would
gather, and sooner or later, we ourselves would become the objects of interrogation. Who could be trusted? It was always but a short step from foreign body
to foreign agent.

Witness, folk doctor (supplier of Ben-Gay, Japanese oils, tiger balm, stomach sedatives), protector, advocate, provocateur, spy, judge, cover, American,
alien, devil's advocate, monster, recording angel, fate-as-observer—the roles
and the game were unknown. We soon found ourselves implicated in stories
within stories within stories, the meaning and ramifications of which we remained ignorant to the very end. It was impossible for anyone to believe that
someone could end up in Gaza by chance or sheer curiosity. The notion of
accident simply did not exist in a world where every rock and tree had long ago
accrued massive meaning and virtual textuality.

5. The Disciple (HAHAHA)

It was Yusuf who set up the meeting for us. Not much was then known about
Ahmad Yasin, founder and "spiritual leader" of Hamas, but he had a reputation
in Gaza for asceticism. He owned nothing, people said, and slept on the floor.
Some believed he possessed preternatural powers.

On the day of the interview, we hired a "special," as Gazans call a taxi with
a single destination, and soon found ourselves lost in the labyrinth of pink and
green shacks of the refugee camp of Jorat-Askalan, some of which had been
constructed so that their cinderblock components spelled out *Allah* in six-foot-
tall letters. The driver finally stopped a passerby on the street to ask for the
whereabouts of the sheikh. The man happened to be a member of the Islamic
Jihad, a rival faction renowned for military operations that were commonly
credited with having ignited the intifada. Upon hearing that we were about to

interview Yasin, he proffered an Imperial cigarette and an introduction to Fathi ash-Shaqaqi, the leader of the Jihad.

"It burns Imperialism," he remarked, as we drove away, referring to the cigarette—presumably, the Jihad as well.

We finally arrived at the sheikh's modest home, where a group of old men sat in a circle of plastic chairs, waiting their turn for an audience. Gaggles of solemn, bearded young men passed in and out of dun-colored cinder boxes set in the rear of the compound.

No one raised a rock or even an eyebrow at our arrival. One of the young men greeted us with little ceremony and plunked us down among the old men, who glared at us a few moments before going back to their prayer beads. We sat so long that we wondered if we'd been forgotten—or purposefully ignored. Suddenly, two of the grim young men appeared from nowhere, pushing a wheelchair containing a little bundle wrapped in blankets—the sheikh. The chair bogged down in the deep sand. The sheikh tottered and swayed.

Since a childhood accident, the sheikh had been confined to a wheelchair. "His entire body is in constant spasm," Mahmud az-Zahar, a big wheel in Hamas, had told us weeks before. "Nothing works but the brain and the genital system. But he thinks very, very clearly." He paused. "And he has very many children," he said smilingly, invoking images of a randy Middle Eastern Strangelove.

In the flesh, the sheikh looked more like a crippled gnome. His tiny body was hidden by the blankets except for his outsized hands, which flapped listlessly on the coverlets. Someone had put little zip-up carpet slippers on his feet. The face didn't match the body. It was not unhandsome, and, except for the mouth, which was fixed in a friendly dolphin smile, seemed relatively unaffected by the accident. He had sharp blue eyes and strongly vertical teeth of Ultra-Brite quality, which were countered by a soft and fluffy beard, gnomelike, and skin as fresh and unwrinkled as a newborn babe's. It was a face both cruel and faerie at once.

The arrival of their sheikh caused the old men in the chairs to rise. "*As-salamu alaikum*," they said. Peace be upon you.

"*Wa alaikum as-salam*," the sheikh squeaked back in a voice like a Talking Barbie.

We wondered if these were the fabled communists who came seeking the sheikh's boon. By the cut of their suits, they seemed more like well-fed merchants. After the initial greetings, the sheikh spoke very little. The fat old men addressed the grim young men, and the grim young men whispered to the sheikh, who would mumble or squeak a little in response. This went on for some time until one of the grim young men picked up the sheikh in his chair and carted him off.

A short while later, one of the bearded young men came out to tell us that the sheikh would receive us, but where was our translator? The young man seemed rather put out. "Why have you come without a translator? The sheikh does not speak English." One of the fat old men rematerialized, introducing himself as Ibrahim. The translator would not arrive until the afternoon. Would we like to come home with him and have lunch?

The sheikh may have been a simple man, but Ibrahim was not. Not for him the thin beard and long robe of the Islamist. He wore a three-piece brown suit that he filled out nicely, plenty of gold on his fingers. His car was a low-slung, 1970s-vintage Oldsmobile, black and sleek as a killer whale. He pulled out a pack of Kents, an expensive brand in the Strip. We cruised out of the camp in smooth American luxury.

Ibrahim's home was a three-story affair set in a nice section of Gaza with paved streets and graffiti-less walls. Ibrahim escorted us upstairs to his front porch and sat us down in rattan chairs interwoven with strips of red, white, black, and green plastic, forming the forbidden motley of the Palestinian flag.

"Welcome," he said, offering us anise-flavored cookies and tea so hot and sweet it made your teeth ache. "Make yourselves at home," he said, and then disappeared.

He returned about twenty minutes later. "How is everything?" he inquired. "Are you comfortable?" He smiled and sat down. We smiled, and soon were being grilled.

It went like this:

"There is one question I'd like to ask you."

"Yes."

"Tell me, this interview you are doing, will it be published in the Israelienne press?"

"We're not exactly journalists. We're collecting material for a longer work. Maybe a book on the role of religious movements in the intifada."

"I see. . . . You said you both met with Dr. az-Zahar last week?"

"Yes. He said we should become Muslims."

Hahaha. "And this project, which government is funding it—the American or the Israelienne?"

"Neither. We wish it were funded. It's out of our own pockets."

"Really? But perhaps you have some help from some other organizations? Maybe from a Jewish organization?"

"O no, we're strictly nonpartisan."

"Christian?"

"My father is a minister."

"And you?"

Umm . . .

"Not that it matters."

"Of course not."

Hahaha.

"Really, believe me. It does not matter if you are Jews, Christians, or Muslims. Once you come to my home, you are my guests. I am obliged to treat you well. It is from Islam. Our Prophet Muhammad, God bless Him and grant Him salvation, compels us to treat our guests well. . . . So you are not Jews? . . . You are sure? . . . Well, never mind. As I said, it does not matter anyway."

If Ibrahim's job had been to find out if we were spies, he could not have chosen a more counterproductive tack. But that was not his job. He simply wanted to have a little fun with us, as did the countless strangers who would stop you on a street corner or a deserted hilltop and barely before saying hello, assault you with questions like "Do you love Yasir Arafat?" or "What do you think of Palestine?" or "Is it true that the Jewish control all of the American Congress?" One man upon hearing that we wanted to write about Gaza, inquired, "Do you want to write, or do you want to believe?" as if the two were mutually exclusive projects. Perhaps they were.

Ibrahim's questions remained. Who were we? Why were we there, and why did we linger? What did we want?

We ourselves could no longer say.

6. A Minor Jihad

It did not take long for Ibrahim to announce his verdict—innocent until proven guilty—for immediately after the interrogation, he set us down on a crushed red velvet sofa with one of his sons to watch a video, a Soviet-bloc production filmed in Jebalya, one of the poorest and most desperate of the refugee camps in Gaza. Another one of Ibrahim's sons was in many of the scenes, chucking rocks at Israeli soldiers about his own age, his face masked by a keffiyah.

"Look," Ibrahim cried as proud as any father showing off his son's barmitzva video, "See him there?! See him!"

After the vicarious intifada, Ibrahim announced that we would have lunch. He led us back outside and into the killer whale. The son hopped into his own little Mitsubishi, and we were off again. "I thought that we might eat lunch in my other house . . . with my other family," he said, looking at us to see if his statement was having the desired effect. We did not disappoint him. Yes, it does take a lot of money he told us, but business was good.

"What sort of business?" we asked.

"Jewelry and gold."

"Jewelry and gold are good business in the Gaza Strip during the intifada?"

"Well, really most of my business is in the Gulf and Europe."

The second house turned out to be much bigger than the first, but it was in a poorer neighborhood on the outskirts of Shatti Camp on the Gaza seaboard. We were taken to the roof, where to the south you could see the Ansar military prison and beyond that a sandy coast curving toward Egypt. To the north, the smokestack of the Ashkelon power plant stood like an exclamation mark above the vanished homes to which no one in Gaza would ever return. We sat under an awning of palm fronds and sipped cola, while a little boy in a turquoise sweatshirt reading SELF-CONTROL ran round and round us with a black plastic pistol, bang bang.

After lunch, Ibrahim dropped us back at the sheikh's house, and someone led us into a bare room, where men were lounging against the wall. After a while, a female arm holding a tray of tall glasses poked itself through the half-closed door. The men propped themselves up, and the tray was taken by a disciple. The female arm disappeared as quickly as it had appeared. Two glasses of warm goat's milk, the favorite afternoon pick-me-up of the sheikh, were set down before him like a votive offering. The sheikh sipped and sucked the milk like a famished babe.

A disciple maneuvered him out of his wheelchair and laid him on the floor, which was of poured concrete softened slightly by a thin mat. A photograph of a miracle hung above his head—a split watermelon in which God had signed his own name in the pulpy red flesh.

Yasin spoke good English, but had called for a translator. The young man was a disciple of a different order than Ibrahim. He was tall and mannered, watched his words. He was one of the many young men in the Strip who saw Islam as his way up in the world.

It was the translator rather than the sheikh who answered most of our questions. It was as though his mouth were somehow magically connected to the brain of the sheikh—a ventriloquist and his puppet. Even when Yasin said nothing at all, well-rehearsed formulae spilled out of the translator. At times, he would catch himself, eye the sheikh for approval, and then proceed, or the sheikh would interject with a little apothegm like "God only knows," or "A man changes every day."

It was through the voice of the translator that the sheikh said that he would accept one state for Muslims, Christians, and Jews, as long as that meant not giving up any part of Palestine. No Muslim could ever give up any part of Palestine, he said, and any division of the hallowed land was acceptable only as a tentative solution. His potentially reconciliatory remarks were further countered by impolitic statements about the selfish Jews who loved themselves and wanted to live all alone, and considered themselves a people chosen by God and everybody else a slave, and stern scriptures like "So fight on the path of God till they are killed and you are killed"—an unmistakable call for jihad.

For Yasin, jihad was a "fard 'ain," a duty incumbent upon each Muslim. This was the standard understanding among the Muslim Brothers (the parent organization of Hamas) even though, traditionally, jihad has not been seen as a fard 'ain, but rather as a "fard kifaya," a duty understood as being fulfilled as long as some members of the *umma*, the Muslim community, are pursuing it. Some of the Brothers' more radical rivals go so far as to call jihad "the forgotten precept," thereby sanctifying it as a "sixth pillar" of Islam.

Mahmud az-Zahar, then Hamas spokesman, had earlier elaborated for us the difference between "the minor jihad" and "the major jihad." The major jihad, he'd explained, involves strengthening one's will and self-management as "a true Muslim," whereas the minor jihad involves the defense of land, money, or honor[2]—a distinction dismissed entirely by 'Abdullah 'Azzam in *Ilhaq bil-qawafila* (Join the Caravan), where he argues that jihad means "combat with weapons" and only combat with weapons:

8. The word *jihad*, when mentioned on its own, means only combat with weapons, as was mentioned by ibn Rushd, and upon this the four imams have agreed.

9. The implication of "fi sabil Allah" (on the path of Allah) is jihad, as ibn Hajar has said.

10. The saying, "We have returned from the lesser jihad (battle) to the greater jihad (jihad of the soul)," which people quote on the basis that it is a *hadith* [an early Islamic "Tradition of the Prophet"], is, in fact, a false, fabricated hadith that has no basis. It is only a saying of Ibrahim ibn Abi 'Abala, one of the successors, and it contradicts textual evidence and reality.[3]

Jihad in the sense of combat with weapons, all Islamists seemed to concur, was the answer to the "Zionist Nazi attack" of the Jews, and not "that which is called a 'peace solution' and 'international conferences,'" to quote again from the movement's covenant. The PLO is thus wasting its time, involved in "the folly of follies." Indeed, international conferences are "only ways of setting the infidels in the land of the Muslims as arbitrators; and when did the infidels do justice to the believers?" for "the Jews and Christians will not be satisfied until you follow their religion"—the latter part, a quotation from the *sura*, or Qur'anic chapter, entitled "The Cow" (2:120). "The Palestinian people," the covenant asserts, "are wiser than to be so manipulated about their future and their rights and self-determination as in the wise hadith: 'The people of ash-Sham [lit., "north," the name traditionally applied to the area now encompassing Syria, Jordan, Palestine/Israel, and Lebanon] are the scourge of Allah in His land, who take revenge for Him against whomsoever of His servants that He wishes. It is forbidden for hypocrites to take from the faithful except that they die with pain and suffering.'"

7. The Gharqad Tree

The sheikh spoke voce ipse only once during our meeting, and that was at the mention of a bizarre tree called the *Gharqad*, traditionally believed to speak in oracles and said to grow in the graveyards of Mecca. The tree makes an appearance in a section of Hamas' covenant devoted to showing that the movement is but the latest link in the long chain of jihad waged by the Brothers. Clenching their argument on the necessity of holy war, the anonymous authors of the text, which surely included Yasin, close with an eschatological prophecy attributed to Muhammad by the renowned collectors of hadith Bukhari and Muslim: "Hamas strives for the fulfillment of Allah's promise as the time grows long and the Prophet, Allah bless Him and grant Him salvation, said, 'The Hour will not come until the Muslims fight the Jews (and the Muslims will kill them), until the Jews hide behind the trees and rocks and the trees and rocks will say, "O Muslim, O Servant of Allah, Here are the Jews, Come and kill them!" except the Gharqad Tree because it is a tree of the Jews.'"

As "the Hour" approaches, Muslims and Jews, according to a related tradition, will be arrayed "east and west"—directions that, not surprisingly, were reinterpreted during the intifada as references to the east and west banks of the Jordan River, the river constituting both the natural and legal boundary separating Jordan's east bank from Israel's west. In a last determinative battle, the Forces of Light would finally prevail, and all of creation would turn against the Jews, even the land itself. Their only ally would be the Gharqad Tree.

Hearing the sheikh speak, one could imagine whole orchards of Gharqads, evenly spaced, each harboring within its thick and gnarly branches a fugitive Jew, like the bags of possessions that the Bedouins dangled from desert trees. Or perhaps there were only a very few of these trees, and their branches were weighed down to the ground by millions of people trying to climb upon them or just touch them, like the trees of the Golan where fat hyrax sat in huge numbers, burdening the branches till they swept the ground, or broke off.

"What is this tree?" we asked.

The sheikh advised us to ask the Jews about the tree. They kept them in their houses, he said. Before the Last Day, he said, the Man with One Eye, the Antichrist Liar, would come. He would tell people that he was a prophet, and spread scientific superstitions all around.

"Why is that?" we asked.

"I don't know," the sheikh said. "The Prophet told us this."

"Are we in the Last Days now?"

"You have nothing to fear," he said, "if you believe in God, the Angels, the Books, the Prophets, all of them . . . The Last Day as well."

For years thereafter, we would seek to find the mysterious tree, as if we ourselves had been infected by the bizarre literalism that Hamas was so adept at promulgating. Why did we actually have to see and touch the tree for ourselves? What did we want to believe or dispel, remember or repress? We persisted on this quest for years, asking everyone we met if they'd heard of the magic talking tree. At its mention, people would smile strange Mona Lisa smiles, and their eyes would widen as if we'd touched upon a fantastic secret, and we would be told with some excitation to go here or there, and we would find the tree.

Some said the Israelis planted the tree around their settlements in the West Bank and Gaza, thereby creating magic mandalas protecting them from attack; others said the tree was planted around important Jewish centers like the Israel Museum and the Knesset. Some said the tree grew outside Herod's Gate; others claimed that the tree was actually not a tree, but a bush that could be found outside Jerusalem's Jaffa Gate, one of several conjectured sites in Muslim eschatological belief where Jesus, his face dripping with pearls, will one day return to earth and slay the Dajjal, following a final battle between Muslims and unbelievers that, some believe, will take place directly below Jaffa Gate at Sultan's Pool—a spot sometimes referred to as the Field of Blood, because the level of gore, it is said, will reach the bridle of a horse. (One of the major figures in classical Islamic eschatology, the Dajjal is the Muslim variant of the Antichrist of Christian tradition. He is the great Deceiver, the One-Eyed Man, the commander of the great Jewish Army that at the end of time will march, seventy thousand strong, out of Isfahan, Iran. Even before the intifada, the figure of the Dajjal was equated by many Islamists with the Jewish Moshiach, the Messiah, as when the highly influential Pakistani Islamist Malauna Maududi claimed in the 1960s that "the stage has been set for the emergence of the Dajjal who, as was foretold by the Holy Prophet (PBUH), will rise as a 'Promised Messiah' of the Jews."[4] By the late intifada, the equation was commonplace in the West Bank and Gaza. When the Lubavitcher Hasidim in the early 1990s began to refer to Rabbi Menachem Mendel Schneerson as the Messiah, the claim had considerable effect on Palestinian Islamists. Some actually began to include Schneerson on their list of False Prophets, referring to him as "the Antichrist Liar.")

Others ascribed a purely symbolic meaning to the Gharqad Tree. According to one allegory popular during the intifada, the Gharqad Tree represents "the collaborator who doesn't want to say 'Here is a Jew!'" to quote Sheikh Isma'il Jamal, the imam of Jericho's main mosque and a Fatah supporter. Indeed, the Gharqad Tree symbolized all the forces of the world believed to conspire with the Jews against the Muslims.

If you tried to find reference to the obscure tree in the Qur'an, you would come up with nothing. It is simply not mentioned. In the hadith, there are a few references to the tree. One of them appears in a story in which Muhammad and his Companions are discussing predestination in a graveyard known as the "Valley of the Gharqad":

> We were in the company of the Prophet in a funeral procession at Baqi al-Gharqad. The Prophet came to us and sat down, and we sat around him. He had a small stick in his hand, and he bent his head and started scraping the ground with it. He then said, "There is none of you, not a created soul, but has a place written for him in Paradise or in Hellfire."

The association between the Gharqad Tree and graveyards is an old one. Most classical sources assert that the Gharqad Tree grew in profusion—and was harvested—in the graveyard of Medina, which was known as "the place of the Gharqad."

The classical authors suggest that the Gharqad is a member of the Osage family, or perhaps the spiny Acacia. Like the Gharqad, the Acacia tree is liberally endowed with thorns and is used by the Bedouin to this day as an organic safe for their belongings, which they hang in its branches. Indeed, the term *gharqad* once signified a protective hedge of spiny branches and was used to demarcate plots of land in Palestine. Whatever its species, most interpreters agree that the Gharqad Tree is simultaneously useless and dangerous. It provides no shade. Its thorns are vindictively poisonous. The fearless few who attempt to remove its leaves (for the purpose of enhancing the effects of henna) are afflicted with pustular wounds that heal only very slowly. According to some, the tree yields no fruit at all. According to others, it produces a yellow-colored fruit that is hollow and inedible. With the revival of the tradition of the Gharqad as "the tree of the Jews" during the intifada, one can see that the sinister characteristics attributed to the tree increasingly began to function in Islamist thought as a pseudo-natural analog of the Jews themselves.

The Gharqad Tree has become such a powerful trope in the Muslim-Jewish and Palestinian-Israeli struggle over Jerusalem and "the Holy Land" that Islamists around the globe now commonly refer to the tree exclusively in terms of the Jews of Jerusalem and Palestine. Thus, the Pakistani Islamist Amin Zafrullah Khan, in a book review disseminated on the website of the Muslim Student Association in 1996, quotes the hadith favorably, specifying for the sake of his readers that the Gharqad is "a species of thorny tree still preferred by the Jews in Palestine." Another example can be found in a communiqué issued that same year by the American Islamic Group to explain a grenade attack on an Egyptian hotel carried out by the Jam'iyat al-Islamiya. "NOTE," the document reads, "the Gharqad is a thorny plant that grows in Jerusalem."

The tree has, notably, also become well known among Israeli Jews, especially Orthodox nationalists, who include the hadith in their high school curriculum—a move that many Palestinian Islamists interpret as evidence that the Jews innately recognize the truth of the Islamic traditions foretelling their demise. For both Israelis and Palestinians, the spiny Gharqad has gone from an obscure reference in a little-known hadith to a major player in the battle for Jerusalem and the Holy Land—indeed, the fate of the world.

Many years after our interview with Yasin, we found the tree—the real, live thing. We were visiting a Hamas sheikh who had invited us home to discuss some Islamic eschatological traditions we'd earlier brought up at a roundtable at the Islamic University of Gaza. We drove to the sheikh's house at the appointed hour with another sheikh whom we'd also met at the university and a guy named Dieb who had been assigned to take us there. The younger sheikh was about our age, and on the way over, he suggested that we begin our discussion in the car before we arrived at the elder sheikh's house. We could ask him questions, he said, from the back seat, and he would be happy, more than happy, to answer them.

He was saying that Muhammad had the strength of forty men so that when he kissed one of his nine wives during Ramadan he could easily control himself when a little dog suddenly appeared in the middle of the road, and Dieb swerved so as to slightly miss him. "Why do you care about a dog?!" the sheikh exclaimed. "There's Bosnia! It's just a dog, so why?" Dieb was silent. "Because God made him," came a voice from the back, speaking on behalf of the poor creature that had just narrowly escaped the fate of becoming a pancake. We soon recognized it as one of our own. "Yes," the sheikh said from the front seat, perhaps thinking that he'd just made a major public relations error of some sort (you know those Americans and their crazy ideas about animals), "Prophet Muhammad, Allah bless Him and grant Him salvation, once told a man who brought water to a dog in his shoe that he would go to Heaven as a result. And once, he told a woman who did something bad to a cat that as a result she would go to Hell!"

And so, with no hard feelings, we arrived at the older sheikh's house, whereupon the older sheikh immediately announced that he had to go to the mosque to pray, and hurried off. When he returned, we sat down and discussed the hadith of the Jassasa, the female spy of the Antichrist—a hadith that mentions various places in Palestine and is often cited as proof of the fact that the Antichrist, the Dajjal, is alive.

The story of the Jassasa brought to mind other eschatological traditions, such as the Gharqad Tree. We asked the sheikh why the covenant of Hamas was concerned with such things. "Because there are Jews," he replied, simply. The hadith on the Gharqad Tree had been put in the document, he said, "to prepare the people for the final battle." Most of the Jews, he said, would be killed in that battle, which would take place in Palestine. The Dajjal would witness it. Palestine would then become an Islamic country, and the only Jews who would survive would be those who left the country.

The Dajjal, he wanted to make clear, was alive now. As in the hadith of the Jassasa, he lived on an island in the sea. Perhaps in the Bermuda Triangle, someone in the room added. There would also be a second battle, the sheikh said. At that time, those Jews who had survived the first battle between the Muslims and the Jews would become "the army of the Dajjal," and they would fight the Muslims at Jaffa Gate in Jerusalem. And Jesus would kill the Dajjal at that gate, and after that, Jesus would say, "I am Muslim," and then all . . . or most of the people would become Muslim. The sheikh decided to reword what he'd just said. Jesus, he said, would kill the Dajjal, and people would say, "Our god is dead," and then they would follow Jesus the Muslim (given that God cannot die). Even the Jews. Everywhere there are Jews, said the sheikh, there is *fasad*, corruption. But no one knows whether the Dajjal is Jewish or not. What is known is that seventy thousand Jews from Isfahan in Iran will be his followers. Maybe, said the sheikh, Jews will come from Russia, America, and the Arab countries and will go to Isfahan. Whatever. The Dajjal was definitely human and was alive. The Jassasa, the hairy spy of the Antichrist, could see him.

The two sheikhs decided to do their prayers. Dieb prayed too. They prayed a few inches away from us. The younger sheikh made a great show of it all, chanting loudly. Dieb had almost completed his prayers when the older sheikh noticed a little speck of dirt just above his right ankle, and remarked on it. "Where? Where?" said Dieb, twisting and turning, trying to locate the offensive stain. "There . . . there," said the sheikh, pointing and wrinkling up his nose. Dieb said, O my goodness and such, and hurried to the bathroom, where you could hear him washing. He returned and began his prayers all over again.

In the meantime, a young man appeared out of nowhere. He eyed us suspiciously for awhile, finally breaking the ice by saying of the elder sheikh, "Sheikh Riqb is a terrorist." He laughed. In the terrific silence that ensued, Sheikh Riqb shot him a withering look before suggesting lunch, which soon appeared as though magically.

The hot bread, hummus, and olives were good, but the sheikh made it very clear that he was offering us this repast only because it was an obligation imposed upon him by his faith (the Prophet, he noted, had said to treat one's guests kindly)—a burst of honesty that, we must admit, put a damper on our appetite.

The conversation turned somehow to Christianity, one of Sheikh Riqb's "specialties." (Sufism, another deviation, was the specialty of the younger sheikh.) Sheikh Riqb actually had a copy of the Gospels in his house. He also possessed a thousand-year-old book entitled *Between Christian and Muslim*. He had heard that there were actually three hundred—indeed, perhaps three thousand—books that had been excluded from the Gospels. He spoke excitedly of *The Book of Barnabas*. No one had actually seen this book, he said, much less read it. It had been smuggled out of, stolen from, the Vatican, which had suppressed it because it prophesied the coming of Muhammad.

After lunch, the sheikh took us out into his backyard, where it just so happened he had a Gharqad Tree, the very thing. He proudly led us to it. The tree was massive and thorny, a fact that the sheikh ignored so keen was he to offer us a souvenir of our visit with him. He bravely tore off two branches of the tree and gave them to us, wrinkling his nose with distaste, and saying, "If a Jew comes here, I will kill him."

8. The Evil Incident

In the popular legends that float around the Bank and Strip, much is made of Yasin's paralysis. Indeed, the accident is commonly viewed as the source of his power. Truly great men, as they say, always bear the signs of great affliction, and these signs are consonant with and proportionate to the particular form of power possessed. Thus, great poets are always preferably blind, as are great singers and great orators, but whatever their disability, it should be sensual in nature. Great military leaders preferably walk with a limp or wear an eye patch, but whatever their disability, it should have been gained during the course of war. Great religious leaders can suffer almost any handicap, provided that it bears witness to the idea of the triumph of spirit.

There are countless versions of how the sheikh came to be confined to a wheelchair, but perhaps the most reliable account appears in a 1991 biography written by 'Atif Ibrahim 'Adwan,[5] a professor of political science at the Islamic University of Gaza, with whom Yasin himself seems to have cooperated. When Yasin was a boy, according to 'Adwan, he and his friends liked to hold religious sports contests on the beach of Gaza. They would stand on their hands and see who could stay upside down the longest. One day, Yasin had sustained the contortionist position for the entirety of an hour when he suddenly fell to the ground. When his friends tried to stand him up, they found that his body had become completely rigid. They frantically massaged his limbs with olive oil and water to no avail, and finally carted him off to a foreign aid agency, which was unable to do anything for him. "The evil incident," as 'Adwan calls the fateful fall, would leave Yasin paralyzed for the rest of his life, and would eventually seal his political power with an aura of stigmatic charisma.

The para-normalcy of the accident is highlighted in reverse by the sheikh's felicitous if not auspicious birth in 1936. Yasin's mother, 'Adwan tells us, received a vision in her pregnant sleep in which she was informed that Allah would give her a great son, and that his name should be Ahmad, meaning "most laudable." Despite the fact that Yasin's father was not fond of "Ahmad" and wanted to name the baby something else, the mother insisted on this name, and it was the name the child was given. The mother suffered great pain during labor, and is said to have hidden under the stairs, where she muffled her cries so well that no one besides the father knew that she had given birth.

Yasin's birth was taken as a sign not only because of the mother's vision and the newborn's glowing health, but also because of the more elementary fact of his sex. Yasin's father had married four women in succession with the express purpose of procuring sons. His first wife, who had previously been the wife of his eldest brother, unfortunately produced only a daughter, so, according to 'Adwan, Yasin's father exchanged her for another man's wife. This woman was Yasin's mother.

Yasin's father died before Yasin reached his third birthday, and the eldest male of the family subsequently became head of the house. The family is said to have been well-off, and life was good until the Arab-Israeli war of 1948 broke out. Prompted by the Egyptian Army, the family left behind ninety dunams of land in and around the village of al-Jura, planted with fruit trees and vineyards. They fled a few kilometers south to Gaza, and like so many others, ended up in one of the refugee camps established by the United Nations.

Yasin was then only twelve years old, but in the tradition of the lives of the saints, he already spoke like a judge and holy man, even when conversing with his own mother, as in the following dialogue found in Ahmad Ziad Ghanima's comic-book hagiography for children, *Ahmad Yasin, Sheikh of Palestine* (no place or date of publication listed):

> "Why are we leaving our house, O my mother?"
> "Because, O Ahmad, when the criminal Jews arrive at our village, they will kill us."
> "Where are our brothers? Why don't they rise up to defend us?"
> "They have forsaken us, May Allah forgive them, except for a small portion of them who are resisting the Jews with courage."

The boy then launches into a small sermon indistinguishable from those he would later deliver as a sheikh: "On the Day of Resurrection, Allah will call them to account for their negligence, and they will be forsaken in the time of our victory, and Allah will compensate the sincere holy fighters of Islam with the greatest of compensations, according to what they have given out of sacrifice and heroism."

In school as well, the boy was known for his zeal for jihad and self-sacrifice. He often outdid his teachers in enthusiasm, and according to one piece of apocrypha, he foretold the day when the Muslims would sell everything they owned in order to buy weapons to wage jihad against the Jews, thus echoing the famed sheikh 'Izz ad-Din al-Qassam, who had sold all of his belongings to buy himself a rifle.

After graduating from the Palestine Secondary School in Gaza, Yasin sought employment as a schoolteacher. He was a religious man, and because all the schools supported by the United Nations Relief and Works Agency were controlled by what 'Adwan calls "Communists," he ended up teaching in a government school, whose administrator, it so happened, had a son who was crippled. Impressed by Yasin, the administrator recommended to his absentee superiors that the young man be hired, omitting from the requisite papers the fact that he was crippled.

Yasin soon gained distinction in his new post not only as a teacher but also as a religious guide. He often took his students to the mosque, where he read the Qur'an to them, expounded on the hadith and showed them how to pray and do their ablutions. He made them learn by heart the Fatiha, the opening chapter of the Qur'an, as well as the *shahada*, the witness of faith. In class, it is said, he never missed an opportunity to call his students to Islam and exhort them to jihad. In addition, according to Ghanima, he urged them "to instill the spirit of jihad in [their] relatives in preparation for the conclusive battle between Islam and the Jews, because the battle to expel the Jews will take place between the faithful servants of Allah and the cowardly Jews."

These extracurricular activities were met with some parental resistance. Providing his readers with yet another lesson on the perfidious nature of Palestinian secularists, 'Adwan recounts for his readers the story of a high-ranking Palestinian officer working for the Egyptian military government in Gaza who became absolutely furious at Yasin because he encouraged his son to frequent the mosque in defiance of his wishes, and "in defiance of the customs of his society." The officer lodged a complaint with the headmaster of the school, but Yasin remained at his post, gaining ever-increasing notoriety.

Yasin's successful recruitment of youth was considered no small matter in Gaza, where the majority of the population is under the age of fourteen. The Muslim Brothers took note and elected him to the inner circle of the Brotherhood, where he replaced Isma'il al-Khalidi, the leader of the Gaza Strip. Yasin took on his new task with the same enthusiasm and perseverance that had marked him since he was a boy. He tirelessly toured the mosques of the Strip, speaking to small groups of young men, and at the end of every meeting, it is said, he succeeded in leaving behind a new leader for the movement. According to a connect-the-dots children's book entitled *Who Is He?* featuring mini-biographies of famous Muslim personalities, including the American boxer Muhammad 'Ali, it was at this critical moment that Yasin expanded his domain of influence. He began to preach in the mosques, "warning people about the consequences of the occupation and spurring them on to jihad."

When it came time for him to take a wife, Yasin delegated his elder brother to arrange the marriage. Along with Yasin's mother, the brother selected the daughter of a near relation, but Yasin refused the match. He desired another and insisted upon having her for his wife. The girl's father hemmed and hawed, and eventually offered his elder daughter instead. Although it is said that the elder daughter was more beautiful and more intelligent than her younger sister, Yasin insisted on his first choice. They were married and set up house in Shati' Refugee Camp. The years that followed were tragic. Child after child was born to them only to die shortly after birth. "The sheikh was blessed by his wife with a young man who was named but died," 'Adwan tells us, "and then she blessed him with another, and they named him in honor of the preceding brother, but he too died, and then she blessed him with a girl, and she remained alive, and was married in 1978. After that, she blessed him with his son Muhammad, who was nicknamed Abu-Muhammad, and two more sons followed who were named 'Abd al-Hamid and 'Abd al-Ghani. She also blessed him with seven daughters, most of whom died."

9. The Brotherhood

Founded in Egypt by Hasan al-Banna in 1928, the Muslim Brotherhood could trace its activism in Palestine back to 1936, the year of Yasin's birth and the year in which a major revolt had broken out against the Jews and the British. The revolt was unsuccessful in military terms, but it laid the foundation for all future uprisings, including the intifada. Some forty years after its conclusion, Yasin would choose to name the military wing of Hamas after 'Izz ad-Din al-Qassam, a Syrian Arab who had preached fiery jihad and organized bands of guerillas in the Haifa hills. Al-Qassam had been killed by the British in 1935, almost half a year before the outbreak of the revolt, but in popular memory, he had led it.[6]

In the years following the 1936–39 revolt, Egyptian brothers recruited and trained fighters for the Palestinian cause, and in 1948, a number of them volunteered to fight against the nascent state of Israel even before the Arab armies had declared war. The movement gained sympathizers, particularly in the Gaza Strip, where many of the Egyptian volunteers had fought. At the close of the war, some stayed in the region, which remained in Egyptian hands. The appeal of the Brothers was magnified by popular revulsion against the corrupt and self-serving regime of the Egyptian King Farouk, who was commonly held responsible for *an-nakba*, "the disaster"—a reference to the Arab defeat.

Despite its long history in Palestine, the Muslim Brothers did not truly begin to reap the fruits of its labor until the overwhelming victory of the Israeli army in the '67 War. Pan-Arab nationalism had long ruled in the West Bank and Gaza Strip, as in the Arab world as a whole, but with the '67 defeat, the nationalists fell from grace, quite literally overnight. The enormity of the defeat was almost impossible to comprehend. Many read in it a divine judgment on the aggressively secular Arab leadership; some even deemed it a just reward for the Jews, who were perceived as faithful and pious, if misguided.

The Brotherhood had long argued that a successful jihad against the Jews was possible only after the "House of Islam" had been adequately prepared. Casting itself as "the Islamic alternative" to the nationalist parties, the organization, accordingly, began to erect an impressive infrastructure of mosques, schools, libraries, and clubs. The heart of this infrastructure was the Islamic Center, which Yasin founded in Gaza City in 1973 as a front organization for the Brotherhood. The center comprised not only a mosque but also a clinic, a training school for nurses, and a sports club for youth. The same year that Yasin founded the center, another Israeli-Arab war broke out when Egypt led a surprise attack on Israel. Anwar Sadat code-named the attack "Badr," a reference to the decisive Muslim defeat of the Meccans in the seventh century, which was commonly seen as a miraculous event. It was a sign of the growing religiosity in the region that many attributed the Arab victories in the war to Islamic faith. The Palestine Liberation Organization began to entertain the idea of a political rather than military solution to the conflict, and the idea of a Palestinian state alongside Israel soon coexisted precariously with the old policy of the liberation of "all Palestine." The Brotherhood denounced these changes as capitulation and surrender.

Six years after Yasin founded the Islamic Center, the Israelis granted it a legal license, which allowed the Islamists a freedom denied their nationalist rivals. In 1978, the Islamic University of Gaza was founded, and it quickly became a major channel through which the Brotherhood could disseminate its doctrine among the youth of the Strip. Israeli acquiescence in the religious and political activities of the Brotherhood continued unabated throughout the late 1970s and 1980s.

It was more than just a blind-eye policy. Believing that a strengthened Brotherhood would weaken the PLO's influence in the territories, the Israelis were reported to have gone so far as to channel funding to mosques and various Islamic institutions in the territories, knowing full well that they were controlled by the Brotherhood. There were even rumors that they armed the Brothers against the nationalist groups. The nationalists thus claimed that the Brotherhood was little more than an Israeli puppet; the Brotherhood, in turn, argued that the nationalists were agents of a Jewish plot whose true aim was the extirpation of Islam.

The struggle between the two blocs reached a climax in the 1980s, when what had largely been a war of symbols suddenly turned very real. In 1980, thousands of Brothers took to the streets of Gaza ransacking and burning "leftist" institutions, including the offices of the Palestinian Red Crescent Society. The Israeli Army intervened only after a mob had surrounded the house of Dr. Haider 'Abd ash-Shafi, head of the Red Crescent Society and a well-known Communist and PLO supporter, and threatened to kill him. Between 1981 and 1986, violent clashes between the Islamists and the nationalists took place in all the major universities of the Bank and Strip. Scores were injured.

The intifada erupted in 1987. With the population mobilized and looking mainly to the PLO for direction, and younger members of the Islamic movement chafing at the bit, Yasin and the Brothers abandoned their former gradualism and entered the fray under the name "the Islamic Resistance Movement," or "Hamas," an acronym possessing the meaning of "zeal." The turnaround was remarkable. It did not take long before the intifada was being presented by members of the organization in terms of jihad.

Hamas gained support among Palestinians disenchanted with the nationalist parties, and battles between the two blocs soon raged. Claiming that it had initiated the uprising, the movement called for strike days and marches of its own, issued a comprehensive covenant rivaling that of the PLO, and began to produce massive amounts of propaganda, which soon made it a major voice on the Palestinian street. It had something to say about virtually everything, from blue jeans to jihad, from "the role of the Muslim woman in the liberation battle" to the distinctions of "Islamic art," from sexual conduct to spies, from Zionism to the reclamation of Palestine, from martyrs to the Last Days.

Most interesting was the way the movement harnessed ecstasy, directing it into very narrow channels of "proper" expression. It strictly proscribed the usual configurations of pleasure, and backed up its injunctions with the threat of force. Singing and dancing were prohibited, as were fancy clothes, Egyptian belly dancers, Tel Aviv bars, family picnics, and "shameless weddings." Proffered in their stead were Islamic study groups and sports teams, Islamic morality plays and Islamic anthems, sermons on jihad and martyrdom, Islamic demonstrations.

Under constant surveillance by Hamas-sponsored "morality squads," women soon abandoned their American jeans for long black skirts and capes and kept their heads and mouths covered. Those who disobeyed were suspected of collaboration with Israel and were punished and humiliated. Taxi drivers took down the shrines to "Marlene Monroe" and "Madona" that had occupied their back windows for years and peeled off the familiar stickers of Arab seductresses in blue veils (puckered lips clearly visible) from their dashboards. Various dens of iniquity were closed; others, burned to the ground—the party palaces on the Gaza beachfront and the so-called bars, liquor stores, and gambling halls (the words often indicating only that a storekeeper kept a bottle of arak under the counter) of Palestine Square, which now occupied the place where a couple of thousand years before had stood the famous and very naked Gazan Venus. In a few short years, the fundamentalization of Gaza was a fact, and it was Ahmad Yasin who oversaw the transformation.

10. Splits in the Brain

Despite its swift rise to power in the West Bank and Gaza Strip, Hamas did not become a topic of debate outside Palestine until the early 1990s when, seemingly all of a sudden, journalists and academics, consultants and political accountants, think-tank analysts and would-be players in the game of foreign policy began to ask, Who are these people and what do they want?

There were two basic schools of thought, both obstinately ideological. According to the first, Hamas was a pragmatic political organization that followed its interests like any other political organization. Toward that end, it built schools, libraries, orphanages, and infirmaries, and provided much-needed services to the inhabitants of the West Bank and Gaza—services that other Palestinian political bodies largely ignored or left to the UN and foreign charities. It prided itself on honest and straightforward dealings; and as a result, even a number of international organizations, it was said, often chose to channel funds to the Palestinians through it rather than through the PLO, renowned in equal measure for waste, nepotism, and corruption. The organization offered a daily self-maintenance system, a regimen both corporeal and spiritual, a "complete way of life," in the words of its proponents—indeed, the promise of personal salvation.

Many young men in the Bank and Strip, possessing neither money nor the requisite connections, saw in it a spiritual ladder to an often worldly success; indeed, the organization was chock-full of doctors, lawyers, scientists, and engineers, and it controlled many of the professional unions in the territories as well as a number of university student councils. Despite its violence and radical ideology, Hamas, according to advocates of the first school, was essentially a practical political group with the practical aim of gaining power. As such, it could be co-opted and domesticated. People should watch what it did, and largely ignore what it said.

Proponents of the second school, in contrast, argued that Hamas was antipolitical to the hilt, the very id of the Palestinian body politic. Through its various pedagogic institutions, it indoctrinated children with visceral hatred. It carried out vengeful executions, often without any real evidence. It fostered emergency modes of behavior and action, in which people easily lost sight of what they were doing. "The destruction of Israel," the movement never tired of saying, was "a Qur'anic inevitability," and one of its favorite means of speeding up the process was by blowing up busloads of men, women, and children, Jewish and Arab alike. From suicide bombings to Boschian fantasies of dismemberment to the End of the World, it reveled in the demonic. The movement's ideology, a sticky mix of blood and flowers, was encapsulated in bywords like "Our goal is liberation, and our policy is spilling blood" and "Our road to certain victory is religion and blood." Hamas, argued proponents of the second school, was, in essence, totalitarian, and its ideology should be taken seriously, that is, literally. Was it too much to see that people sometimes said what they meant and meant what they said? Indeed, weren't Hamas' actions proof of such a congruence? For most members of the second school, Hamas was completely outside the pale, and there could be no dealings with it. For a smaller subset, the movement was completely outside the pale, and accordingly, must be dealt with.

In actuality, of course, Hamas was neither an organized bunch of zealots willing to slit your throat at a moment's notice nor a benevolent society run by a knitting circle of kindly old men. Although the movement contained both zealots and do-gooders, the vast majority of Hamas' followers and sympathizers were neither. What the rank-and-file seemed to live and die for, in the end, was neither hospitals nor politics nor ideology nor religion nor the Apocalypse, but rather an ecstatic camaraderie in the face of death "on the path of Allah."

These ties were often cemented by less-than-benign factors, kindness and cruelty being allotted along the lines of "us" versus "them," as in the Hamas graffito, "Our answer to the Zionist practices must be/ 'Your prisons will not frighten us/ Our jihad is to victory or martyrdom/ Our dead are in Paradise, while your dead burn in Hell,'" a sentiment we often found reduced simply to "Our dead are in Paradise, while yours burn in Hell"—a message that manages to transpose the conflict onto an even higher terra sancta, suggesting on some level the wish for resolution, while on another the desire for the conflict to live on forever, unimpeded by the mere facticity of death. The slogan owes its origins to a hadith in which Omar bin al-Khattab, one of the early Muslims who became dissatisfied with the terms of a peace treaty that had been signed with the Bani Quraish, asked Muhammad, "Won't our people who have been killed in battle go to Paradise while theirs will go to Hell?" to which Muhammad answered, "Yes." "Why then," the man asked, "should we accept this humiliation?" and Muhammad answered, "I am only the messenger of Allah." The same theme is found in the Qur'anic sura "Repentance" (9:73), where we read, "O Prophet! Strive against unbelievers and the hypocrites! Be harsh with them. Their ultimate abode is hell, a hapless journey's end." Associated with the us-to-Paradise, them-to-Hell theme, and often coupled with it, is the "they-love-life, but we-love-death" theme, which is found throughout intifada media. Israelis, it is commonly asserted, are deathly afraid of death; Palestinians, in contrast, are said not only not to fear death, but to love it passionately.

All the seeming contradictions within and surrounding Hamas indicated perhaps not so much paradox as "splits in the brain," a phrase coined by Mary Khass, Gaza's most well-known feminist. She was describing an Israeli settler whom she'd once met, a scientist who believed that God sent spirits down to earth to help the Jews in battle (he claimed to have seen such a spirit with his very own eyes), but the phrase applied equally well to many of the followers of Hamas. Indeed, it seemed an apt description of lots of people involved with and interested in the Israeli-Palestinian conflict, some of whom were acutely aware of the perfidious splits of heart and mind from which they suffered, while others sutured them up and forgot all about them—and who was to say which of the two was the more dangerous? The very heart of the conflict was schizophrenia, and what made Hamas a primary locus of interest was its spectacular exaggerations of this fact. In these spectacles, people thought they saw something writ large, and that something had, most essentially, to do with the problem of Good and Evil, their capacity for transforming themselves into each other.

11. The Miracle Sheikh

On May 18, 1989, a few months after our interview with him, Yasin was arrested, along with 250 members of his organization—a move reportedly made at the behest of the United States, which had hoped to encourage PLO-affiliated groups to accept Israeli peace proposals. Two IDF soldiers had been kidnapped while hitchhiking and subsequently killed. Yasin was implicated and sentenced to fifteen years in jail.

It was there, in an Israeli prison, that the sheikh became larger than life, as if his very absence from the scene were the source of his transformation from juridical to charismatic authority. His vatic gifts became the means for his survival as a political power: He was everywhere and nowhere, heard but not seen—the perfect oracle. His words appeared and disappeared on the walls as if ghostwritten, as in the graffito, "In order to forbid evil, you must ask what is this evil worth?" and "Ahmad Yasin said: 'He who is not able to marry has no right to whoredom, and he who is not able to return the entirety of his land does not have the right to surrender an inch of it'"—an equation that held special significance for the thousands of young men in the territories unable to pay the huge dowries required for marriage.

While Arafat was called "the symbol," Yasin was touted with a certain one-upmanship as "the greatest symbol of the intifada." Testifying to his emblematic power were his many titles—"the throbbing heart of the intifada," "the sheikh of the intifada and its pride," "the warrior sheikh," "the professor," and "the jihad professor,"—many often combined into one message as in the following salutation, "Greetings to the Sheikh of the Intifada, the professor Ahmad Yasin Hamas/ A vow to Islam not to surrender for victory sprouts when watered by blood." As with saints of old, virtually no details are proffered that might distinguish him from his predecessors or contemporaries.

He was sometimes virtually identified with his organization, as in "Hamas Ahmad Yasin" or with Palestine, as in "Your boundaries are the river and the sea/ Theirs are all the prisons"—a message reminiscent of the popular intifada slogan "Palestine is ours from the river to the sea," which in the hands of the Islamists became "Palestine is Islamic from the river to the sea." Similarly, he was often linked with the holy sites of Jerusalem, his face sometimes superimposed on al-Aqsa Mosque. In October 1990, a street leading to the mosque was dubbed "Ahmad Yasin Street"; a perpendicular byway, "Hasan al-Banna Street," a reference to the Egyptian founder of the Muslim Brotherhood.

The two leaders were often coupled in Hamas media. In one poster in our collection, their portraits float against a fluorescent sunrise of hot pink, orange, and yellow. Between them sails a rendition of *safina al-khalas*, "the Ship of Salvation," a traditional design based on the story of Noah in the Qur'an. (Arab calligraphers often transmute verses from the holy scriptures or the *basmala*— the invocation "In the name of Allah, the Compassionate, the Merciful," used by pious Muslims to initiate any significant act—into the shape of the ship. For Palestinians, the figure possesses the additional meaning of *safina al-'auda* or "Ship of Return," a reference to their longing to return to homes lost to Israel in 1948. The symbol was brought to life in dramatic fashion in February 1988, when the PLO chartered the Sol Phryne—dubbed "the Return"—to carry 130 Palestinian deportees to Haifa. The ship was disabled by an explosion, reportedly set by the Israeli intelligence agency, the Mossad, as it sat in the harbor of Limassol, Cyprus.) The hull of the ship is composed of a Palestinian flag across which is written "the Muslim Brothers." Another Palestinian flag flies from the mast. The ship's five sails feature the five-part motto of Hamas and the Brothers—a pentad meant to recall "the Five Pillars of Islam" (bearing witness to the unity of God, prayer five times daily, almsgiving, fasting during the holy month of Ramadan, and pilgrimage to Mecca).

The sheikh was often depicted with the sun, or occasionally even conflated with it. In one poster we recorded in the West Bank town of 'Ajjul, he appears on an orange horizon like a rising sun. The metaphor is made clear in writing. Above his head appear lines attributed to him, "And I will light the earth with my faith," the letters of which are delineated as emanating rays. Casting shadows below him is the continuation, in partial rhyme, "Soon I will return from my imprisonment," while trees and bushes around him spell out *harakat al-muqawama al-Islamiya hamas*, "The Movement of the Islamic Resistance, Hamas."

In the vast majority of media devoted to him, the sheikh is drawn from the waist up, a face without a body, in sharp contrast to those who act in his name—the mujahidun, the holy fighters of Islam, who are often depicted as bodies without faces. Sometimes, the fighter is depicted with no head at all, as if doubly to stress that he is pure body, myth in action, embodied imperative. The paralysis of the sheikh only accentuates the fact that it is the young militants of his movement who constitute his body, the means by which the sacred commands[7] he espouses and represents are fulfilled.

The sheikh's handicap is not glossed over in these media, however—far from it. His paralysis is made into a symbol of strength, as in this poem, which appeared on a poster put out by the Battalions of 'Izz ad-Din al-Qassam: "You were born a giant/ and a giant you will remain./ You are free/ while the Arab world is paralyzed." The sheikh was often attributed with action-at-a-distance powers that managed to grow ever stronger with each new setback. One poster depicted the disembodied "giant" with his arm so supernaturally extended that he was able to stab an IDF soldier while sitting in his wheelchair, displaying the same disinterest with which, it is said, he had listened to his life sentence being read by an Israeli judge.

The veneration of Yasin might be seen as somewhat endearing were it not for the fact that his was the name that served as the imprimatur for virtually every operation and suicide bombing carried out by the Qassam Battalions. Demanding the release of the sheikh before or during an operation was virtually de rigueur during the intifada, a ritual not dared omitted. Once the magic name was uttered, almost anything could be done.

Consider, for instance, the following excerpt from a Hamas leaflet, which mentions the names of two suicide bombers, who, unbeknownst to us at the time, would later become a focus of this book:

> In the name of Allah, the Compassionate, the Merciful

> "So fight them so that Allah may punish them by your hands and put them to shame and help you against them and heal the hearts of the believers."[8]

> Pertaining to the Jewish man you seized and then killed

> Praise be to Allah, Lord of the Worlds, Prayers and peace on the Lord of the Messengers, and so:

1. Our people arrayed for war in Palestine:
We in your mujahid Battalions, "the Battalions of al-Qassam," write to you after Allah, Mighty and Majestic, granted us victory through the killing of three soldiers, two of them in Deir Balut and the other in Beitunia, in order to make plain the truth, and so that the Sons of Zion understand that there can be no life between us and them. For they are killers of the prophets and shedders of blood and occupiers of the land, while we are the soldiers of Allah who inflict calamitous torture upon them, Allah willing. Allah is with us, and we will never cease our operations:

At exactly 6:00 p.m., a group from your mujahid Battalions set out and gained entry into Jerusalem by means of a stolen car that had had its color and license plate changed. It then stopped near ar-Ram in the Jabah area, when a soldier requested a ride but then refused the lift, and in order to allay his suspicion, we said to him that we didn't want to go to his area. Then soldier 3, Yaron Chen, who was born 19/2/72, came running up and shouted, "Are you going to the Golan area?"
(And he mentioned the name of the location.)
    So we said to him, "*Ken.*"
    (Yes.)
    And after he got in, inasmuch as it had been determined that he would be kidnapped and exchanged for Sheikh Ahmad Yasin, May Allah protect him, we began raining blows upon him. But another soldier, in a car driven by a woman, witnessed this and opened fire on us, but Allah decreed that the car of the woman would halt perhaps due to her fear. After that we sprayed the soldier in the face with tear gas, which we had with us, so that he would not be able to summon help. He started trying to break the window, so we gave him two shots in his head from a 5 mm pistol. Afterwards, we strangled him until we were sure of his death.
    After half an hour, we decided to burn him like they burned the bodies of our two martyrs Mahir Abu-Surur and Muhammad al-Hindi, May Allah have mercy upon them. So we burnt the car while he was inside of it. And we managed, by the grace of Allah, to capture his weapon, which bore the serial number 413102 and was of the Galili type. And likewise his personal possessions and his identity card, the image of which is clearly reproduced in this leaflet, and everything else in his possession, which was only one shekel, May Allah's curse be upon him.

Since 1988, Hamas has killed or injured many hundreds of Israelis and has tortured and killed hundreds of Palestinians—collaborators and political opponents, women and misfits—and then gone on to talk about these acts in a way that can only be described as sadistic. Great satisfaction is sometimes taken in the knowledge that even if the victims aren't killed outright, they are at least maimed and mutilated for the rest of their lives. Yasin reigned over all these operations as unseen commander and guiding force. He was the indestructible father—the father returned to his rightful place of honor, every father rejected by his son as impotent and paralyzing—and in gratitude, the street boys of the intifada laid body after body before him, like so many mice brought in by the cat to please its master. In the ever-accumulating pile of corpses, the full extent of Yasin's power could be witnessed. The commander lived, his commandos died, and their deaths instantiated and sealed his power—a hard, cold exchange not much softened by the fact that Yasin himself was often treated as a "living martyr," an honorific awarded those who have vowed to sacrifice themselves.

(Even after death, the martyr is spoken of as alive, as in the Qur'anic verse, "And do not think that those who are killed on the path of Allah are dead; Nay, they are alive and with their Lord, well provided for." The most ubiquitous of tributes paid to martyrs of the intifada, nationalist and Islamist, the verse reproduces a speech Muhammad delivered in the early days of Islam to his followers, who had just suffered a serious military defeat after a number of victories, assuring them that the fallen were in heaven, and rebuking the *kuffar* or "unbelievers" who had taunted the followers with the claim that had they heeded their words and stayed at home, "they would not have died nor would they have been killed.")

That the "miracle sheikh" remained alive against all odds did not, however, ensure his power in a culture in which suicide had become a gift and revelation; sacrifice, a powerful antidote to the primal anxiety that permeated the very air of Israel and the Palestinian territories it had ruled for a quarter century. Yasin, above all, knew this. He had watched carefully from his prison cell the rise and fall of the preeminent Palestinian symbol of nine-lives survivalism—Yasir Arafat, former Muslim Brother, head of the PLO, president of Palestine, and the sheikh's major political rival.

12. The Mechanical Waving Hand of a Keffiyah-Clad Manikin

In the summer of 1994, Arafat suddenly materialized in the sands of Gaza after an absence as long as the occupation. Thousands of Palestinians thronged the dusty streets of the newly autonomous realm, hoping for a chance of glimpsing "the Old Man," as he was then affectionately called. People waved palm branches, olive branches, branches of flowers. Little girls were dressed in their finest for the occasion; they matched the walls that surrounded them, which had been freshly painted in pastel pinks and blues, fluorescent yellows. Little boys wore fatigues and T-shirts reading "Produce of Palestine" and held in their arms Kalashnikovs as big as themselves and saluted. Older boys sold nut-covered halva; bright, rainbow-striped coconut; pink "girls' hair." Hornets glued themselves into the sweets, sucking and clinging as if unto death.

Packed like sardines in a stolen Israeli Mazda, the latest acquisition of Yusuf's good friend Jamal, who had recently bought it from a high officer in the PA, and who had to hotwire it each time it was driven, we rolled along the major artery connecting the major cities of the Strip in a caravan of black limousines and military trucks loaded with Fatah dignitaries and youth wildly chanting, "With spirit, with blood, we will sacrifice ourselves for you, O Abu-'Amar"

(Arafat's nom de guerre, meaning "the Builder"), while PLO soldiers fired their guns into the air. Making their way in-between were slower-going vehicles—cars, taxis (inevitably Mercedes), tractors, horses, anything that could move. Jamal kept one hand pressed against the horn, and the other close to his not-so-secret girlfriend crushed beside him—he considered her something of a feminist and referred to her as "Hanan Ashrawi," the well-known Palestinian Christian political activist. She was dressed in the traditional black guna, but underneath, she revealed, slightly hitching up her skirt, were sexy black embroidered tights and white high heels.

Occasionally, Jamal would spy a woman out the window of the car and yell at her, "You are so beautiful!"—something for which on any other day he could theoretically be killed, or at least badly beaten up. As we approached each of the many checkpoints set up by the PA for the occasion, he would slow down ever so slightly and flash our Harvard "OFFICER" i.d. cards authoritatively through the open window in the face of a policeman recently brought over from Iraq or Tunisia and then roar with laughter as the policeman unwittingly waved us through.

After a while, we pulled over to the side of the road and waited. Something was about to happen. He was coming! He was coming!! Then, nothing. We waited longer. He was coming! He was coming!! And then, suddenly, he was coming. Several sleek, black limousines appeared out the dust and roared past the crowd with such speed that they almost knocked people over. And there he was, Yasir Arafat, Abu-'Amar, the symbol, the leader himself, perched atop his limousine, smiling and waving, as he whizzed past wide-eyed children, ululating women, and IDF soldiers (some of whom flashed V-signs as he passed), young men and old men, past the PFLP black-flag demonstration for Palestinian prisoners, past the Israeli flags and banners that read "Kill the murderer" in Hebrew, Arabic, and English that settlers had erected near the overpasses, which had been surrounded by electric fences for the occasion.

The surprising thing was how much the man looked like himself, or rather like the hundreds of images of him that had circulated throughout the Bank and Strip during his absence, when his face had embellished everything from telephone poles to boxes of candy. Everything he said was considered worthy of being made into a proverb to be chanted at demonstrations, spray-painted on walls, inscribed in the notebooks of schoolboys. "If you want to be human, you must be a true revolutionary," the message he sent to the people of Jenin upon the death of Fatah military leader Mahmud az-Zaraini, is one such example. "O mountain, you will not be shaken by a wind" is another. The latter is, of course, a poetic tribute to Palestine, but in the eyes of many Fatah loyalists in the Bank and Strip, it could just as well have applied to Arafat himself, who was commonly referred to as "the symbol," a title suggesting that his significance was based neither on military success nor charisma but rather on a capacity almost royal in nature.

The guy was basically immortal. Every time, he managed just to walk away from the scene of death—the bullet-pocked buildings, the smoking remains of a fallen plane—unscathed and looking younger than ever. Resurrection is, of course, a contagious phenomenon, and with his return to Gaza, many said that Arafat was soon going to announce that his former deputy Khalil al-Wazir, best known by his nom de guerre "Abu-Jihad," had survived his 1988 assassination by Mossad agents in Tunis. He was alive and would soon show his face! Exhilarating mythologies of the Elvis variety floated around the territories for a day or two and then died away, revelation fast becoming a form of embarrassment, only to be replaced a short while later with yet another rumor.

One rumor had it that a Palestinian policeman who'd recently been killed by his friend had actually been shot by a settler, and the Palestinian Authority had covered up this fact. The story not only fed the conspiracy hunger of the time but also lent content to the deep distrust of any sort of authority. Lots of people seemed to believe that the PA was in deep cahoots with the Israelis. Indeed, Arafat and Rabin were soon going to embrace, according to another rumor, and afterward the Palestinian leader was going to say to the Israeli leader, "We are one people!" This was, in fact, the greatest hope of the guy who told us the rumor, his secret fantasy. He used to work with Israelis, he said, and they would say to him, "Why don't you unite with us and fight with us? Why don't you have the Israeli mentality? You can be our army!" He had kept silent, he said, but had thought to himself that they were right, that teaming up with the Israelis would be the smartest thing the Palestinians could ever do.

On walls up and down the Strip from Gaza City to the Egyptian border, Arafat remained a symbol of victory and the hope of return. His body was composed of land and trees, and balanced precariously on his arm was an orange map of Israel, the West Bank, and Gaza Strip, signifying the long-cherished goal of regaining "all of Palestine." He was seen as heralding victory, and a popular verse from the Qur'anic chapter entitled *al-Fatah* appeared on the walls—"We have given you a resplendent victory [*fatah*]" (48:1), *fatah* being the Arabic word for "opening," as in "opening a land for Islam" as well as the name of Arafat's organization. Shabab managed to scale the "Welcome to Gaza" arches that towered probably forty feet or more in the air and tear off the Hebrew lettering as a gift to the leader—one imagines the crowd below cheering as they did.

Within days of the homecoming, the tide began to turn, as if people were afraid of their own optimism. You began to hear the leader openly mocked. He was called all kinds of things. Some said that he would be allotted two or three months, and then would be unceremoniously killed. The king must die! Many began to doubt that they'd even seen the man, insisting that the figure they'd welcomed home could not possibly have been the real thing. They'd seen only the mechanical waving hand of a keffiyah-clad manikin, a giant wind-up puppet, flying by at seventy miles per hour on top of a fancy black limousine. It was all a little like the thick plastic blowups of the president's head you could buy at the kiosks on Omar al-Mukhtar Street, which from afar looked like balloons but when untethered went nowhere. It was, as Yusuf liked to call it, "the time of the apricot"—a saying people used to signify a great time that never quite arrived.

13. Soldier in Chinese Hat, Planning Escape

The road is nicknamed "the Curves" for it takes you to the oasis city of Jericho from Nablus, Jenin, Tulkarem, and all points north by the most circuitous route imaginable, at points seeming almost to fold in on itself like an accordion and collapse. Even before the peace accords had been signed, the Israelis had begun work on the road. It was now newly paved and widened a bit but still perilously narrow with gorges on one side, sheer cliffs on the other. Pieces of plastic bags, baby blue and baby pink, had caught in the small round bushes scattered across the landscape below, where they announced themselves triumphantly, "I'm a girl!" "I'm a boy!"

Going round one of the famous curves one day shortly after Arafat had returned home, we were almost flattened by an oncoming truck. 'Ali noted dispassionately, as though nothing extraordinary had just transpired, that there had been many accidents on this road. In fact, he said, it was a dangerous road in a dangerous area. Among other things, a scorpion was said to lurk under every rock. A few minutes after he said this, we stopped the car to get some air, flipped over a rock, and lo and behold, there sat a small desert specimen the color of amber, so bright and clear that it could have passed for a plastic toy had it not immediately positioned itself in attack mode, unfurling its long segmented tail high in the air, the stinger at the tip seemingly quivering in anticipation.

We were on our way to Jericho to meet a blind and fiery Hamas sheikh often calling for jihad. Earlier, we'd called a telephone number that the sheikh had given us. It was the number, we now discovered, of a clinic located next to Hisham's Palace Hotel in the heart of the city.

"Is Sheikh Harb in?" we asked.

"No!" someone said, and hung up.

Nevertheless, we decided to go to our appointment at the appointed time. When we arrived at the sheikh's office, the woman behind the desk said she'd never heard of a Sheikh Harb.

She was a little paranoid. Indeed, by this point in the intifada, everybody was a little paranoid. Disguise and subterfuge had practically become art forms. You couldn't trust anybody. You couldn't trust people even if they looked, talked, and walked like what they said they were.

Strangers, especially those not easily pigeonholed as aid workers or journalists, had by this point become not a little suspect. The *ajanib*—a word that suggested something to be avoided—with whom Palestinians were most familiar were Israeli soldiers and the invisible but greatly feared agents of the Israeli Shin Bet. Palestinians were particularly fearful of what they called *musta'ribun*,[9] "those who pretend to be Arab," a reference to Israeli Special Forces who caught wanted Palestinians by dressing up as Arabs, using keffiyahs and mustaches and, less frequently, veils, embroidered dresses, fake eyelashes, and lipstick. Some said they also occasionally pretended to be journalists. They liked to drive around in white Peugeot 504s, cars so popular among Palestinians that they constituted almost nationalist symbols in and of themselves. Sometimes, it was only the smallest of details that enabled their identification. When one guy on an early videotape of the Qassam Battalions is asked if it's easy to recognize Israeli Special Forces, he notes that the hairs of the fake beards they wear, unlike those of a real beard, consist of one length only! Occasionally, their props and disguises were so authentic that their own people were unable to distinguish the real from the fake, and killed each other in incidents of "friendly fire."

After a while, a man in a white lab coat came out from the back of the office, and said he was sorry but Sheikh Harb had gone to Qalqilya to the zoo with some children. 'Ali simply couldn't believe that a sheikh would stand people up to go to the zoo of all places. What should we do now? Go back home? Sniff the breeze at the Seven Trees Restaurant? 'Ali suddenly remembered that one of Yusuf's cousins, a Palestinian soldier recently brought over from Iraq to serve on the PA police force, happened to be stationed right down the road.

The soldier's quarters were part of an old, yellowish UN building, covered with dust blown off the Judean desert, surrounded by an ancient wall composed of mud and rock. Inside, someone had painted a broad and solitary slash of new white paint across one of the walls as the backdrop for a Palestinian flag. Two cheap mattresses and a Styrofoam mat occupied the floor, while a small army of PA uniforms hung upon the walls. Scattered about the room were various and sundry items—a Kalashnikov, two red plastic chairs, an antediluvian fan, olives in a jar, rounds of pita, a half-eaten watermelon. Yusuf's cousin greeted us warmly, even though he was half asleep. Perhaps we'd even awakened him.

He offered us seats on a littered bed while he took out a kelly green mirror, cracked to the hilt, and carefully combed his hair and rubbed Ultra Sol cream on his face. It was high noon, and he explained that he couldn't go out unless he wore sunscreen. A bomb or something had exploded in his hands when he was stationed in Baghdad—he'd spent three thousand dollars on an operation to repair the damage to his face. For extra precaution, he wore a red-and-white keffiyah and a conical straw hat that made him look as though he should be planting paddy somewhere warm and wet and tropical. We chatted as he groomed himself as though it were the most natural thing in the world.

Finally, he checked himself out in the mirror, and deeming himself presentable, came to us with two oranges, two pears, an apple, and some plums, all delicately floating in a thin layer of water on a tin tray. He sliced them open with a knife, and peeled them for us. It was a sweet and noble gesture from someone who only the week before had been found fighting over a boiled porcupine (it was said to taste like lamb), someone who went for three days at a time with nothing to eat but stones, as he called the hard, stale bread and harderyet cheese that was his daily ration.

Mahir had been in Iraq during the "Great Gulf War," when the missiles had fallen around him like "steel rain," and like so many others, he had fled. There was nothing one could do. Before, during, and after that war, he said, the people loved Saddam—Saddam and his distinctive face. He himself, he said with great conviction, would die for the man. Why? Because he had challenged the West and Israel all by himself. Arafat had said to him, I put our fate in your hands. And Mahir admired him for the way he'd rebuilt Baghdad after the war, the way he'd thrown up walls with nothing in between them, just shells whose innards were to be supplied later.

The people of Baghdad, he said with a strange pride, survived only because of prostitution. It was as if nothing, he said, for a man to come home and find his mother, or his wife, or his sister piled up in bed with a stranger. In fact, the man himself had, in all likelihood, offered the women to any and all who could pay. After serving time in Iraq, Mahir had been sent to Libya to fight for Qaddafi in his war for uranium in Chad. "Just like a prostitute," he said.

But O! life had been good in Baghdad. He had been paid $50 a month, which amounted to a small fortune on the black market. Now that he was in Jericho, the PA, in contrast, gave him around $150, which sounded like a lot more, but really wasn't—it wouldn't even pay for cigarettes if he smoked them. Arafat, that "son of a dog," had promised him $400 per month. He was still waiting for it. While soldiers like him had to make do with hard bread and cheese, the table of their commanding officer, Hajj Isma'il, was so well laden, he said, that there was not one place on which you could place your hands if you could be so lucky as to sit at it.

Around two in the afternoon, we all decided to go eat lunch at a chicken restaurant in downtown Jericho. Driving there, Mahir turned to us and said, "I hope to see you some day in Iraq." It was an assertion of a kind of power and authority, as if to say, I have known great things—if only you could see what I was before. At the restaurant, Mahir gulped down his food, taking plates of chicken rolled in purple sumac and shoveling the food into his mouth. During the past week alone, he said, he had gone for three whole days without eating. When he had been a prisoner in Iraq, during the Gulf War, he said he'd resorted to eating snakes. Rats as well—there were plenty of rats in Iraq then. The coalition forces had airlifted them there, dropped them into the country in order to decimate the crops. He had seen it with his own eyes. Things weren't much better now in Jericho, and Arafat was doing nothing about it, and was going to do nothing about it. When the president had visited Jericho shortly after his homecoming, some of the Palestinian officers, Mahir said, had gone to speak to him about the poor conditions under which they were living. Arafat had sent them away and cursed them. "What do you want?!" he had said. "I have brought you back to your homeland!!!"

Mahir was planning his escape already. He was no warrior-fida'i keen on sacrificing himself. His body was soft and supple and small; his face, kind and gentle. He had no desire to fight, no desire to become a martyr. On the contrary, he firmly believed in the power of death, the sheer and utter factuality of it. He would sell his old gun, which he said was worth a pile of money, and leave Gaza through the tunnels to Egypt. Although his family was Palestinian, and he had been born in Saudi Arabia, and was proud to say that he had been on the hajj four times (his mother had made the pilgrimage eight times; his father, twelve), he considered his home to be Egypt. And how was that, we asked? Because of something that had happened before he was even born. His father, he said, had refused the bride chosen for him by his father, Mahir's grandfather, and instead had married an Egyptian woman of his own liking. Since that time, the two men had refused to speak to one other.

After he'd first arrived from Iraq, Mahir said, he had gone to visit his old grandfather, who lived in Gaza, and had said to him bravely and with conviction as if to wipe away the past, "There is no longer any need for us not to speak to each other. We are all family." The grandfather agreed, and the very next day, as if compelled to repeat what he had done with his son some twenty-odd years before, brought Mahir a girl to marry. Naturally, Mahir refused the match, and he and the grandfather had not spoken since.

Everyone had had too much chicken to eat as we rolled back to the camp. Mahir asked if we could possibly smuggle him into Jerusalem so that he could see the city through the window before he escaped to Egypt. Isn't that forbidden? we asked. Yes, he said, but so many others had done it. He started to open the car door, but then turned. I have been very happy with you, he said, smiling, before he walked away, the Chinese hat bobbing ever so slightly as he went. That was what he had wanted to say from the beginning.

14. The Sweet Girl

By the time of Arafat's homecoming, Yusuf had pretty much returned to his former self, moved into his own place downtown, and had three small children. The new place, the property of an uncle, was called "the duck house" because for years it had housed the family's stock of ducks and other birds. The ducks had all been eaten, particularly the ill-tempered specimen who launched at visitors' legs, flapping and snapping, and all that remained were a few rabbits and a couple of the beautiful birds that Yusuf had raised since he was a boy—Egyptian pigeons, pigeons from Ashkelon and Jenin, lovebirds, multicolored canaries, *drari Hindi*.

Constructed of concrete blocks encrusted with sea animals and pockmarked from the great battles of 1967, the house consisted of five rooms, three of which led out into a walled garden shaded by lemon trees and lufas, and dotted with the cacti and succulents that Yusuf so loved and that we brought him periodically from Jerusalem. The place was completely unprotected. None of the doors to the rooms could be locked, and IDF soldiers had an inexplicable penchant for kicking in the iron gate that led into the enclave. Thieves had once scaled the walls and carted away Yusuf's singing birds. The back room was the only room in the house that could be secured, and there Yusuf kept locked away his two most prized possessions. The first was a finely crafted *oud*, a musical instrument whose strings were picked rather than strummed. The second possession was an electronic keyboard that featured 150 buttons including *fellahi* (peasant-style), *biladi* (nationalist), Ayubi, Dixie 1, Dixie 2, reggae, and funk. You could intersperse these transcultural beats by pushing other buttons like *tablah* (traditional Arabic drum) and *zaghrut* 1 and 2, slight variations of the wild and piercing celebratory ululations of women, which sounded somewhere between a war cry and a mourning wail. Theoretically, you could play Dixie peasant style punctuated by zaghruts.

It was stultifyingly hot that afternoon, and we sat in the back room, the coolest in the house, discussing Arafat's return, swigging tap water from Eden Spring bottles (thirst, we'd read somewhere, is actually a late sign of dehydration), watching interminable videos of recent family weddings, and chitchatting with the various visitors who drifted in with the sand every half hour, seeking reprieve from the heat and boredom. Ahmad, a blind singer, arrived, and soon, accompanied by Yusuf on the oud, sang a song of Um-Kulthum, whom Yusuf compared to the pyramids of Egypt: "Sing for me, slowly . . . slowly . . . slowly . . . slowly . . . Sing for me and take my eyes . . ."

"And she took his eyes!" Yusuf interrupted, and the two blind men laughed.

A former intifada activist who was in the process of planning his dead brother's revenge dropped by and displayed some boredom-nullifying stunts that he had learned in prison. (Now that the Israelis were gone, half of the population seemed to be engaged in the settling of scores). He fashioned a flume out of paper, made a spitball out of one end, and sent it hurtling to the ceiling where it stuck along with several others that seemed to have abided there for some time. Hurray, hurray! As an encore, he took two forks and placed a half-shekel piece between them and adroitly balanced the arrangement on the edge of a glass, to the tune of "Santa Claus Is Coming to Town," which emanated from a toy on the patio that had gone berserk. Hurray, hurray! everyone cried.

Not long after, a man appeared at the door. He was bearded, decked out in white robes, white pants, white cap, . . . very Muslim Brother, very Hamas. The man was nervous and aggressive, and soon a minor argument broke out between him and another guest over the name of the plums we were eating.

Were they Santa Rosa or Laila? The Islamist insisted that they were of the latter variety.

"We say *laila helwa*," he said, turning to us. "*Laila* is also the name of a girl, so *laila helwa* means a 'sweet girl' . . . which we are now eating."

Watching the man speak in this way, we suddenly realized that it was Yusuf's brother-in-law Muhammad, whom we hadn't seen in years. Muhammad's first wife had bore him no children, and so a marriage had finally been arranged with Yusuf's sister, who was half his age. We had attended the wedding.

Once recognized, Muhammad insisted that we come home with him then and there.

The long-time manager of an Israeli rug factory in the town of Rishon leZion, Muhammad was privy to special deals on carpets, and his house was hot and thick with them. The linoleum floors were carpeted. The chairs were carpeted. The cabinets held countless brochures advertising various carpet-making machines and stacks of carpet samples in neat black binders. Muhammad was very proud of these things, and we admired them, one by one. Later, we drank tea and talked with Nuha, played with her three children, reminisced about our days together in Gaza, the days when she had read Mahfouz and dreamed of going to college (she could never be fully convinced that such an endeavor was an option for her or for any woman).

It was now long ago.

"What's it like outside?" she asked us. It was a stock question, and we replied with a stock answer, but it soon became clear that she wanted to tell us something. She had barely left the house for the past several years, she said with a matter-of-factness beyond pity. She was not allowed to leave. She lived her life behind a heavy iron door that opened only when Muhammad came and went, or when his first wife, who inhabited the ground floor of the house, made her daily visit. The first wife was there now. She was dressed in black, and wore lots of gold jewelry around her neck and a huge cubic crystal on her finger. Her voice was deep and husky. Nuha's little children called her Mama.

When we finally stood up to leave, Muhammad produced a last-minute revelation for us—a photograph of himself holding a Kalashnikov in one hand and a Qur'an in the other. Actually, it was a cliché of a fantasy—that of the Islamic warrior—which anyone, even the manager of an Israeli rug factory, could fulfill at the local equivalent of an Olan Mills studio.

"*Ba-ru-da!*" 'Gun!" exclaimed his small son.

Muhammad beamed and led us out. The iron door shut behind us with a thud of finality.

Outside, the night was balmy and sweet and smelled of guava and night-blooming jasmine. It was the way Gaza smelled in our memory, which had managed to distill the essence over the years, subtracting from it the stench of accumulated trash and rats and tear gas.

A voice descended from above: "Good-bye, good-bye."

It was Nuha. She had waited on the balcony a long time for this moment, and as we drove away, she waved and waved into the night, a small, steady benediction on the girl she once was.

15. The Antidote

Some three years after Arafat's homecoming, Ahmad Yasin would also return home to Gaza, the result of the most spectacular bungle in the history of Israel's foreign intelligence operations—a botched assassination attempt on the life of Khalid Meshal, the Hamas political chief in Jordan thought to be behind two recent suicide bombings in Jerusalem in which twenty-one Israelis had been killed. The story runs like a James Bond movie in which none of Q's inventions get to do their ignominious work—the fake passports, the synthetic opiate, the high-tech delivery system, the black syringe of antidote wielded by an Israeli doctor, who, according to one member of the royal Hashemite family with whom we spoke shortly after the incident, happened to be blonde and female.

The chain of events[10] seems to have been something like this: On the morning of September 25, as Meshal was headed for his office in 'Amman, he was approached by two men on the street—one blonde, the other dark—who, according to several eyewitnesses, struck Meshal near his left ear with a strange device wrapped in tape, and then fled. Meshal's bodyguard and driver chased after them. A green Hyundai was awaiting the attackers, and, like stunt men in a B movie, the two leapt into it while it was still moving. The bodyguard trailed them in a taxi. In less than a mile, the two men jumped out of the Hyundai. The bodyguard followed suit and after a bloody fistfight, succeeded in wrestling one of the attackers to the ground. Soon, a crowd gathered. There happened to be a plain-clothes policeman in the group, and he arrested the two. They carried Canadian passports, but did not request to see Canadian Embassy officials.

A couple of hours after the attack, Meshal began to vomit and was taken to the King Husain Medical Center, where it was eventually concluded that he had been poisoned; doctors, however, could find no point of entry for the toxin. A delivery system would never be found.

The Jordanian king remained ignorant of the incident until Israeli Prime Minister Bibi Netanyahu telephoned him later in the day, requesting that he meet with Dani Yatom, then head of the Mossad, the Israeli Institute for Intelligence and Special Tasks responsible for human intelligence collection, covert action, and counter-terrorism—and the subject of countless Tom Clancy-like novels. Yatom was said to be a not infrequent visitor at the palace, and these visits were often spur-of-the-moment, so the request did not strike the king as particularly odd. At their meeting, Yatom reportedly informed Husain that what had transpired earlier in the day had indeed been an assassination attempt.

The king was furious. He immediately ordered the Mossad to close its base in Jordan and soon expelled the handful of agents who had long worked out of the Israeli Embassy with Jordanian permission. He insisted that if Meshal died, the Israeli Embassy would be closed and the two captured agents put on public trial. He demanded an antidote for the poison. Netanyahu hemmed and hawed. As a last resort, the Jordanian king appealed to U.S. President Bill Clinton to intervene, and finally, under U.S. pressure, Israel agreed to identify the drug it had used on Meshal and to provide the antidote for it, which was in the hands of a backup member of the Israeli team still in Jordan—a doctor who was holed up at the Intercontinental Hotel, one of the fanciest lodgings in 'Amman, whose bookstore specialized in anti-Semitic works such as *The Protocols of the Elders of Zion* and Henry Ford's *The Eternal Jew*, which were sold alongside tourist guides of the royal kingdom. Within a couple of minutes, the antidote had done its work, and Meshal was saved from certain death.

The mystery drug turned out to be Fentanyl, an opiate dozens of times stronger than morphine. First synthesized in Belgium in the late 1950s, the drug is used for medical pain relief, particularly that of terminally ill patients. Its most famous user was perhaps Timothy Leary, who used a transdermal Fentanyl patch after he was diagnosed with cancer. (William Burroughs visited him, and reportedly expressed great interest in more recreational uses for the drug, which on the street eventually became known by a myriad of names— Apache, China Girl, China White, Dance Fever, Goodfellas, Friend, Tango & Cash, TNT, King Ivory, Jackpot, He-man, Great Bear, Murder 8, Poison.)

The weekend after the attack, Netanyahu—who later admitted to Ehud Barak, then leader of the Israeli opposition, that he had personally directed the Meshal operation—flew to 'Amman to apologize personally to King Husain. The king refused to see him, and sent his brother, the crown prince, in his stead. The Canadian Embassy recalled its ambassador from Israel in protest against the fraudulent use of its passports. Meshal lived, and later claimed that it was not the antidote that had saved him, but God himself.

In the end, a secret deal—never formally acknowledged by King Husain— was struck. Jordan would release the Israeli agents and, in return, Israel would release Sheikh Yasin as well as a few dozen other Hamas detainees. The question was, would Yasin accept the deal? Here, after all, was a man who said he enjoyed the solitude of prison life, and, according to his wife, Halima, who came to visit him there twice a week, said over and over again that he wanted nothing more than the next world.

16. A Babe in the Womb

In the wake of the Oslo Accords, Sheikh Yasin told an interviewer for the magazine *Dar al-Haqq* that an Israeli intelligence officer had come to him and said:

"Would you accept an airline ticket to the destination of your choice in exchange for the corpse of Sadon?" (a reference to the IDF officer kidnapped and killed by Hamas in 1989).

"I said to them: 'I am paralyzed, I cannot walk, and you want me to search for the corpse?'

"They said: 'We'll put a car and a chauffeur under your disposal.'

"I said to them: 'I refuse all of this. I would prefer to stay here one hundred years rather than get out of prison in exchange for a corpse.'"

In the end, the sheikh agreed to be released in exchange for a vial of antidote.

From a Tel Aviv airstrip, he was flown by Jordanian royal helicopter to the King Husain Medical Center in 'Amman, where he was visited by both Yasir Arafat and King Husain. At 4 A.M., citing the sheikh's poor health, the Israeli army announced his pardon—a pardon that allowed him to return home to Gaza.

Upon his return, a hungry cry rose up in thousands of throats—"With spirit and blood, we will sacrifice ourselves for you!" It was the same ritual chant that had greeted Arafat years before, but the differences between the two homecomings were palpable and telling. Whole families had stood on the dusty streets of Gaza to witness the return of Arafat—husbands and wives and children; the crowd that greeted Yasin was almost entirely male. Separated from their husbands and sons, fathers and brothers, as if at the Wailing Wall, women danced again, but this time behind chain-link fences on the sidelines of the action rather than in the heart of the public squares of Gaza. The men were bearded rather than clean-shaven or mustached, and they flashed the one-way sign of the religious rather than the universal "V" of the nationalists.

And then, of course, there were the two old men themselves, longtime competitors for the heart of Palestine, who according to a strange fate, had somehow ended up changing places. Yasin, religious leader and longtime advocate of military gradualism, was now the symbol of a militant, apocalyptic spirit; Arafat, the old warrior, was now the symbol of political compromise and military gradualism and a revolution that was dead. Dressed in fatigues, Arafat had stood before the crowd on his day of return and addressed it like a conqueror; Yasin, in clerical robes, was carried onstage, a swaddled totem tendered by dozens of eager hands. He was surrounded by murals of Yahya Ayyash, "the Engineer," the bomb-maker for the suicide squadrons of Hamas who was killed by the Israelis with an exploding cell phone in 1996; 'Amir Sirhan, who in 1990, stabbed an IDF soldier and Israeli policeman; and 'Imad 'Aql, a top-level military leader of Hamas who was the subject of numerous videos and a book published not long after his death by the press of *Filistin al-Muslima* in London in 1994. ('Aql must have seemed a strange choice to many. He had become the subject of a huge controversy after he brutally killed a Palestinian police officer in a revenge attack, and then was himself killed by a guy named Ashraf Kahail, who, in turn, was later captured by Hamas, interrogated, and killed. On one video produced by Hamas, Kahail names dozens of nationalists as collaborators, thereby initiating one of the nastiest scandals the Gaza Strip has ever seen.) Yasin spoke in a voice so small and thin that it had to be amplified and repeated, word for word, by a disciple to the crowd below.

In a bold, deflationary gesture, the ailing sheikh later likened himself to "a baby returned to his mother's womb"—a fantasy of womb and grave, succor and engulfment, that held inestimable charm for a people who had just spent the last ten years in a state of delirious excitation only to return in the end to the rule of an old and corrupt order, almost as if the intifada had never happened at all. He is said to have cried in his robes—an almost unthinkable thought in the machismo world of the young militants who worshipped him—and in his tears could be read the sadness of a nation that fully embraced its infirmity as the sign of a secret greatness.

With his return, no one could doubt that Yasin was a major symbol of greatness-in-infirmity; he was the mutilated king. People began to think about both the man and the movement with renewed fervor. There was talk that the higher echelons of Hamas had lost control over the Battalions, and that a general split between the pragmatists and the radicals within the movement was imminent. There were two major questions on everyone's mind. Would, could, and should Hamas be coopted by Arafat's Palestinian Authority? And now that Yasin had returned to the land of the living, would he be an inciting or moderating element?

In the months that followed, Yasin showed himself eminently capable of both. On the one hand, there were the photos—Yasin and Arafat sitting side by side, Yasin and Arafat kissing, Yasin and the Israeli rabbi and settler-leader Menachem Froman holding hands—as if a religious equivalent of the famous handshake between Arafat and the late Rabin on the White House lawn. The meeting between the sheikh and the rabbi seemed promising, touching even. Clasping Yasin's hand in his, Froman read aloud a letter from Chief Sephardi Rabbi Eliahu Bakshi-Doron, who called upon the sheikh as a fellow "believer in God" and asked him to prevent any further shedding of blood. Froman also delivered Yasin a letter from Yehuda Wachsman, whose son Nachshon had been kidnapped and killed in 1994 by Hamas militants demanding the sheikh's release from prison. Yasin thanked Froman for his visit, but in response to Bakshi-Doron's call, said that he could not commit himself to stopping the violence. He would have to pass the letter on to Arafat.

Who knew what the sheikh really thought? He was as unpredictable and mysterious as the Qur'anic chapter from which his name was ostensibly derived. On some days, he would say that a truce between Israel and the Palestinians might be possible under certain conditions; on others, he would issue a call for jihad. On some days, he said that he supported Arafat and the Palestinian Authority; on others, he said that he categorically opposed the Oslo Accords, defended suicide bombings, and insisted that Hamas would use any means within its power to achieve its goals. As soon as one mask fell, another was revealed.

The sheikh said he was sick; everybody said he was sick. It had been said for many years, making the sheikh one of the slowest-dying people in the world. A photograph in the *New York Times* in October 1997 showed him being given water by a disciple. The caption below read, "Sheik Ahmad Yassin, spiritual leader of Hamas, back home in Gaza after his release by Israel, is so frail he drinks only with help." Barely half a year later, however, the sheikh, under the guise of needing medical treatment abroad, left Gaza to tour and fund-raise in the Arab capitals for four months. He returned home in June 1998 with a reported ten to fifteen million dollars, and tens of millions of dollars more under pledge.

In Damascus, he predicted that "the Zionist entity" would be eliminated within the first quarter of the new century, bringing to mind the quirky but popular numerological predictions of fellow Hamas leader Bassam Jarrar, who had pinpointed 2022 as the fateful year. Upon his return, Yasin talked again of Israel vanishing from the map, and called on Arafat to join him in a renewed armed struggle—challenges that perhaps could no longer be taken as signs of "irony," "political ambiguity," or "shrewdness," as the commentators liked to put it. It was as if money had made the sheikh giddy. He dropped the defenses of silence and prevarication, and spoke instead like a millionaire who could say anything he pleased. The "soldier of Hamas," as he liked to call himself, a man renowned for his asceticism, would in later years be seen driving around the camps of Gaza in a specially outfitted brown Range Rover, which some said was a gift from the Saudis, while others insisted it was from none other than Arafat.

"A great man," wrote Canetti, "is one who disposes of millions." If the sheikh's dollars were largely virtual, they nevertheless pointed to the fantasized millions under his command—martyrs and suicide bombers, unborn children in the camps and cities of the Bank and Strip, exiles dispersed to the four corners of the globe, the masses of the Islamist revolution in "Palestine and all the world," as Hamas liked to sign off on its leaflets—the seed, as he saw it, of a great Islamic umma arrayed for battle in well-formed lines that stretched out across the desert as far as the eye could see.

Six years after returning home from his tour of Arab countries, the sheikh finally attained what he had long said he wanted more than anything on earth. Shortly after the dawn prayer in a Gaza City mosque not far from his home, he was struck to the ground by a missile fired from an Israeli Apache helicopter. He was hit directly—the missile, it is believed, passing straight through his body. By the time most photographers arrived on the scene, all that remained were two wheels of his chair, circles in a pool of blood. Strangely, they had been damaged only slightly by the massive blast, and in the wire photos that soon made their way around the world, men hold them up for the camera and look through them.

17. The Crazy Girl

There is a tree that grows in Gaza that Yusuf said was called *al-majnuna*, "the crazy girl." Its huge blossoms are an unnatural, shockingly hot orange that cascade downward in flaming clusters—the exuberant botanical analogue of, one imagined, some sort of insanity or sexual excess. We dutifully recorded the tree's existence in our notebooks, laughing a bit at the zany name. We later brought up the tree with other people, but no one had ever heard of it. Mr. Yusuf, it seems, had made the whole thing up.

"One could easily claim that the joke is on you," a friend observed, "except that you do not see it." Perhaps indeed, the joke was on us. Perhaps we had learned nothing from our ridiculous quest. In the years that followed, as we settled under the shadow of Hamas, watching videotapes of suicide bombers made sometimes but scant hours before their deaths and mulling over the meaning of hundreds of bloody slogans and documents, we would sometimes think of the crazy girl and feel a sudden pang of hope and fear.

PART TWO

The Portfolio

18. The Dark Room

One day, we received a phone call from Yusuf. It's not a good time to come down now, he said. Maybe next week things would be better. The family was having problems. In particular, a young man who'd once invited us to have lunch with him and his family kept calling the house, asking for us. The family found it very strange, the young man calling and calling. He must be a collaborator—why else would somebody keep calling like that? Only many years later did we discover that one of Yusuf's brothers was the driver for the Black Panther, Fatah's strike force during the intifada. It was very simple—the family hadn't needed anything else to draw attention to itself.

After that, we moved into a compound at Sha'ria Mala'ika—Angel Road—in the Old City of Jerusalem at the juncture of two of the four worlds encircled by the ancient walls. It was really a little cave of sorts, set at the street level of five centuries ago, now ten feet or so below ground. The structure consisted of two mildew-ridden domes whose walls and ceiling constantly rained flakes of antediluvian whitewash like snow, and was kept locked and bolted behind double gates, as if the Crusaders might come again at any minute. For extra protection, broken bottles and shards of multi-colored glass had been cemented atop the walls where they caught the sun in deathly rainbows.

It was from this base that we first began collecting the political ephemera and underground media of the intifada. We hadn't started out with the idea of a "collection"; we'd simply begun taking photographs of the graffiti that covered every square inch of the walls of the Old City as a way of trying to understand the intifada, then in its heyday. The streets of the West Bank and Gaza soon exploded with other media that we collected as well, often taking them out to Ali's house on the weekend where we would translate them and discuss their meaning over endless rounds of sweet tea, RC Cola, and TIME ("This Is My End") cigarettes, sometimes accompanied by a small crush of neighbors and visitors.

One day, out of the blue, the Armenian watchmaker who owned the compound and lived in the house next door came home from work and told us that his wife—indeed, all his long lost relatives from Jordan—would be returning home to Jerusalem, so we would have to leave. We hurriedly looked around for a new place. One man, with great excitement, showed us an apartment in the Muslim Quarter of the Old City that appeared to have been bombed at some point. We considered it—it was, like the man said, cheap, a good deal, but then it did have holes in the roof. In addition, it had no front door. There was not even a door jamb. Anyone and everyone were welcome. Then a Jewish woman who lived near the shuq told us she had a place for rent. It also seemed very nice until we drew back a curtain in the bedroom and, behold, there sat a little old lady on a chair, two feet away, like a stage prop from Psycho—who looked up and said "shalom" to us as if such an arrangement were the most common thing in the world. Finally, someone told us that an American photographer was returning home to marry—perhaps we would be interested in her place. It was very nice.

The house was located in Matzkeret Moshe, one of the first Jewish neighborhoods to be built outside the Old City of Jerusalem. It was but a stone's throw from the *shuq*, the Jewish market, so close you could almost taste its wares— tomatoes red as rubies, orange sherbet mangoes, olives of every color and stage of desiccation (could there be that many shades of green?), onions, corn, watermelons, and cucumbers, all stacked in rows, neat as tacks; Iraqi bread; tofu made by militant Jewish hippies in West Bank settlements; cardamom, za'tar, heavy bunches of purple sweet basil ("so you will have something sweet to smell on the Sabbath"); kebab, kubbeh, cow udders roasted brown; bad cigarettes.

The shuq was an entire kingdom unto itself. The spice man sold sacks of saffron tendrils, golden turmeric, magenta sumac (and, at the back of his stall, spicy movies), while the fish man (down the steps, follow the smell) was involved in commerce equally forbidden—bags of unkosher, pink shrimp from the seas of Gaza, sold under the counter to those in the know. The bread man sang a bread song virtually medieval—*everything's hot, everything's hot, come and get it*. There was also the Evil Eye man, the pastry man, the fruit man, and the halvah man, amongst others. And presiding over all with the air of a West Point sergeant was the pickle man—IDF buzz cut, steel-rimmed glasses, glance even steelier—whose brusque right-wing political commentary and supremely positioned stall at the main entrance of the market made him a favorite of beat reporters, who might begin a story with "According to a pickle seller in the market . . ."

To the south of the clamor of the shuq, Matzkeret Moshe stretched out in odd geometries—the original straight-as-an-arrow courtyards and houses of whitewashed stone with pan-tile roofs having been augmented over the last hundred years with zany shacks of tin and concrete, talismans against the Evil Eye, winding flagstone paths, and bomb shelters at every corner, all shaded by ancient eucalyptus trees dispersing in the occasional breeze an almost chemical perfume somewhere between mint and turpentine. Red and white, red and white, with small bursts of green as far as the eye could see.

The photographer's house had a dark room tacked onto it, cantilevered out over a flagstone courtyard, held up by a precariously angled stilt of negligible proportions. Inside, we felt as though we were dangling above the abyss; there was nothing beneath us. Through the thin walls, we could hear everything outside—*Hasidim* praying for rain in the *shtiebl* (tiny synagogue) down the street; children shrieking in the playground below; yellow-eyed Egyptian cats raging rooftop battles above our heads; the couple across the way talking sweet talk over breakfast (a mere ten feet or so separated us); the old woman downstairs sweeping the flagstones, pausing now and then to blow antique kisses to God.

On many an afternoon, we'd retire there to develop and print the film we'd shot earlier in the week. Closing the door, we'd turn the dial to the renegade Israeli station Abie Nathan's Voice of Peace, "broadcasting from somewhere in the Mediterranean," or Jordanian radio, which liked to alternate paeans to the late King Husain with daily English lessons administered via American-style pop.

"Ooooh ba-by, I love your way, ev-eree-day. Want to be with you night and day," the radio English teacher would repeat after Peter Frampton, enunciating each syllable so distinctly that English began to sound like another language. The song's close would bring with it an exposition, which would go something like this: "It means he loves her. . . . It means he likes everything she does. . . . It means he wants to accompany her in the morning and in the night."

We'd laugh a bit, as we washed our new prints under the citrine glow of the dark-room lights, the little box on stilts perhaps quivering ever so slightly. The temperature in the tar-covered shack often exceeded 100 degrees, far above the limit for properly developing anything, so we'd plop ice cubes swaddled in plastic into the steaming Dektol. And when at last our endeavors would pay off and an image materialize in its final bath of water and sweat, it was never exactly what we thought it would be. Beyond the possibilities of overexposure and underexposure, the technical vagaries and miscalculations, there was always a surprise in the photo itself or something we now knew that changed the photo, or how we felt about it—something that had happened in the interval between taking the picture and actually seeing it.

Here, for instance, is a shot of the "Welcome to Gaza" sign at the entrance to the Strip. It was taken through fire, masked shabab having lit a pile of tires in the middle of the street as a lure for the soldiers. We can feel the heat, smell the burning rubber, the adrenaline and fear, as they surround us, shove us into the taxi, slam the door behind us, and then for good measure stone us mightily as the driver, laughing like a mad hatter, speeds away. The picture now elicits the faint vertigo that often accompanies the memory of inassimilable things.

And here is the poster we were photographing in Bethlehem the time we got caught between the soldiers firing and the shabab fleeing. We remember looking at the poster, studying it for awhile, and then deciding to take a picture of it, and suddenly we turned around and saw that we were the only living things on the entire street, everyone else having somehow managed to notice the masked men, the soldiers gathering at the corner, and the sound of breaking glass, and run for safety inside the shops, slamming the heavy, anti-Evil-Eye blue metal doors behind them—everyone but us. We remember the preternaturally loud crack as the bullets started flashing out of barrels a few feet from our heads, the helpless feeling as we froze in position, too startled to move. Someone else looking at the photograph of the poster, so calm and immobile, would see nothing of this.

And here are some snapshots of Martina immediately prior to the Gulf War. Mira has just left. The Israelis have just handed out gas masks, and she's gotten hers. We convince her to try it on for us. The thing is monstrous—bug-eyed and pig-snouted. No one looks at it too closely—it's like the emergency directions aboard airplanes—why torment yourself? It's Saturday, a holy day, in West Jerusalem, and we all go out to the shuq, which is empty except for the occasional hasid shouting "*Shabbes! Shabbes!*" at the unlucky unpious. From a distance, Martina looks like an alien mutant as she tromps across hacked-up cauliflower heads and squashed strawberries, pausing now and then to pose in front of the closed-up stalls. She's passing the one with the hand-drawn portrait of Menachem Begin. Now, she's nearing the spot where the taxi on the Jerusalem-Gaza route would let us out as if from the moon, and we would be so happy to escape the rats and curfews, guns and tear gas, heat and haze, that we would feel like clicking our heels in the air or kissing the ground. We look more closely at the sequence, each of us, in turn, cocking one eye to the prints like a bird, and, in a flash of perception mixed with memory, suddenly spy the zany telltale—she has on high heels—a gas mask and high heels, can you believe it?

The dark room is not the only repository for what we eventually begin to call "the archive." The entire apartment has been transformed into something of a mini warehouse with materials stacked on the floor in tall towers, scattered across desks, stuffed in boxes, drawers, and the backs of closets, spooled in canisters, balanced precariously on chairs. The project has virtually taken over our lives. We spend all our time now collecting media; translating rhetoric that all the Arabic courses in the world couldn't possibly have prepared us for; tracking down arcane allusions to ancient battles, martyrs, and heroes; picking the brains of anybody and everybody who'll talk with us. It's gotten easier. Unlike in the early days, we now know the Script—when people are sticking to it, when they're divulging from it, what it might mean.

Huge canvases hang from tacks on the walls—one is supposed to keep painted canvases unfolded and unbent, we've been informed—and were you to visit, you might have to sleep under a painting of almost life-size exiles walking across a bridge of skulls and bones above a torrent of blood or something of that order (a fact that did not stop many from visiting, but neither did it contribute to small talk and sweet dreams).

The stuff is everywhere—invitations, accusations, exercises in the untranslatable.

Plays, leaflets, directives, graffiti by the dozen.

Martyr cards passed around by kids in the West Bank and Gaza Strip as if baseball cards.

Murals hung not so long before in the mosques of Gaza City.

Posters—a mujahid commanding the faithful; a tree hung with the dead bodies of Israeli soldiers, as if Christmas ornaments; red poppies sprouting from land irrigated with the blood of martyrs; an exploded Egged bus smoldering on a road littered with broken bodies; a bomb detonating in a shower of apocalyptic orange, a foreshadowing of the End of the World.

Inventories of the dead and soon-to-be-dead.

Videos of the last words of boys hell-bent on Paradise. Videos of their funerals. Videos of the interrogations of collaborators, punctuated by clanging pots and pans, roosters crowing, donkeys braying, babies crying—an entire homey peasant world, ostensibly oblivious. We have dozens of such videos, all variations of the same story:

The Collaborator Ashraf Kahail
The Collaborators Muhammad Abu-'Eid +'Abd-Fatah Muhammad Ilwan
Commemorative Celebration for the Martyr Ibrahim Salama
Commemorative Celebration for the Martyr Muhammad Abu-Musameh Taha, Bani Suhaila
Commemorative Celebration for the Martyr Yasir al-Hasanat
The Hero-Martyr 'Imad Kilab, "the Jerusalemite"
Jihad Ibrahim 'Asfur, the Greatest Example of National Unity
The Martyr of the Battalions of 'Izz ad-Din al-Qassam
The Martyrs of the Battle of the Egyptian Border
The Martyr Ra'id Dhar'ib from Rafah

And here is a Christmas card from the little town of Bethlehem featuring on its cover a "child of the stone," as Palestinians call the children who grew up during the intifada, splattered with simulated blood, and, inside, the perversely cheery greeting, "Happy Holidays."

Gifts—a brass finjan, the frontispiece of a Palestinian woman's dress, a plaster recreation of the Dome of the Rock bedecked with Stars of David.

A holographic Miracle Jesus bought in the Jerusalem shuq—look at him from one angle, and his eyes jerk open; look at him from another, and they close tiredly on the world. It's horrible the way you animate him without want-ing to. You catch yourself looking at him out of the corner of your eye until he blinks. Finally, you can't take it anymore and put him inside the closet door.

(Jerusalem is full of such paraphernalia—alarm clocks that produce the call to prayer, red strings from Rachel's Tomb—remnant of some ancient men-strual ritual, Baba Sali knickknacks, rabbi trading cards, Qur'anic keychains, Egyptian scarabs, amulets of every description, vials of holy water, water from the Jordan River, holy soil from the Holy Land—all co-existing in sometimes happy confusion, the indiscriminate pantheism of pilgrim capitalism.)

Keychains featuring V-signs, the Dome of the Rock, and the map of All Pales-tine (which includes the West Bank and Gaza Strip as well as the state of Israel).

A poster of Sheikh 'Abdullah Yusuf 'Azzam, patron saint of the Battalions of the Martyr 'Izz ad-Din al-Qassam, depicted with gun in hand and a pukul cap perched jauntily on his head, commanding boys to their deaths with the serenity of a minor god.

The video still of an automated arm and fist stabbing a prostrate IDF soldier.

A cluster of blue eyes to be worn around the neck against the Evil Eye.[1]

A flattened box of "Palestine Wafers" featuring the visage of Abu-Jihad, mastermind of the first intifada, assassinated by the Mossad in Tunis in 1988.

The poem of a suicide bomber. The favorite book of a suicide bomber. The favorite audiotape of a suicide bomber.

A Ship of Salvation[2] made out of toothpaste tubes by a Palestinian prisoner in an Israeli detention camp.

Brightly colored maps of the refugee camps of Gaza and the West Bank.

Genealogies of the Prophet.

Newspaper clippings.

A book on karate favored by intifada activists.

A tape of whirling Sufis.

Diagram of a Kalashnikov.

Copy of a prison newspaper.

The phone numbers of now-forgotten persons.

Acceptance notices, rejection notices (people tended to see what they wanted to see, some insisting on flowers where there was blood; others on blood where there were flowers).

Painstakingly coded notes, the meaning of which is now indecipherable.

Files too big to be opened.

Objects that but suggest the phantasmagoric universe from which they came.

19. Walls, Maze, Prison

Here's a snapshot that evokes that universe if only because it captures so much sheer space, so many worlds and subworlds. It was taken from the roof of Yusuf's house in Deir al-Balah, where people seemed to spend half their time during the intifada—shooting the breeze, escaping the heat and mayhem and teargas of the world below, shouting "Allahu akbar!" or just listening and watching and waiting for God knows what to happen. We were always waiting, it seems.

In the far distance, a thin blue line of ocean can be seen, another world beckoning, while below, the city resembles a maze—a thick conglomeration of cinderblock in which the houses are jammed so closely together and are so windowless that the effect is that of walls within walls, streets being formed by the outer walls of houses within which there are yet more walls. All the sights and sounds and smells of this city bespeak one thing—revolution. It's a virtual Richard Scarry BusyWorld turned upside down.

Every wall is awash with slogans—daubed, brushed, scratched, and sprayed—that appear and disappear overnight, the words of unseen ventriloquists—"Strike, strike by Molotov . . . after the stone, the Kalashnikov!" "Yes to martyrdom and immolation . . . no to disgrace." "Kill . . . blow up . . . destroy!"

Music is playing on a tape player. One song[3] sounds like this:

Palestinian blood has been flowing since the feet of the new Tatars set foot on a land blessed by Allah; so, from Kufur Qassem to Deir Yasin to Jerash and 'Ajlun, to Tel az-Za'tar to Sabra and Shatilla, to the Shaja'iya incident to the slaughter of 'Ayun Qara, this torrent will not be stopped except by a torrent of revolution and giving.[4]

The blood flowed and covered the land—and daylight filled the world
The scoundrels have taken Palestine—who will bring revenge?

In Sabra, a wound is bleeding—and flowers are wilting
In Tel az-Za'tar—the garden of the revolutionaries is growing

In Black September—a fire broke out in the camps
The father went, the brother went—and what happened to us happened

They said, Husain,[5] and they said, Fahd—they counted many men
They said, Qabous, and they said, Mubarak—they counted many men

I said, What a pity—Mighty Jerusalem, liberated by midgets!
I said, What a pity—Mighty Jerusalem, liberated by midgets!
I said, What a pity—Mighty Jerusalem, liberated by midgets!

The blood flowed and covered the land—and daylight filled the world
Scoundrels have taken Palestine—who will bring revenge?

Communiqués are blowing through the streets. They announce strike days, "days of the Palestinian flag," the latest slogan to be written on the walls, the most recent martyr. Instructions are being broadcast from the minarets of mosques. Shabab walk the streets, shouting messages through hand-carried loudspeakers. Strike-force members police the shops, forcing clerks to lock up on strike days, and schools, where they announce the answers to exams on loud-speakers. You never see the faces of these guys, only their eyes, peering through the crude peep holes they jag into masks of cloth, paper, and garbage bags.

The teachers are afraid of them, these young men with knives and guns, swords and hatchets, and soon agree to grade their charges' schoolwork ac-cording to "revolutionary criteria." Even kindergartners are not exempt from the fervor. Along with the usual nursery rhymes, they are taught songs and chants like this one, which was performed for us in a school in Khan Yunis, with the teacher directing:

> My father brought me a present
> A gun and a machine-gun
> When I grow up, I will join the Liberation Army
> The Liberation Army told me how to defend my homeland
> Victory, victory over America and Israel!

The teacher stands at the head of the class. "What is the name of our country?" she asks. "Palestine!" the children reply in unison. "Who is the en-emy who stole our country?" she asks. "The Jews!" exclaim the children. "What shall we do to them?" she asks. "Strike them with stones!" the children scream.

After school, children pour into the streets for a lethal version of catch-me-if-you-can. They roll tires into the middle of the street, set them on fire, and then run for their lives, taunting the soldiers with stones and curses as they go. Or they parade through the streets, chanting about martyrdom, as if spec-tators of their own deaths:

> O mother, my religion has called me to jihad and self-sacrifice
> O mother, I am marching toward immortality; I will never retreat
> O mother, don't cry over me if I am shot down, laid out on the ground
> For death is my path; martyrdom, my desire.

Soon, a stone or Molotov will be tossed at the soldiers. Someone will get ar-rested, or beaten, or shot.

Inside the houses and shops and mosques are photographs of martyrs, martyr calendars, martyr shrines, martyr cards, close-ups of wounds incurred in dem-onstrations. Doors, walls, ceilings, mats, and furniture are painted in the colors of the Palestinian flag, or depict scenes from the intifada. Laid out on tables are prison memorabilia—stones elaborately carved with lapidary verses, photo frames constructed out of Elite Chocolate wrappers and toothpaste tubes, prayer beads out of olive pits, bracelets out of the canvas of IDF army tents. Buried outside are caches of weapons, wrapped in plastic.

Videos are playing, featuring the latest martyr—his last words and call for others to follow in his footsteps. On other sets, news footage of the latest street demonstration is being shown over and over again, with scenes of the wounded being carted away in ambulances. A leaflet has decreed the day to be a "day of the Molotov cocktail." The clocks all read in "Palestinian time," rather than "Israeli time."[6] Outside, someone has hoisted a flag atop a telephone pole, and yet another crowd of people has formed, and is chanting, "With spirit, with blood, we will sacrifice ourselves for you, O martyr!"

Outside this echo chamber, this exhaustion of resources, there is nothing. You get the feeling that you do not see and hear what everyone else does. Something is missing.

20. An Entire Cosmology

The display suggests an entire cosmology. It's huge—over thirty feet in length—and is composed of twenty or thirty hand-colored mimeographs that have been taped together end on end.

It's 1992. The intifada is going strong, and people still believe on some level that victory over Israel is possible. "Truly," as the Islamists liked to say, "a nation whose sons vie with each other for the sake of martyrdom does not know defeat." The idea that people might die for nothing had simply not yet seeped into consciousness, and for some, it never did.

That is why the two men in the central panel of the display are shown crouching atop a blue Star of David, the major symbol of the state of Israel, loading their pistols, while in the row of panels above them, the theme of promised vanquishment is repeated again in the form of more armed men standing victoriously atop the star, which is cracked and bleeding. A grenade occupies one corner and a soldier's helmet the other—the detritus of victory, means and end.

In another of the panels, a map of All Palestine has been stood on its end next to a Kalashnikov rifle, and nestled within the map is a shabb masked in a keffiyah. Members of strike forces often referred to themselves as *mulaththamun*, "masked ones," avenging Ninjas, as in the half-rhyme, "For every masked man, a keffiyah; for every collaborator, an axe." Barbed wire spikes outward from the shoulder of the shabb in gnarly intricacies, while nearby can be seen a depiction of the Dome of the Rock and the shabb's death oath:

> I swear by the One who made fast your mountains
> and set your clouds in motion, O Palestine,
> that I will erase shame
> in every house
> and from my blood and bones I will weave
> banners of victory for Islam

Using body parts to form images and words was a common device in the iconology of the intifada. Recalling an ancient Arabic technique of writing, the simple calligrammatic figures meld object and word, the concrete and the abstract, into a single indivisible unit. Human skulls are piled atop one another to form the word *Hamas*, or they are used to form a ladder, as in the slogan, "At your service! I will make from our skulls a ladder for your pride," or a bridge, as in "We will make from the skulls of the traitors a bridge/for the revolution to cross over." Torches are fueled by human blood rather than oil. Kalashnikovs stack up to form the name of a particular faction. The blood of martyrs is transformed into stones in the hands of street fighters. Blood streams from the back of a boy-martyr to form the byword, "The intifada continues." The word "freedom" is formed from miniature bombs ready to explode in the face of the reader.

Visceral imagery such as this abounded in all the media of the intifada—images of spitting, shaking, shuddering, riding, cutting, writhing, stabbing, thrusting, bleeding. The very word chosen by Palestinians to describe the cataclysmic changes wrought by the intifada relies on the body in this way, derived as it is from the verb *intafada*, meaning "to shake; to shudder, shiver, tremble."

The next panel in the series is occupied by the figure of Sheikh Yasin. "O Ahmad Yasin," reads the tribute, "You are our imam/ Your gigantic faith fortifies us/ You, O Ahmad Yasin, have taught us/ that prison is a vacation and pride/ that man is made of his positions/ his unyieldingness, his . . . decisions." Another panel features the map of All Palestine, which resembles a crude dagger or an exclamation point—a reminder of the Islamists' insistence that Palestine is *ard al-muqaddis*, or holy land, "a land of the Islamic Waqf for the Muslim generations until the Day of Resurrection," as it's put in the movement's covenant, and until victory arrives, not a *shibr*, or "hand's breadth," of it can be relinquished. Still more of the panels feature other major emblems of Hamas—the Dome of the Rock; crossed rifles; an open Qur'an inscribed with the Muslim Brothers' motto, *Wa'iddu*, "And prepare," the imperative that begins verse sixty of chapter eight of the Qur'an; a mosque encircled by an evil serpent; an Islamic Ninja. The Ninja is dressed, typically, in Islamic green and poses with an M-16 and Qur'an. Hanging from his belt are a knife and grenade, which further accentuate his status as a "lover of death." He peers from his mask, brandishing his weapon, or explodes out of a grenade, while beneath him lie the skulls and bones of the dead, floating in pools of blood.

Whereas the Ninja figure owes its origins to the popular Ninja movies that play almost nonstop across TV screens throughout the West Bank and Strip, the serpent dragon,[7] sometimes of the fire-breathing variety, coiled tightly around the Dome of the Rock or the globe, is probably borrowed from the revolutionary art of Iran, whose influence became more prominent in the posters of Hamas after the 1991 expulsion of a number of the movement's leaders to the snow-clad slopes of Marj az-Zahur, Lebanon, an Iranian-influenced Shi'a stronghold in the south of the country, following a Hamas-sponsored campaign of "stabbing operations" carried out against Israelis on the streets of Jerusalem. In the West Bank and Gaza, the deportees were quickly made into heroes with songs, poems, and paintings created in their honor.

In one such poster, an Islamic eagle lifts the flap of an exile's tent, revealing a black despair within. In another, drops of red blood form patterns in the snow. In yet another, a group of deportees trudge onward through the icy cold, their shoulders hunched in harsh determination. They march across a bridge composed of Israeli skulls, inscribed with Stars of David. A river of red blood runs beneath them. In the background, white snow falls beneath two black suns.

The dragon may also be derived from the illustrations accompanying Western conspiratorial and anti-Semitic works, many of which have been given an Islamic slant in intifada media. The connection is made explicit in one poster in our collection made in celebration of 'Eid al-Fitr, the Feast of Breaking the Fast, celebrated at the end of the holy month of Ramadan, a popular day for carrying out armed attacks. A bald eagle wearing a medallion inscribed with the word *Islam* clutches in its talons a bleeding snake crowned with a red Star of David. The blood falls on the Dome of the Rock, which is cradled in a tree. The roots of the tree are irrigated by pools of blood, on which float the skulls and bones of the dead.

Written below the configuration are words uttered shortly after the creation of Israel in 1948 by "the imam, the martyr" Hasan al-Banna.

> The state of Israel will persist!
> It will continue to exist until Allah abolishes it by Islam
> Like that which he has abolished before

In case the message is still unclear, the authors have added the popular Hamas slogan, "Truly, the destruction of the state of Israel is a Qur'anic inevitability," which is derived from the title of a book by Sheikh As'ad at-Tamimi, the former imam of al-Aqsa Mosque and one of the founders and leaders of the Palestinian Islamic Jihad. The slogan is followed directly by verse 104 of the chapter of the Qur'an entitled "The Night Journey" (or "The Tribes of Israel"): "For when the last promise comes," reads the verse, "we will gather you together from a motley crowd"—words widely taken as a prophecy of the ingathering of the Jews and the destruction of the state of Israel.

21. A Question of Style

Here's a message that brings to mind the question of style, the connections between style and ideology, style and violence. It was posted in the West Bank village of Jiljilya by Fatah *mulaththamun*, dressed in snappy brown jumpsuits, beekeeper-style headgear, and matching red-tipped hatchets slung low on their belts, the ultimate fashion accessory. It is written in English, and reads, "I love to kill Jews," and thus departs from the traditional nationalist practice of calling the enemy "Zionists."

One simply can't imagine the Islamists posting such a message. Although not averse to directness per se—one thinks of messages like "Peace with the Jews leads to Hell" and the almost comic "Did you know that the director of the BBC is a spiteful Jew?"—when it came to killing, the Islamists generally avoided direct, unadorned confessions of bloodlust, preferring instead to authorize their operations with Qur'an and ahadith.

In the early years of the intifada, it was easy to distinguish between nationalists and Islamists. Their lexicons were different. Their conception of the world was different. Their style, a word almost impossible to define, was different, and it was not a trivial difference, as the word might suggest to some, but rather held radical implications, style being inextricably intertwined with content. Pick almost any topic, and the difference between the nationalists and the Islamists would quickly become manifest.

Whereas the Islamists called for jihad, the nationalists used less-loaded terms like *al-kifah al-musallah*, "armed struggle," and, less often, *al-harb ash-sha'bia*, "popular war." They liked to draw the map of All Palestine in what was then the forbidden mix of black, white, red, and green—the colors of the Palestinian flag—or cover it with a keffiyah, as though land and shabb had been mapped onto one another, the loss of Palestine correlating with a sense of lost personal wholeness. Sometimes, they surrounded the map with weapons or melded it with weapons or drew it in blood or in tears.

The nationalists loved biladi, folksy songs about the land, the time when the people were one with the land. The land was a flower, as in the children's rhyme, "If the rose is the most beautiful of flowers, then Palestine is the rose of the Arab world." It was heart, wound, key, mother, witness, green tree, crown of hearts, "bosom" of the world. It was "plowed by fingernails." Its grass "moaned." Its trees—olive, pepper, lemon, fig, and cypress—talked and almost walked, bowing down in awe to the glorious mujahid people of Palestine. It was said to possess eyes, waist, chest, bosom, hair, a "perfumed spirit." It was a giant. It was a "volcano of blood." It was said to be angry.

Shepherds roamed its hills with flock and flute, as in the lines invoking the pastoral figure Zarif at-Tul by the Fatah-affiliated Sharaf at-Tibi Band, "O shepherd, O you who take your flock out early in the dewy morning/ How beautiful is your flute letting fall the sweetest melodies, the flowers spreading smiles around you." Peasants harvested its wheat, a common symbol of martyrs, and were often referred to in sacrificial language reminiscent of martyrs, as in this excerpt, also from the Sharaf at-Tibi Band, in which the peasant is said to "irrigate" the land with his blood:

> O fellah [peasant], the land . . . the land
> O fellah, the land . . . the land
> Never neglect it, by Allah
> Defend it like your honor
> Defend it like your honor
> With your blood, you'll irrigate it, by Allah

The Islamists didn't care for this type of thing at all, melding as it did nationalism and a soft and fertile folk culture, even though many of them had grown up within such a culture. They considered nationalism, especially secular nationalism, an "ideological incursion" (to quote from Hamas' covenant) advanced by foreign powers to weaken the Islamic world. They preferred to call Palestine *ula al-qiblatain*, "the first of the two qiblas," a reference to the time, early in Islam, when Muhammad and his followers followed the custom of the Jews in orienting their direction of prayer (qibla) toward Jerusalem—a direction that was later changed from Jerusalem to the Ka'ba in Mecca, the central shrine of Islam and the second qibla. The Islamists also called Palestine *ard al-Isra'*, a reference to Muhammad's Night Journey from Mecca to "al-Aqsa," an event that constitutes one of the chief miracles in Islam, and *ard al-Masra*, "the place of the Isra'." Although Arafat would later copy the Islamists when speaking of Jerusalem, for most of the intifada, such references generally characterized Islamists, not nationalists.

The Islamist ideal was neither peasant nor shepherd but rather the hajj, the religious pilgrim who relinquishes his earthly possessions in order to fulfill the commands of God, as in the following graffito we recorded in Deir al-Balah Refugee Camp, a message that, notably, makes no direct reference to the political, instead relying on the resonance of religious acts easily translated into the political realm. The implications of the cultic practice of stoning Satan would have been lost on no one:

> Hamas welcomes those who journeyed from the soil of the homeland, leaving behind them the most precious of their possessions for a love raised above all other loves, which is the love of Allah and the Messenger. The hajj accepted into the grace of His Lord has no other portion but Paradise. Hamas calls on the sons of the Muslim people to fulfill the command of Allah and to take refuge in Him, following the example of our noble pilgrims. How urgently our mujahid people need to realize that before them are the dangerous temptations of Satan and the necessity of resisting them and of following the example of the pilgrims who have _____ [illegible] the stoned Satan.

Another Hamas poster in our collection features the religious formula *Labaik*, "At your service" or "Here am I," used by pilgrims to address God as they approach the Ka'ba on the hajj. "At your service, Islam of heroism. All of us will sacrifice ourselves for you," reads the poster, whose centerpiece is an Islamic green crescent inscribed with the major slogan of Hamas, "Islam is the solution," while below, a fist wielding the map of historical Palestine as a weapon bursts forth from barren ground next to the slogan, "Our al-Aqsa, not their Temple."

As these messages suggest, Hamas saw personal rectification, if not salvation, as a necessary prerequisite for the success of a wider, political reconstruction and gained considerable power through the melding of the two. Everything else was deemed a distraction. Worse, it was said to be *jahaliya*—a term referring to the time of "ignorance" before the arrival of Muhammad. Following the Islamist thinker Said Qutb, who applied the term to contemporary political and social structures he considered un-Islamic or anti-Islamic, Hamas uses the term in its covenant in a section entitled "The Role of Art in the Liberation Battle":

> Art has orders and standards by which it is possible to know [the answer to the question], Is this art Islamic or jahaliya? The crisis of Islamic liberation demands Islamic art, which elevates the spirit and does not favor one side of man over another side but rather elevates all sides in balance and harmony.
>
> And man is a miraculous and wondrous being made from a handful of mud and a puff of spirit, and Islamic art addresses man on this basis whereas jahaliya art addresses the body and favors the side of mud.
>
> Books, articles, publications, sermons, epistles, poems, odes, songs, plays, and others—if they evidence the characteristics of Islamic art, then they are necessities for ideological mobilization and for nourishing the continuation of the journey and refreshing the soul. For the road is long, and difficulties are many, and spirits can flag. And Islamic art renews vitality, and inspires the movement, and kindles in the soul good qualities and sound management.

Despite its dedication to purist goals, the "Islamic art" of Hamas managed at times to be both austere and stimulating—a difficult feat to carry off, one might be inclined to think. Unlike the songs and military marches beloved by the nationalists, many of which were similar to their counterparts the world over, the chants and anthems of Hamas were devoid of music except for the hypnotic beat of drums. Nationalist graffiti were often florid designs rendered in the colors of the Palestinian flag—a style epitomized by the work of what we began to call "the Beit Hanina School," named after the upper-middle-class, largely nationalist Palestinian suburb of northern Jerusalem. In contrast, Islamist graffiti were generally more wordy, images being initially restricted to the triad of mosque, fist, and banner but quickly expanding as the intifada went on. The nationalist-oriented artists disallowed almost any Islamists into their closed circle as inferior, but the Islamists, despite the much-touted Islamic ban on graven images, often had a flair for painting, whether rendering scenes from the intifada or commuting Arabic letters into almost psychedelic swirls. The tension and overlap between excitation and spiritual exaltation was nowhere better expressed than in a face mask we saw featuring the rallying cry "Allahu akbar!" formed out of hot pink sequins—a wacky marriage of religious formula and belly-dancer kitsch.

More commonly, Hamas activists declared a zealous suspicion of all things sensual—indeed, pleasure, in general—associating it with nationalist decadence, as when a singer on the Islamic Jihad audiocassette *The Call of Jihad* bemoans the nationalist pastime of folk song and dance, suggesting that it has diverted the attention of the umma from its proper goals—a song whose breathy repetition of the name of God reminds one of a Sufi chant, or *dhikr*:

O our nation, where is honor? Where dignity and freedom?
Where the fervor for glory? Where the proud souls?

> In the name of Allah—Allah, Allah
> In the name of Allah—Allah, Allah
> In the name of Allah—Allah, Allah
> In the name of Allah—Allah, Allah

They taught us only dancing, and they taught us only singing
They made us learn all kinds of dancing—shaking and dabka [folk dance]

> In the name of Allah—Allah, Allah
> In the name of Allah—Allah, Allah
> In the name of Allah—Allah, Allah
> In the name of Allah—Allah, Allah

The Islamist condemnation of merrymaking often took stronger forms. In the following communiqué from the Gaza Strip, for example, Hamas demands cessation of what it calls "shameless parties," a reference to traditional celebrations featuring music and dance that had been common before the intifada, and promises violent punishment for those who continue to hold them:

> In the name of Allah, the Compassionate, the Merciful
> This is a communiqué for the people
>
> The Islamic Resistance Movement, Hamas, demands that you, O people of the camp fortified for war, cease from making shameless parties, which the enemy tries to spread. And those who make such parties will be punished violently, and Hamas will not be silent this time or ever out of loyalty to the blood of the martyrs, the wounded, and the prisoners. Allahu akbar. And thanks be to Allah.

The threat is full of Qur'anic terms and allusions that empower and authorize it. It is addressed, for example, to *an-nass*, "the people," a formal term often found in the vocatives that initiate verses of the Qur'an, rather than to *ash-sha'b*, its secular analogue. In the next line of the document, *an-nass* becomes *al-murabitun*, "people fortified for war," a term derived from the Qur'anic root *rabata*, used to refer to those who fight according to the prescriptions of the Qur'an, that is, in closed ranks. Due to its association with Qur'anic-inspired conquest and victory, the term possesses a long heritage. One of the more notable usages of the term occurred in the late tenth century when 'Abdullah ibn Yasin applied it to his followers. A Moroccan brought back from Mecca by the chieftain of the Sanhaja, a Berber tribe in the western Sahara, to teach Qur'an, hadith, and *shari'a* (Islamic law),[8] ibn Yasin warned of the coming of the Day of Judgment, called for the punishment of sinners according to a strict interpretation of Islamic law, and insisted that "the greater jihad" involving the inner rectification of the fighter, must precede "the lesser jihad," prescribed war against enemies. He and his followers went on to conquer Morocco and southern Spain, after which they set about closing down taverns and destroying musical instruments—a mission that today would be fully endorsed by Hamas. The movement insists upon a puritanical code of conduct, and, as can be seen in the following leaflet disseminated in the Gaza Strip in the summer of 1994, often blames what it calls "dissipation" on the nationalists and their peace initiatives:

From Occupation to Dissipation[9]

Following the lifting of the affliction of the occupation from some of the areas of Gaza, young women appeared barely dressed, and the people started to take pleasure in ostentatiousness, and jeans appeared.

And confusion and friction have been noticed between adolescent girls and boys as well as drumming and singing here and there.

And in this way the honor of the martyrs is trod upon, and we forget their blood and the unmarried prisoners and the wounds of the injured, and it is as if Palestine and her al-Aqsa [Mosque] had already been liberated from the dung of the sons of monkeys and pigs [a common reference to Jews in Hamas literature].

And it is clear that the sole possible explanation for this dissipation is the Gaza-Jericho plan . . . and it is as if the occupation has been replaced by dissipation.

There is no power and no strength save in Allah.

We belong to Allah, and to Him we are returning.

The "Gaza-Jericho plan" refers to the 1993 agreement between Israel and the PLO that led to the withdrawal of Israeli troops from the Gaza Strip and the oasis town of Jericho in the West Bank as a first step to the parties holding wider-ranging talks. Hamas attributes all manner of "dissipation" to the plan—everything from blue jeans and flirting to "drumming and singing"—temptation, it seems, comprising the ultimate military strategy and weapon of war.

22. It Doesn't Matter When or How I Am Killed

We started out collecting graffiti, which we should explain is not graffiti as most people probably think of it. When people in the West think of graffiti, they think of subway tags spray-painted in bold, blocky, sparkling letters; anarchy signs; drug slang; love confessions. But that's not what intifada graffiti was like at all. You could ride forever through the towns and villages of the Bank and Strip and never see anything like "David Loves Jenny" among the hundreds of messages that on any given day covered walls, telephone poles, stones, cacti, and bodies. Intifada graffiti was preoccupied with other things—the announcement of strike days, instructions on boycotts and demonstrations, advertisements for one faction or another ("Long Live the PLO!" "Hamas is the solution!"). The intifada was young, and people hadn't yet learned what it was they were supposed to be doing and thinking.

Many of the slogans of the intifada can be traced at least as far back as the Palestinian revolts of 1929 and 1936 and the war of 1948, with comparable and sometimes identical rhetoric to be found in the old poetry on the "oppression" and "tyranny" of the Turks during the period of Ottoman rule in Palestine. A surprising number of messages were concerned with far older events and personages—ancient battles, warriors, prophets, and martyrs. The past, it was clear, was something felt as real and pressing; you could never escape from it, and were condemned—honored, some believed—to repeat it until the end of time.

Here, for instance, is a not atypical piece of graffiti that suggests the uncanny quality of eternal return, referring as it does to an event that took place fourteen hundred years ago. Painted on a wall on the main thoroughfare connecting Jerusalem and Ramallah, in Beit Hanina, the graffito features a map of All Palestine crowned by an open Qur'an, emitting rays like a sun, and the last words of the martyr Khubaib al-Ansari, who had fought in the famous battle of Badr (623 CE), the first major victory of Muhammad and the early Muslims over the enemy Meccans and the paradigm of victory against all odds for Palestinians—nationalists and Islamists alike.

Spray-painted at the top of the graffito is the imperative "And prepare," which initiates a section of the Qur'an in which Muhammad's followers are assured that although outnumbered, they will be victorious in their upcoming battle against the Meccans, a reference to the battle of Badr:

> And prepare against them whatever forces and cavalry you are able to muster so that you may terrify the enemies of Allah and your enemies and others besides them that you know not but which Allah knows. And whatever you shall spend on the path of Allah will be paid back to you in full, and you will not be wronged.

Around the borders of the map are written other sacred imperatives derived from the Qur'anic sura "The Family of 'Imran" (3:199). Counterclockwise, they read, "Be patient and persevere," "Fortify one another," and "Take up your positions." The heart of the map is a clenched fist holding twin banners that bear the credo of Islam, "There is no god but Allah, and Muhammad is the Messenger of Allah." The fist, in turn, is founded upon the Dome of the Rock—a configuration that serves to underline Palestinian claims to Mount Moriah, the ancient site of Solomon's Temple. Everything is symmetrical—there's a split down the center of the canvas, and objects appear exactly in the middle or balanced precisely on either side, as though the whole structure were in imminent danger of collapsing.

To the right can be seen the last words of Khubaib al-Ansari, who, after being captured during the battle of Badr, was sold in Mecca to the sons of al-Harith, a man whom al-Ansari had killed in battle. Before dying, al-Ansari is said to have uttered, "It doesn't matter when or how I am killed as a Muslim as long as my death is for the sake of Allah." The words appeared not only on the walls during the intifada but also in music. They are featured, for instance, on an audiocassette of Islamic anthems produced by the Group of the Guardians (a band based in Kafr Kana, an Israeli Arab village located within the Green Line), as well in the Hamas anthem "O My Homeland," which has Sheikh Yasin repeating them from his prison cell:

> O proud mountain, though shackled in sadness, you will not yield
> O Ahmad Yasin, the night has dissipated because of your patience
> The horses of the call are calling us
> They are bringing us to Ahmad Yasin
> O horses, don't fall back
> Although he is far away, behind iron bars, in his cell,
> it is as though I am with him, hearing him repeat the words of Khubaib, saying,
> "It matters not to me when I am killed as a Muslim,
> on which side my death takes place, as long as it is for the sake of Allah."
> To the Paradise of Eternity, we are going
> We will be with you, insha'Allah

For a long time after we first came across al-Ansari's last words, we puzzled over the phrase "on which side my death takes place," wondering what it could possibly mean. It was a pre-Google world, and we solved the mystery only after a lot of digging. We brought up al-Ansari's name with virtually everyone we met and searched through countless books until we finally hit upon an allusion to the martyr that mentioned that he might have been crucified, or perhaps even drawn and quartered. Still other accounts have him hanged before being speared and mutilated. While dangling from the hangman's rope, he is said to have recited a poem suggesting that God would bless his amputated limbs.

Al-Ansari holds a particularly high place of honor in the Islamic pantheon of martyrs not only because he was one of the first, but because he lent Islamic ritual form to the act of dying in the hands of one's enemy. The first request he made of his captors was for a razor with which to shave his private parts; the second was that he be allowed to pray before dying. His captors granted him both wishes. He prayed a shorter prayer than usual, and is attributed with setting the tradition by which a Muslim sentenced to die in captivity should offer a prayer of two prostrations rather than the prescribed four. (He would have prayed longer, he informed his executors, but he did not want them to think that he was afraid of dying.) His last rites are recounted by al-Bukhari and, today, serve as ceremonial trappings, ritualizations of death, for those who would follow in his footsteps.

Used in similar fashion as the battle of Badr as a harbinger of future Palestinian victory is the battle of Hattin, the name of a hilltop above the Sea of Galilee, where, in 1187, the Muslim armies under the leadership of the Kurd Salah ad-Din defeated the Crusader force of the Knights Templar in a decisive face-off. The battle makes appearance in a song from the tape *Islamic Anthem Festival* 1, which presents the intifada as its return: "Hattin has returned in Balata [Refugee Camp] and Hebron, and its Salah [ad-Din] is a masked child in the camp, suckled at the breast of dignity, so be happy, O Jerusalem, for salvation has come from youth who love death and bullets passionately." A poster we acquired in Gaza City promises a similar recurrence:

Hattin: Salah [ad-Din] wrote it, so don't you see
that we will celebrate our Hattin with the destruction of the Jews
O our people, rise up, for the Lord of the Worshippers
does not wish for us to be humiliated like slaves

Despite his non-Arab origin, Salah ad-Din, who founded the Ayyubid dynasty that ruled over what is today Syria, Iraq, Egypt, and Yemen, has long been used in Arab polemics as a symbol of what is imagined to be the eventual vanquishment of the Jewish state. It took two-hundred years to regain the land occupied by the Crusaders, the argument goes; the Jewish state, in comparison, has existed for a mere forty-five years. Hamas sees itself as the spearhead of such an enterprise, and commonly presents itself as Salah ad-Din's inheritor, as in the following song by the Hamas-affiliated Jordanian Islamic Band:

If the heroes of Hattin
could witness the deeds of our Battalions,
Salah [ad-Din] would get down off his horse and announce,
Here am I, Hamas, our inheritor.

Like Hattin, Khaibar, the last of a series of battles fought between Muhammad's followers and the Jewish tribes of the region for the control of western Arabia, is another historical battle that makes frequent appearance in intifada media. In the time of Muhammad, the oasis of Khaibar was inhabited primarily by Jewish Arabian tribes. At the start of his mission, Muhammad had expected acceptance and support from the Jews, seeing himself in the line of Abraham, Moses, and the great Hebrew prophets of old. Within a short period, however, it became clear that the Jews of the region rejected his claim to prophethood. Matters only worsened when he became a political as well as spiritual leader. In a series of battles fought in the oases surrounding Medina, the Jews were quickly overwhelmed. The battle for Khaibar oasis was the last of these skirmishes. The Jewish males were killed; the women and children, sold into slavery. By 640, the Jews had been exiled from much of the Arabian peninsula.

References to Khaibar abound in Islamist media, as in the popular chant, "In the name of Allah, Allahu akbar /In the name of Allah, Khaibar has come!"

and the sung line, "Khaibar, Khaibar, O Jews, the Army of Muhammad will return!" On one Hamas videotape in our collection, an armed man states that his cell, the Group of the Martyrs, "rose to answer the call of duty, the call of 'Come to jihad,' the call of 'Allahu akbar, the time of Khaibar has come!'" On the tape *Islamic Zajal* 4, the call for slaughter is made explicit. "Intensify it [the intifada] by knife and *khanjar*, and slaughter the Jews, the Sons of Khaibar," the anthem commands, *khanjar* referring to a curved dagger often used as a symbol of Arabdom, and "slaughter" denoting a sacrificial act, specifically, "to slaughter by slitting the throat."

Yet another historical battle referenced in intifada media is the attack launched against Mecca and the Ka'ba by the king of Yemen Abraha al-Ashram in 571 CE, "the Year of the Elephant," the year in which Muhammad was born—an event recorded in the "Sura of the Elephant" (Qur'an 105). The Christian king was said to have employed in the attack elephants, which were successfully repulsed by birds carrying stones. As in the following song, the story is commonly translated into the present with America in the role of the elephants and Palestinians as the stone-throwing birds who, surprisingly, prove victorious against their weighty foe—a reversal of expectations that works in the same way as the biblical story of David and Goliath, which was similarly rewritten during the intifada with a Palestinian "child of the stone" replacing David and Israel replacing Goliath:

> And we are making war with black stones
> so to whom will be the victory, Abraha al-Ashram or Muhammad?
> America will make war on us with airplanes, tanks, and dollars
> and collaborators and incompetents and mercenaries
> and we will make war on them with the sword of Salah ad-Din
> and we will know the duration of the darkness
> It is impossible to blot out the moon of the poor
> It is impossible to extinguish the sun of the bereaved

Perhaps the most well-known allusion to the war of black stones occurs in "Where Are the Millions?" the hugely popular song by the Lebanese Christian Julia Butros. The song contrasts "the generation of truth, the generation of revolution" with "the Masters of the Elephant," and the accompanying video makes clear who is who and what is what with scenes of IDF soldiers beating Palestinian demonstrators interspersed with shots of the Smoking Cowboy of Las Vegas, the flurry of Wall Street, and other signs of American power and decadence.

23. Martyr on a Black Horse

You will never understand anything about the lure of martyrdom, the centerpiece of intifada cosmology, until you realize that someone who has decided to take that path as his own sees himself not only as an avenging Ninja, but also as something of a movie star, maybe even a sex symbol—a romantic figure at the very least, larger than life.

Here, for instance, is a photograph that was posted in Khan Yunis Camp upon the martyrdom of Khalid al-Halabi—a mujahid who was also well known as an artist (he learned to paint in an Israeli prison by looking at art books on the European masters) and philosopher (he wrote a book in prison called *The Philosophy of Truth*—it was confiscated). The photograph exudes a certain self-consciousness. The subject knows he's a striking figure as he races across the sands of Gaza atop a black horse.

The horse is dashing—chestnut undertones, massive vein-studded neck, clean white diamond at the center of her forehead, long forelocks held back off her face by a bridle. She wears a brass triangle with red tassels around her neck as a protection against the Evil Eye, an amulet against anyone who would want to take her away. In the photo, you can see al-Halabi pulling at the reins, his mouth tight and drawn, the horse almost prancing, her lips pulled back, teeth bared; and even though you are only looking at a photograph, you can feel her tempestuousness, her romance—why she was called *Zawabia*, "Storms." When al-Halabi was alive, people liked to recount, the horse would follow him around like a dog. She was the last thing he painted—the two of them, horse and rider, rendered in the webby, membranous style for which he was famous. After his death, the horse, they say, became wild, like a thing possessed, as though she were just waiting for death like her master had waited for his, as though she were neither completely of this world nor of the next.

Here's how it would happen—how, that is, somebody would become such a ghost—what Palestinians liked to call a "living martyr," a person dedicated to death but still alive. First, to prove himself, the person would kill an Israeli or a Palestinian collaborator. After that, his name might be placed on an IDF black list, and he would be "hunted" by undercover squads who often dressed as Palestinians in order to trap their quarry. He would no longer wear a mask, his identity being known, nor would he continue to live at home; rather, according to West Bank legend, he would live in one of the many limestone caves that dot the countryside. People would bring him food and water. Everyone would speak his name. Cards would be printed with his picture on them, his face surrounded by guns and roses, to be given to friends, relatives, and fellow activists, or sold on the street to admirers as memorials and souvenirs, as in this "certificate for self-sacrifice" for Mahmud az-Zaraini, former West Bank commander of Fatah's Black Panther:

Name: Martyr with a stay of execution

Date of birth: I am as old as the revolution

Occupation: Fida'i ("self-sacrificer")

Summary of above: Certified for self-sacrifice for the homeland

To the right, the name *Mahmud*, drawn in a keffiyah design, tears through and initializes a bleeding wound in the heart of a map of All Palestine, as if the name itself were capable of staving off the impersonality of death and language. At the top of the card is inscribed the accolade, "The martyr of Arabitude and the homeland, Mahmud," which is followed by a poem popular long before the advent of the intifada, which Palestinian prisoners say was often written on the walls of their cells:

> I will be patient until patience is worn out from my patience
> and I will be patient until Allah decrees my condition
> and I will be patient until patience knows
> that I will bear stoutly that which is more bitter than patience.

In a cutout photograph to the left, az-Zaraini can be seen pointing to a cactus and, simultaneously, to himself, thereby presenting himself as the poem's incarnation. The illustration is also a pun of sorts, *sabr* ("patience") and *subar*[10] ("cactus") being cognates. Behind him is a black panther, his group's totem, which upon his death will be engraved upon his tombstone.

The martyr was said to live forever in Paradise, his sins wiped clean. Indeed, a special place was reserved for those who killed and were killed fi sabil Allah, as it is written, "In Paradise there are a hundred levels, which Allah reserves for the mujahidun on His path; the distance between two levels is like that between heaven and the earth"—words attributed to the Prophet Muhammad by Bukhari.[11] Moreover, according to a hadith quoted favorably by 'Abdullah 'Azzam, the martyr immediately sees his assigned station in Paradise.

Living martyrs spoke often of the joy of martyrdom[12] and their hopes of seeing Muhammad and his Companions and their friends and family who were already in Heaven, for it is said that with the first drop of blood spilled, the martyr went straight to Paradise and was reunited with everyone he loved who had died before him. He might be buried in the clothes in which he died, the bloodstains of his wounds serving as witness to his sacrificial death. His body was believed never to decay—indeed, it was said to smell sweet for a month or longer after death. Numerous stories circulated during the intifada to support the belief in the immortal intactness of the martyr's body—stories of roses blossoming on the bodies of martyrs, mothers obtaining fatwas to open the tombs of their sons and finding them completely unchanged, corpses emitting spectacular lights. (A far lesser number of stories expressed doubt and misgiving, as in the tale of the man from Jalazon who wanted to build a stone tomb for his brother, a PFLP hero, following the traditional forty days of mourning, but who actually had doubts about whether he was really the great martyr that people said he was. Seeking proof one way or the other, the man dug up his brother's grave and found only bones.)

As a martyr, not only were you immune to postmortem decay but you were also exempt from the so-called Torment of the Tomb, the interrogation of the dead by the angels Munkar and Nakir, which took place during the eerie time between one's death and one's entrance into the afterworld. Renowned for their blue-black hue, thunderclap voices, lightning-bolt eyes, and iron whips—the descriptions are those of ibn Taymiya—the monstrous twins are said to come and sit by the dead in their tombs after the last footsteps of the mourners have faded away.

If you were a member of Hamas, you might even have experienced a taste of the torment before your death in the form of mock burials. In these dress rehearsals staged by the movement, the would-be martyr, according to some reports, would have to prove his mettle by being interred in an empty grave, either alone or with comrades, where he would recite Qur'anic verses associated with the torment before being allowed to return to the world of the living. Others were, reportedly, locked in dark chambers. More often, initiates would simply be required to do something like walk through a graveyard by themselves.

Sometimes, youth even staged their own brand of rehearsal, as when twelve-year-old Karam al-Kard announced his death on the walls in the form of graffiti.[13] In another example of such rehearsal, 'Ahid Salim al-Habit, a first lieutenant of the Fatah Hawks (the military wing of Fatah), a guy who preferred to be called "Father of War," had his picture taken in a T-shirt with Hebrew lettering, cradling a hand grenade in his mouth like an egg, and then plastered it on the walls of Shati' Camp in Gaza.

The next time around might be the real thing. Awakening not on earth but rather in the Gardens of Delight, the martyr would find himself surrounded by all good things. Rather than the rivers of sewage that run through the camp where he was born, there would be rivers of milk and honey and wine. He would lie on luxurious couches beneath beautiful trees, feeling neither heat nor cold, pain nor sorrow. Seventy-two beautiful women whom "neither man nor jinn has deflowered before" (Qur'an 55:74–75, "The Compassionate") would be his for the taking. He would be given the power "to intercede on behalf of seventy members of his household (to bring them into Paradise and save them from the Hell Fire)," to quote 'Abdullah 'Azzam; and when Judgment Day at last arrived, and the dead of all time were arrayed before the eyes of God, naked as on the day they were born,[14] he would stand tall and without fear.

Until then, his fame on earth lived on. He was awarded posthumous titles like "Prince of Justice," or even "Emperor," and poems were written in his honor. "My lofty goals," begins one such poem, "cannot be diverted by a whip/ Nor by death nor torture nor the jailor/ We will remain hawks ferociously attacking/ Black fate and fire." His every attribute was valorized, as in the following poem, which goes so far as to hymn the martyr's eyelashes:

> Greater than speech
> Surpassing the limits of description
> Stature most noble, head held high, eyelashes that reach for the sun
> Yesterday, a candle shone, crowned by singing
> but its flame will continue burning
> in the spirit of every hero who fulfills the oath

Posters of his image decorated every conceivable surface, and he was the talk of the town, at least until the next martyr took his place. He was commonly referred to as a "bridegroom," with funerary rituals constituting his "wedding," as in the following tribute to Fatah Hawk Anwar Zar'i Suleih (known by his nom de guerre *Abu ar-Ra'd*, or "Father of the Thunder"), which we recorded in the central square of Khan Yunis:

> The Fatah Hawks announce with the utmost pride and revolutionary anger the death of its military leader and the engineer of its activities, the brave hero, the Prince of Justice, Major Anwar Zar'i Suleih, A.[bu-] ar-Ra'd. On this occasion, we call the masses of our steadfast people to the wedding of the martyr, which will begin today and last until 24/10, and we call on you to walk on the road of the martyrs and to go to the house of the martyr in the Kharraba area, where there will be a lunch for the bridegroom, the Martyr A. ar-Ra'd.

The martyr's "bride" was commonly said to be Palestine, as in the nationalist graffito, "My country is my bride, and her *mahr* [bride-price] is my martyrdom." An Islamist variant, "Blood is the mahr of the precious girls," casts the perpetually virginal maidens of Heaven, or *hur*, as brides. In all cases, the mahr is a gift of blood rather than gold. Likewise, blood often takes the place of the traditional wedding henna.

Less frequently, the martyr himself was treated as the bride, a practice with deep roots in Palestinian mourning and martyrdom songs, as in the following Fatah song, which a group of children sang for us in the West Bank town of Bethlehem:

> Fatah the revolution, Fatah the fire
> Abu-'Amar announced it
> He closed her eyes and laid her
> hand to put henna on it
> His waist is thin,
> and he's covered with a *mandilla* [shawl]

The appeal of nuptial imagery for the martyr-to-be, who was often unmarried and childless, can be seen in those messages that present death as an unabashedly erotic consummation, as in the following Hamas graffito, which we recorded on the entranceway of a cemetery in Jenin, the West Bank. "This is Jenin," reads the wall, "today leading its knight in procession to his bride/ Wedding and exaltation await him in Paradise. The virgins of Paradise are in ecstasy, calling, O Omar/ Glad tidings, glad tidings: Paradise and eternity."

24. Terror in Their Hearts

Is it an arm or a tree? Difficult to tell. The configuration terminates in a hand closed around a serrated dagger, but the base consists of a mangle of veinlike roots that feed off a pool of blood formed by the dripping dagger and an axe that has been driven into what looks like a trunk. The hand's index finger—or "trigger finger," as many Islamists prefer to call it—is raised heavenward, composing the *shahida*, the one-way sign of the Islamic Movement, and ends in a sun.

One supposes that the strange humanoid tree is meant as a symbol of Hamas and, in a wider way, Islam—both are often talked about as if mighty trees—for surrounding it are the identifying markers, "The Islamic Resistance Movement, Hamas" and "Islam is the solution," the major rallying slogan of Hamas and the Muslim Brotherhood. Given the bloody knife, the figure seems also meant to symbolize jihad, and indeed, in the accompanying texts, the movement claims ownership to two recent armed actions and reiterates its opposition to talks between the PLO and Israel. The poster was, notably, hung in Palestine Mosque, Gaza City—one of the largest of the mosques controlled by Hamas in the Gaza Strip. Its imam, Sheikh Ahmad Bahar, was a frequent critic of the Palestinian Authority, and it was from this mosque that worshippers set out in a demonstration in November 1994 that resulted in the death of twelve of them and the wounding of over a hundred more at the hands of the PA police—an incident that followers of Hamas refer to as "the Gaza Massacre."

Written to the left of the figure can be seen the basmala, which is followed by a lengthy headline in blood-red script, "Three Cowardly Jews Killed and Numbers Wounded in Lightning Bolt Operations in Tulkarem and Ramallah. One of our Lions Martyred, Another Wounded, Three Escaped." The Qur'anic verse that follows (9:14, "Repentance")—"Fight them so that Allah may put them to shame at your hands and bring you victory over them and heal the hearts of the believers"—refers to Muhammad's nullification of a treaty made by the first Muslims with a party of unbelievers who later violated the contract's terms. In light of Hamas' counsel that the Oslo accords are illegal according to Islamic law, and accordingly, jihad must continue, the meaning of the allusion would surely have been missed by no one.

Further contrasting the differences between Hamas and the PLO are the lengthy greetings that follow the Qur'anic citation—"O upright masses of our people. . . O mujahid heroes . . . O patient free men . . . O honorable men arrayed for war . . . O distinguished men in a time of slavery . . . O proud men in a time of kneeling and begging . . . O descendants of al-Banna and al-Qassam . . . O valiant leaders of glory and pride." Of these, the reference to the "descendants of al-Banna and al-Qassam" is meant to position Palestinians firmly in the camp of Hamas, while the invocation "O distinguished men in a time of slavery, O proud men in a time of kneeling and begging" can be read as a pointed rebuke against the PLO, which is commonly accused by its Islamist rival of having forsaken the goal of reclaiming Palestine by arms and having betrayed the Palestinian cause by recognizing the state of Israel. The rest of the text continues the rebuke, contrasting Hamas' continued dedication to the injunction of jihad with the shameful "surrender" of the PLO:

This is the road . . . and this is the banner

And this is the language that the enemies of Allah and mankind understand.

The language of bullets and bombs . . . No to the shameful language of destructive negotiations!!

Indeed, O free men, you have heard the voice of bullets . . .

Indeed, O honorable men, you have heard the whistle of bullets in Jerusalem and Tulkarem . . . The operations were like thunderbolts and made laughingstocks of the Jews . . . They set terror in their hearts and made them anxious and made them fear the Youth of Truth and the Lions of the Battalions . . . These are the men who have taken upon themselves the vow to hunt the enemies of Allah, May He be glorified and elevated, until victory is granted by Allah or martyrdom on His path.

O upright men . . . These are the talks that we present to you so that you might shout at the top of your lungs . . . No to the negotiations of surrender! . . . No to paltry autonomy . . . No to destructive and rotten positions. No to begging and slavery. Yes, a thousand times yes, to the whistle of bullets . . . Yes, a thousand times yes, to resistance until the alien occupation is expelled . . . Yes, a thousand times yes, to the Battalions of might, eternity, and pride . . .

Written across both panels of text in large crimson letters are the words, "This is the language that the Jews understand!!"

The idea that armed operations make "laughingstocks of the Jews" and "set terror in their hearts" is an important one and is repeated numerous times throughout intifada media, especially in the media of Hamas, where the ability to inspire fear in the enemy is commonly presented as a major measure of success in and of itself. "Here is the answer to the struggling sons [of the Palestinian people] who have not heeded the heroes of the surrender conference," reads a leaflet released by the Qassam Battalions in May 1993 and disseminated in Gaza; "Here! Here are our heroes, kidnapping soldiers in the Strip and taking their weapons and stabbing them until they die . . . in order to spread terror and fear in their hearts."

Likewise, fear and terror should be felt by all those who become "a traitor to Allah, His Messenger, and the Muslim umma," to quote the popular book *Martyrs of Palestine*. Here, however, the coding is somewhat different in that the punishing hand could be read as that of God himself. "Verily, we are warning these people that they are standing on a narrow bridge; it will shake them with many shudders," writes Muhammad 'Abd al-Qahir Abu-Faris, playing on the root of the word *intifada*. "On the first of these," he continues, "their hearts will quake, and they will stare forth, their bellies shuddering with fear, for they will be facing a day when the hair of children will turn gray with terror."[15]

As these examples make clear, one of the most important fantasies involved in Hamas' fearful tableaux is a reversal of power, the bringing down to size of the enemy. Hamas mujahidun are commonly portrayed in the movement's media as massive Herculean figures towering above dwarflike Israelis. In one poster in our collection, a single Hamas colossus stands tall while numerous Lilliputian

Israelis scurry for cover around his feet; in another, a terrified and childlike Israeli soldier struggles in the King Kong grip of an al-Qassam "giant." In other visuals, the process of diminution becomes one of infantilization, as when an Israeli soldier is shown awakening beneath a Hamas ghost, screaming for his mother, or a kidnapped soldier is described as having lost control of his bodily functions before he was killed.

Similar reversals can be found in a communiqué issued on June 4, 1994, from "the operations room" of the Qassam Battalions announcing the group's responsibility for a revenge attack carried out shortly after the "Hebron Massacre." The operation took place at a critical juncture in peace talks between Israel and the PA, and on a major Israeli holiday—yom ha-Atzmaut (May 14), the day on which David Ben-Gurion declared the state of Israel in 1948 and the end of the British Mandate. The document is particularly important as it was one of the first to lay out a new policy of carrying out suicide attacks against "soft" Israeli targets with the express aim of causing high civilian casualties—a policy that had a number of repercussions, including a significant loss of leverage for Arafat in peace negotiations with Israel:

> In the name of Allah, the Compassionate, the Merciful
>
> "Nay, we hurl truth against falsehood, and then it disappears."
>
> A military announcement emanating from the operations room of the Battalions of 'Izz ad-Din al-Qassam
>
> To the leadership of Israel:
> You turned 'Eid al-Fitr into a black day so we swore to turn your independence holiday into Hell. This is our first reply to the Hebron slaughter . . . . The next four are en route.
>
> The Battalions of al-Qassam announce the death of Doctor Ra'id Zakarna.
> O our Palestinian masses in this holy land:
> Immediately after the disgusting slaughter that Doctor Barukh Goldstein carried out, which changed 'Eid al-Fitr in the lives of our people, the operations room of the Battalions of al-Qassam swore to reply to this attack with five violent attacks. We chose the passing of the forty-day [the traditional period of mourning] anniversary of the Hebron slaughter and the beginning of the Israeli leadership's celebration of their false independence holiday to carry out the first attack so as to transform their holiday into a hell of tears and screaming and death.
> Thus, the hero-martyr Ra'id Zakarna, a steadfast son of Qabatiya, stepped forward to drive the booby-trapped car, which was carrying 157 kilograms of explosives, and smash it into bus number 348 yesterday at 12:10 a.m. exactly on Wednesday, 6/4/1994, resulting in the killing of nine of the passengers on the bus and the wounding of fifty-two Israelis, twenty of them gravely, and the rest doomed to spend the remainder of their lives with mutilated faces or amputated hands and legs.

The document goes on to request that Arafat stop negotiations with Israel and to demand that merchants in the Bank and Strip conserve their supplies "because an atmosphere of true war will reign over the Zionist troops and enemy leaders in the coming time." The Battalions, the text asserts, will force Israel out of "Gaza and Jericho and Hebron without preconditions," and this will be "a first stage on the road to the liberation of the Bank and the Strip." The document ends with guaranteeing "Mr. Arafat the position of the presidency if he adheres to that which Allah sent down and the glorious Islamic law."

Typically, the document incorporates a confusing mix of genres. Take away a few phrases from the penultimate paragraph of the text, for instance, and it might pass for a news report in which who, what, where, and why are answered in quantitative detail, yet it is precisely those phrases that remain with the reader. They are central rather than secondary to the meaning of the message. Indeed, the rhetoric is so sadistically charged that one might be excused for thinking that the mutilation and dismemberment described was a major source of libidinal satisfaction in and of itself.

Throughout Hamas literature, properties are commonly transformed, as here, into their opposites. Bullets possess a "voice"; machine-guns "chatter." Blood becomes a precious fertilizer. A holiday becomes "a hell of tears and screaming and death." A killer is awarded the title of "doctor." Suicide-murder is transformed into bravery, celebration into horror, horror into celebration, negotiation into surrender, the victim dead into cowards, corpses into gifts, life into death, death into life.

25. We Are Worth Nothing without a Machine-Gun

He'd been walking around the neighborhood with the gun for some time. Yeah, for sure, he'd like to have his picture taken. He poses, holding the weapon at a nonchalant angle, the strap taking most of the weight. It's made of wood, this M-16, but from a distance, it looks like the real thing—so real that the guy better be careful. A number of shabab have already been shot when IDF soldiers mistook their fake guns for real ones.

Relatively few shabab possessed real guns during the first intifada. They made do instead with fakes ones fashioned out of wood or nails or even banana stalks. They studied diagrams of AK-47s and argued over the make and capacity of various weapons featured on Hamas videotapes, discussing the finer points of their usage, debating the merit of one model over another. These tapes offered detailed lessons on everything from how to load a gun to how to make explosives, as in this excerpt from an early tape of the Qassam Battalions:

> This is an oxygen canister filled with sulfur and gunpowder from bullets. Close it tightly so that no air can enter. Be sure to leave no air inside the

bottle. It's also possible to fill it with TNT, either in part or in whole. We attach a piece of wire, lay it out for thirty-five meters. Attach the wire to a twenty-four volt headlight from a car. First, we break the glass, so when we connect it to the battery, the tungsten wire will ignite and make a spark. The sulfur inside it will start to burn, and the result is a tremendous explosion, which can bring down an entire building. This is a twenty-four volt battery that can be made at home. All the twenty-four volt batteries sold here are for cars and are big, and carrying one in your hand during an operation is difficult, so we use radio batteries to produce the electricity. These two wires attached to the battery must be connected to the bomb. They must be kept away from it until the time of the explosion. You must lie [lit., "sleep"] this way when you connect the wires [he demonstrates, lying on his side], and you should be thirty-five meters away.

The lesson being offered here, the masked instructor tells us, is "for the sake of knowledge and not for manufacturing." He warns viewers not to try to reproduce what they've just seen at home, for many mistakes can be made. "If some of the powder is left on the screws," for instance, he says, "the friction caused in closing it will make a spark, and it will explode." Later in the video, crouching on his knees with the stock of his rifle placed against his shoulder, he offers the viewer another lesson—this one on "hunting":

There are many ways to hunt. This is how we shoot. If you are using your right hand to shoot, your left hand should be in this position at this angle. The butt should be placed against the chest. Line up the sights, both front and back. If you want to kill someone—say there is a Zionist—direct the gun toward him and line up the sights on his chest. You want to shoot him in the chest or the heart. You have to direct your aim above the belly, and this is the position of sitting in order to hunt. Your hand will be on the trigger, and you must be ready and sit up straight.

He then displays parts from Barettas, Galilis, Kalashnikovs, and Uzis. All those present seem anxious to handle the instruments. Even when they are not directly involved, they can be seen in the background, touching and stroking them, admiring them.

Almost no one during the intifada thought of the gun as a mere tool for revolt; it was, rather, an object worthy of reverence in its own right. It was the ultimate power fetish, able to confer on its owner an aura of mastery, even identity, as in the line of a song of the Fatah Hawks, "We are worth nothing without a machine-gun." Power, few doubted, came from the barrel of a gun, as in the graffito,

By the points of daggers and knives, the road of victory will be ours
With the tears of bereaved mothers and orphans, we will draw the map of the homeland
From the barrels of guns, we will take back our rights and forge our glory
We write to the world that we are a Muslim people
Passionately we love death, and we scorn bullets

The word we've here translated as "passionately" is traditionally used to speak of romantic love. Although there is a little bit of death in erotic love, and the erotization of death no doubt made the idea of martyrdom more palatable to the teenagers and twentysomethings who participated in the intifada, the idea of being in love with death is a strange one perhaps for everyone but students of literature. The equation of death and power and an almost sexual passion was objectified not only by the gun, but also the mask, which made of the eye a weapon and lure—a conflation evidenced in the sung line, "Your eyes sparkle like a Martine [rifle], by Allah."

26. Children, but They Are Men and Heroes

Here is a collection of posters of Palestinian children, bought in a shop not far from where we lived in the Old City that exhibit what can only be called bathos. There's a little blonde boy, perhaps five years old, perhaps six or seven, dressed in rags and a black-and-white keffiyah. He points a pistol toward the camera, holding it with both hands, and even with both hands, it is too heavy for him. The little face is grimaced, angry and hurt. "I don't want this . . . but!!!" reads the legend.

In another of the posters, a dark-haired boy wearing a red jacket and matching Ninja headband peeps out from behind a rock with a pistol in his hand, which he holds close to his face, finger on the trigger. Behind him is another child's disembodied hand, the fingers forming a V sign. "Piercing eyes," the inscription reads, "a hand clutching the burning ember without trembling . . . . Let his impossible face challenge."

And here is a blonde girl wearing red lipstick and earrings. She stands next to a red rose, her hands held palm up, helplessly, beseechingly, above the legend, "We were born here between water and fire, and we will be born a second time in clouds." Still another poster features another blonde girl, this one in a keffiyah, her hands weighed down with bicycle chains, with the title, "Freedom is in chains, a prisoner/ Welcome to death as long as I am a prisoner," and to the left in small print, the jarring, inexplicable title, "The little girl of geniality."

Here were the children who would reverse a "black" history, as in the following message from the West Bank village of Issawiya, in which the graffitist draws upon "Children Bearing Rocks," a poem by Nizar Qabbani, the Iraqi poet best known for his scathing, often earthy political verse lampooning Arab political leaders and structures. Later put to music by the Syrian-based Palestinian group "The Lovers," the poem paints the children of the intifada as a force that, sooner or later, will obliterate an era of injustice:

> Ah, O time of prostitution, O time of betrayal,
> You will be conquered by the heroes of the stones
> No matter how slow is history

"Children of the stones" was no mere figure of speech. The age of many of the boys, less often girls, fighting on the streets of the intifada was astonishingly young, as was the age of those who became casualties. The image of the child warrior was fostered by an intense campaign on the part of all the major factions participating in the uprising. Photographs of armed children were everywhere. Brigades of boy soldiers marched through the streets in uniform. The poet Nizar Qabbani wrote of how his generation had relinquished the ability to lead and how it was now up to the children to "make us crazy again." Children's songs celebrated everything from stone throwing to hijackings, as in the PFLP song sung for us by a boy in Burka, the West Bank, "O you of the Kalashnikov, O you of the Kalashnikov/ Move from one port to another/ Teach them the hijacking of ships/ Bottles of Molotovs, bottles of Molotovs," with other stanzas including "Move from one fig tree to another/ Teach them stabbing with knives" and "Move from one narrow road to another/ Teach them the launching of the bazooka." (The same boy, possibly thinking of Qur'an 56:21, "The Event," told us that Paradise was full of nice chickens to eat.)

Even young children joined factions, participated in demonstrations, threw stones at soldiers, and, remarkably, even issued warnings, as in this 1992 graffito signed by the Ashbal Fatah, "the Fatah Cubs," a group composed of boys aged nine to twelve. "We will strike with an iron hand," the message reads, "those who try to spread *fitna* [schism] in the mosque through slander and market insults, which damage the Sons of Fatah and its cadres—this we assure you. And those who are trying to disseminate their opinions must keep them to themselves and not spread schism as this is what the occupation wants. All the people know of Dimuna and 'Ailabun.[16] And they are from Fatah."

Child fighters were not infrequently sanctioned by sacred tradition, as in the Hamas communiqué entitled " . . . Children, but Men and Heroes." Embellished with a drawing of a boy throwing stones, his forehead inscribed with the formula "There is no god but Allah," the document offers "a lesson in the tarbiya of jihad and the love of martyrdom," *tarbiya* signifying the method of education and upbringing of children. Citing the example of Rafa' "the Thrower," a boy allowed by Muhammad to join the Battle of Uhud, the author argues that "he who fits the bill is worthy of acceptance, regardless if he is young or old, a registered soldier or one desiring to be so." Palestinians must raise their sons for battle despite the fact that they are living in an "era in which the [political] systems bring up their sons to celebrate the child of peace and to learn songs of peace by heart."

When such children were martyred, they were almost invariably put forward as models for emulation and as testaments to the brutality of the enemy. Like their elder counterparts, they were typically celebrated with commemorative posters and cards,[17] as in the following example, which was hung from the ceiling of a funeral tent in Khan Yunis Refugee Camp. Signed by the Palestinian National Liberation Movement, Fatah, the poster commemorates the death of a Fatah activist, Suleih, for whose sake his "cub," Abu-Shahmah, was said to have "sacrificed himself." (Abu-Shahmah was killed in a demonstration following the death of Suleih, who is said to have trained him. A double funeral was held for them in October 1992.) The announcement begins with a Qur'anic verse derived from "The Confederates" (33:23) that is commonly used by both nationalists and Islamists to assert the martyr's immortality:

> In the name of Allah, the Compassionate, the Merciful

> The Almighty said: "Among the believers are men who have been true to their covenant with Allah; among them are those who have fulfilled their vow [by dying on the path of Allah], and among them are those who are waiting, and have not changed at all." Allah the Almighty speaks the truth.

> Here are the men of Fatah presenting martyr after martyr, shot after shot, and the waterfall of their blood continues, beginning with the first martyr of al-'Asifa ["The Storm," the externally based military wing of Fatah], the martyr Ahmad Salama passing on to the sheikh of martyrs and their prince, the leader, the martyr Abu-Jihad to our martyr, the hunted Anwar Suleih, for whose sake his cub, the hero Tahsin Abu-Shahma, sacrificed himself. So to the Paradise of Eternity, O our brave martyrs.

> The Shabiba Movement in the area of the High Dam announces with the utmost pride its martyr, the hero Tahsin Abu-Shahma. The High Dam.

Tributes to children often evidenced a process of infantilizing, miniaturizing, and, for lack of a better term, cutifying death, as in the 1991 poster of the Hamas boy-martyr Bassam 'Isa al-Faruz of Dahaisha Camp, the West Bank. The poster features al-Faruz's photograph and the legend, "And I have made from my wounds and my blood a little stream . . . in the plains and the valleys," a line from an old Fatah song to which the word "little" has been added.

A similar process can be seen in a children's coloring book in our collection, which features on its first page a Qur'an; on the last, a connect-the-dots teddy bear; and in between, pictures from what would seem to be irreconcilable domains, with titles like "The Torture of the Muslims," "The Battle of Hattin," "The Battle with Rome," "The Conquest of Jerusalem," and "The Struggle with the Sorcerers." Famous military leaders—Khalid ibn al-Walid, Salah ad-Din al-Ayubi, and Mu'tassam—are juxtaposed with flowers; trees and chirping birds share space with scenes of killing and being killed—a happy cohabitation of blood and flowers, mujahidun and teddy bears, all within a single volume.

If the book contained only battle scenes, under the title, say, "Famous Islamic Battles," one might think nothing of it; as is, however, one must ask what "The Struggle with Sorcerers" has to do with a teddy bear, that preeminent transitional object and proto-verbal symbol. Similarly, what does it mean—the "little girl of geniality" announcing, "Welcome to death . . ."; the little boy practically falling forward under the weight of a gun too heavy for him to bear? Isn't this precisely "enculturation"—the child, the infant as "one without speech," composed of, reconstituted by, big people's words, their nightmares and visions?

But these materials, uniting as they do the kind and the unkind, the benign and the malignant, suggest something more, for the child is made not only to speak the correct formula, present the collective fantasy, but also to carry it out, embody it, indeed, die for it—the kind of generational reversal and extinction of chance that, rightfully, are said to belong among the minor signs of the End of the World.

27. Al-Aqsa Massacre Video

The tourist is standing on the Mount of Olives, filming a standard tourist shot of Jerusalem. Across the Valley of Kidron, the white limestone walls of the city glimmer in the midday heat. It's classic Holy Land picturesque, vaguely medieval—a tableau found on countless postcards and pilgrim calendars, fans in Baptist churches, "Visit Israel" flyers in synagogues.

The first gunshots resemble firecrackers or caps. Suddenly realizing what he's hearing, the tourist mutters, "O my God," and screws a telephoto extender onto his camera. For an instant, we see the Temple Mount through a black tunnel with the glittering Dome of the Rock framed in a small circle of light at the end, like the view through a telescope in a comic book. A moment later, we make out ghostly figures on the plateau. Some are scurrying back and forth, engaged in some kind of activity. Others seem to be hiding behind the Dome. Still others are walking across the expanse as if nothing out of the ordinary is taking place.

At first, the distance between the Mount of Olives and the site known to Muslims as *haram ash-sharif*, "the Noble Sanctuary," and to Jews as *Har ha-Bayit*, "the Temple Mount," a distance of perhaps half a mile, results in sounds as etherealized as the images, but then the tourist fumbles with some kind of switch on the front of his camera, and suddenly, we hear loud and clear what seems to be one of the mosque's imams issuing commands from the minaret.

"Don't fire in the yards of al-Aqsa Mosque!" he screams in Arabic. "Don't strike the Muslims in the yards of al-Aqsa Mosque!" A second imam takes over. He also demands, repeatedly, in Arabic that the police stop shooting. "The Muslims," he says, "will never abandon the mosque even if they all die! We will never abandon this mosque. You will never enter it except over our bodies!" The police must stop firing. "Martyrdom," he says, "is the most exalted thing for which the Muslim wishes."

We cannot see much from the tourist's vantage point atop the Mount of Olives, but the first part of the confrontation is short, lasting only around three-and-a-half minutes. Toward the end, the booms of tear-gas grenades are replaced by staccato pops of rifle fire, and then a few short rapid bursts of what

must be automatic weapons fire, followed in short order by the wailing of si-
rens signaling the arrival of ambulances. Then all is quiet again. Little figures
continue running around on the plateau in all directions, while large crowds of
people can be seen streaming toward the exit gates.

After a few minutes, we see more tear-gas grenades as they arc their way over
from the western side of the plateau, where the Israeli police are deployed and then
fall smoking in front of the Dome of the Rock. All too soon, the crack and chatter
of rifle fire resume. As the situation spins ever more out of control, the gunshots,
which had been intermittent, increase exponentially the way kernels of corn explode in a pan before building to a crescendo of pops and ricochets.

The imams continue to issue demands that the police desist from firing.
"Allahu akbar! Allahu akbar!" yells one of them, "take your hands from our
mosque! It is a mosque that Allah has forbidden to anyone except the Muslims.
O occupation authorities, the signs of the Hour [i.e., the End of Days] are
drawing near! The Hour is coming, no doubt about it."

"To the police, to the police," screams another, "O occupation authorities,
stop firing! Here are the angels cursing you, and here is history cursing you. It
is al-Aqsa Mosque."

The imams—there are six of them who take over the loudspeaker at one
point or another—cannot seem to decide whether to call for people to martyr
themselves or to flee. Sometimes they issue calls for both almost in the same
breath. Here, for instance, is the fifth imam:

> O youth, O girls, don't stand in front of the soldiers. Don't let the soldiers see
> you! O youth, O girls, advance toward martyrdom truthfully. O people, let
> ring out, "Allahu akbar!" O people, it is al-Aqsa Mosque imploring you. It is
> al-Aqsa Mosque asking you for help. It is al-Aqsa Mosque calling you. Who is
> answering? Who is answering?

The tourist's footage ends up on the Hamas video *al-Aqsa Massacre*, where
it is sandwiched between scenes of the event's aftermath—coffins and palm
branches, trails of blood, demonstrations, songs of revenge, news reports, and
even a tour of a morgue where some of the martyrs have been put on display.
One victim has been shot cleanly through the neck; the cameraman lingers on
the wound. "Look what he had in his pocket," says one man, withdrawing a
picture of Arafat dressed in a military cap and placing it on the dead man's
chest. Many of the dead have name tags and small signs hung around their
necks identifying them as martyrs.

The event that quickly came to be called "al-Aqsa Massacre" took place in
October 1990, after the Temple Mount Faithful, a fringe Jewish group devoted to the reconstruction of the ancient Jewish Temple, the so-called Third
Temple, announced its intention to lay a cornerstone on the mount. As in the
year before, the request had been denied by the Israeli police, and the group
had prepared to enact its political theater piece in the parking lot outside the
Dung Gate instead.

This year, however, Palestinian religious leaders quickly called on people to come protect the mount, and Palestinian newspapers featured advertisements for the event. Why this moment was chosen as a point of confrontation is unknown and unknowable. Certainly, tensions were running high. Three years of the intifada had worn people down, although Saddam Husain's invasion of Kuwait had picked them up again, with the Iraqi leader being idolized throughout the West Bank and Gaza as "the purebred Arab knight" and "the vanquisher of America." With hundreds of thousands of American soldiers streaming toward the Gulf and a war looming on the horizon, the shabab were feeling fired up and ready. By 7:00 A.M., hundreds of Palestinians had arrived at al-Aqsa. The Israeli police seem completely to have underestimated the potential for disaster. They did not equip their troops with riot gear; the chief of police, reportedly, even left for a meeting.

No one knows exactly how the confrontation began, but some people remember a woman screaming "The army is coming!" and then a Hamas guy with a loudspeaker yelled, "Pick up the stones! Pick up the stones!" And stones began raining down on the heads of Jews worshipping at the *kotel*, the ancient western retaining wall of the Temple Mount, known in English as the Western, or Wailing, Wall, located directly below the plateau on which al-Aqsa rests. Meanwhile, the rumor spread among the Palestinians on the mount that Gershom Salomon himself, head of the Temple Mount Faithful, was going to storm the site. Instead of retreating, the police confronted the crowd, and against regulations, turned their weapons from manual to automatic. By the end, twenty-two Palestinians lay dead.

It was not the first time the site had been drenched in blood. Indeed, no one spot in the Holy Land was more saturated in gore than this one. The place first receives mention in the Torah, the sacred book of the Jews, in the tenth century BCE, when King David moved the holy cult and the seat of his kingdom from Hebron to Jerusalem. He purchased a threshing floor from a Jebusite farmer, a man seemingly with two names, on an exposed rock on Mount Moriah overlooking the city, intending it to be the foundation of a temple. His hands having been deemed by God to have spilled too much blood, it was not he but his son Solomon who actually built the temple, a structure that stood for 350 years before being destroyed by the Babylonian Nebuchadnezzar in 587 BCE. Seventy years later, when the Jews were allowed to return, they rebuilt the temple on a modest scale. The sanctuary was used for hundreds of years until King Herod launched a massive building project in 19 BCE.

After the return of the Jews from the Babylonian exile, the temple regained its position as the center of Jewish life. It also became a rallying point in times of war. When Judaea was occupied by the Seleucid Greeks, the defilement of the temple became the central focus of the Maccabean revolt. When the Romans replaced the Greeks, the Zealots also made control of the temple a central focus of their campaign. In both revolts, the Maccabees and the Zealots spent as much or more time fighting their fellow Jews as they did fighting the foreign occupi-ers. Though the Jews scored a few victories, their fight against Rome was hope-less. In seventy CE, they were defeated utterly. Hundreds and thousands of Jews were killed or sold into slavery; and in an event that would remake Juda-ism forever, the Romans destroyed the Temple, banned Jews from Jerusalem, and renamed Judaea *Palestine* in order to emphasize that Jewish ownership of the land was no more.

Five centuries later, the Omayyad Caliph 'Abd al-Malik erected an Islamic structure over the rock of Moriah called "the Dome of the Rock." The church that the Byzantines had earlier constructed on the plateau in honor of the Vir-gin Mary was transformed by al-Malik's son into a mosque that became known as al-Aqsa ("the furthest") Mosque—a reference to the miraculous journey of Muhammad called *al-Isra'*. According to the many hadith that preserve the story, Muhammad traveled in the course of a night on a winged steed with the face of a man to "al-Aqsa" where he prayed, and then afterward led the proph-ets Abraham, Moses, and Jesus in prayer. The occasion is celebrated annually in intifada media, where Palestine is often referred to as "the land of the Isra'," as in the slogan, "We will make from the blood of the Sons of Zion an ocean to cover the land of the Isra'."

In 1099, Jerusalem fell to the Crusaders—arguably the greatest trauma in Arab Muslim collective memory. The fall of Jerusalem saw particularly hor-rendous slaughter. Most of the Muslim defenders of the city were put to death, as were the Jews who had taken refuge in a synagogue. The carnage was such that the streets of the city were said to be littered with hands, heads, and feet; in the Temple of Solomon, as the Crusaders referred to the mount, men rode in blood as deep as their knees and the bridle reins of their horses.

In 1187, Salah ad-Din, leading an Islamic army, captured Jerusalem from the Crusaders; and from then until World War I, Jerusalem and the mount remained under Muslim control. Famous throughout the Arab and Muslim world for centuries for leading the Muslims to victory and for liberating Jerusa-lem and al-Aqsa, the figure of Salah ad-Din was seized upon by Islamists in modern times as a model for the modern mujahid fighting against Western neo-Crusaders. He is found throughout intifada visuals, depicted atop a rear-ing horse, sword in hand, in front of the Dome of the Rock. "Jerusalem will return with the sword of Salah ad-Din," reads one graffito from our collection, "so no, a thousand no's, to those who are worn out," a reference to Arabs who have relinquished the idea of jihad.

The Kurdish general also makes an appearance in the covenant of Hamas, where he is mocked by the French General Henri Gouraud upon the latter's entrance into Damascus in 1920: "These incursions took place after Salah ad-Din the Ayyubi drove out the armies of the Crusaders," the covenant reads. "The Crusaders realized that it would not be possible to vanquish the Muslims unless they paved the way through an ideological incursion that would confuse

1. Here, in the Old City of Jerusalem, a Palestinian boy rides through a geography of opposing symbols. On the right, Israeli Border Guards, using a machine especially designed to erase graffiti, have covered over a Palestinian slogan with a Jewish menorah. To the left can be seen the remnants of a message addressed to the Israeli General Security Service, which reads, "Let the dogs of the Shin Bet know that the Popular Front is stronger than all their beatings. We will not be terrorized by the atrocities of the occupation." Israeli Border Guards, many of whom are Druze or Bedouin Arabs, later covered over the slogan with the word *Isra'il*, Arabic for "Israel."

2. During the intifada, keffiyah-clad shabab throwing rocks at IDF soldiers were ubiquitous images on TV screens and in newspapers across the world. This wall in the Gaza Strip features a hand bearing a rock dripping blood. The accompanying graffiti welcome back Fatah cadres from Tunis, Iraq, and Yemen following the signing of the Oslo Accords in 1993 by Yasir Arafat and Yitzhak Rabin, an agreement allowing the return of PLO political and military members from abroad in order to form the basis of a Palestinian government and armed force.

3. This graffito of the Islamic Resistance Movement, Hamas, features the last words of the seventh-century Islamic martyr Khubaib al-Ansari, "It doesn't matter when or how I am killed as a Muslim as long as my death is for the sake of Allah." At the center of the composition is a clenched fist founded on the Dome of the Rock. The figure has been situated within a map of All Palestine, while above, a Qur'an shines like a sun. Spray-painted at the top of the map is the ubiquitous imperative, *Wa'iddu*, "And prepare," which initiates verse sixty of chapter eight of the Qur'an, "The Spoils of War." Around the borders of the map are written three more Qur'anic imperatives (3:199, "The Family of 'Imran"), which, counterclockwise, read, "Be patient and persevere," "Fortify one another," and "Take up your positions."

4. The one-way sign or *shahida*—a fist with the index finger raised
heavenward—is commonly used to signify allegiance to the ideology of the
Islamic Movement. In this graffito posted in ar-Ram, the West Bank, by
"The Throwing Arms of Hamas," the index finger and thumb have been
inscribed with the *shahadatain*, "There is no god but Allah, and Muhammad
is the Messenger of Allah." The "double witness" is uttered by the worshiper
with index finger raised toward the end of the second prostration of the
Islamic prayer cycle.

5. In downtown Khan Yunis, a man pauses to read a handwritten notice announcing a "suicide operation" carried out by Fatah. "Painful Fatah strikes against the occupation and its accomplices," reads the poster. "One soldier killed and three wounded in a suicide operation carried out by a son of Fatah. O masses of our great people, this morning, 9/3/92, the Brother, the Son of Fatah, 'Ala al-Mughrabi carried out a suicide operation against a group of soldiers and policemen in an-Nasser neighborhood in Gaza City, where he killed one of them on the spot and gravely wounded three others. With the utmost insistence and challenge in continuing on the road of struggle, Fatah announces the death of its martyr, the Martyr of Palestine, the Brother 'Ala al-Mughrabi. We first promise Allah and then the masses to continue on the road of giving until victory."

6 & 7. *Fatah* and *Hamas* in the shape of assault rifles.

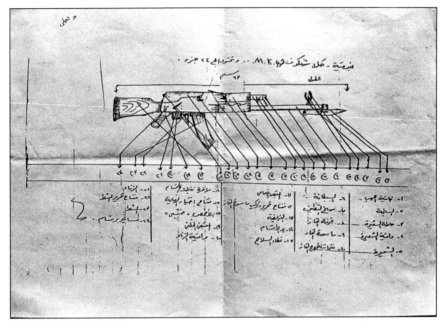

8. Diagram of a Kalashnikov.

9. This detail from a poster over thirty feet in length is composed of
individual panels featuring hand-colored photocopies of the leaders, martyrs,
and major symbols of Hamas. The central figure is of two *mujahidun* of the
Battalions of 'Izz ad-Din al-Qassam crouched atop a blue Star of David, the
major symbol of the state of Israel—a theme repeated throughout the poster.
To the right can be seen a photograph of Hamas leader Sheikh Ahmad
Yasin. Featured in the panel below are a masked youth superimposed on a
map of All Palestine and his oath:

> I swear by He who made fast your mountains
> and set your clouds in motion, O Palestine,
> that I will erase shame
> in every house
> and from my blood and bones I will weave
> banners of victory for Islam

أَضْرِب أَضْرِب بِالمِلْتُوف بعد الحجر كَلاشِينكُوف
حركة المقاومة الإسلامية
" حمــاس "

10. A masked shabb prepares to toss a Molotov cocktail at an Israeli jeep below. Above the figure is written, "Strike, strike by Molotov—after the stone Kalashnikov," a Hamas chant expressing the popular wish to move on to more lethal methods of attack.

11. The deportation of Hamas leaders to Lebanon brought them into daily contact with the Hizbullah and Iranian revolutionary guards active in the area. Almost immediately, one began to see new forms of expression in Hamas media. The new media were more elaborate and technically adept, featuring serpents, dragons, octopuses, bleeding martyrs, and the like, all of which spoke of the influence of Iranian revolutionary art. Substantive changes were also evident in Hamas texts, which for the first time began to include greetings to Hizbullah. In this example, a "Zionist serpent" is depicted wrapped around the globe. Written in the top left corner is the major slogan of Hamas, "Islam is the solution."

12. For many Hamas activists, the words of Dr. 'Abdullah 'Azzam constitute almost holy writ. In this blood-splattered poster issued by the Islamic Bloc of an-Najah National University on the anniversary of his martyrdom, 'Azzam is shown delivering a speech with his index finger raised to form the one-way sign of the Islamic Movement:

If preparation is terrorism
then we are terrorists
and if defense of the land is extremism
then we are extremists
and if jihad against enemies is fundamentalism
then we are fundamentalists

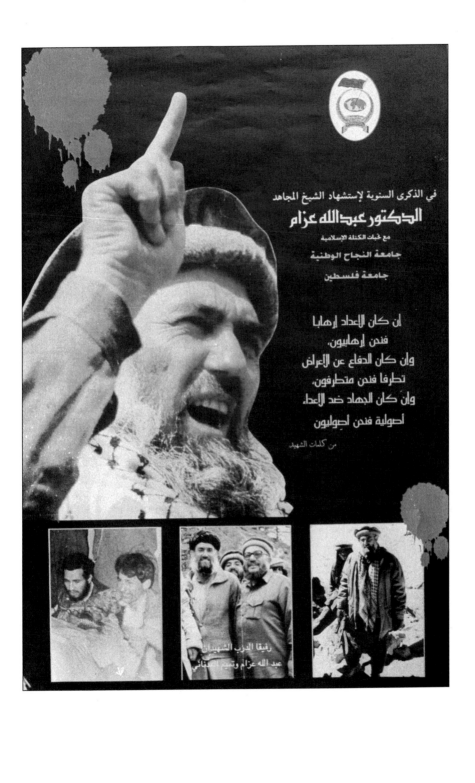

في الذكرى السنوية لإستشهاد الشيخ المجاهد

الدكتور عبدالله عزام

مع خيبات الكتلة الإسلامية

جامعة النجاح الوطنية

جامعة فلسطين

إن كان الإعداد إرهابا
فنحن إرهابيون.
وإن كان الدفاع عن الأعراض
تطرفا فنحن متطرفون.
وإن كان الجهاد ضد الأعداء
أصولية فنحن أصوليون

من كلمات الشهيد

رفيقا الدرب الشهيدان
عبد الله عزام وتميم العدناني

13. In this poster from the Gaza Strip, Sheikh Ahmad Yasin (right), the late leader of Hamas, is depicted along with Hasan al-Banna (left), the Egyptian founder of the Muslim Brothers, against a fluorescent backdrop of hot pink, orange, and yellow. Between the two leaders sails a Hamas rendition of *safina al-khalas*, "the Ship of Salvation." The hull of the ship is composed of a Palestinian flag across which has been written, "The Muslim Brethren." From the ship's mast flies another Palestinian flag, while the ship's sails feature the five-part motto of Hamas and the Brothers:

Allah is our goal
The Messenger is our model
The Qur'an is our constitution
Jihad is our path
Death on the path of Allah is our highest aspiration

Facing page

14. In this poster, three martyrs of the military wing of Hamas are presented to the public. The middle youth wears a T-shirt inscribed with the name of the group and the religious formula, "Allahu akbar, and Allah be praised." Featured in the top right- and left-hand corners is the emblem of Hamas—an orb containing the Qur'an cradled between two crossed swords, beneath which is written the Qur'anic imperative, "And prepare," as in prepare for war. The upper half of the orb is formed by two symmetrical Palestinian flags; the lower half, by a banner reading, "The Islamic Resistance Movement." The figure is topped by a clenched fist emanating rays of light. In the lower right corner can be seen Sheikh Ahmad Yasin.

15. Hamas made frequent use of the "gift" of death in its media, as in the following graffito disseminated in Deir al-Balah under the signature of the movement's military wing. "The Battalions of 'Izz ad-Din al-Qassam," reads the message, "present this first gift to the government of Rabin, by killing two Jews in a citrus factory in Nahal Oz." The reference is to an attack in which two Israelis were stabbed to death in front of their Palestinian employees in a warehouse just over the Green Line in Israel.

Above

16. Two boys in the West Bank village of Beit Rima wearing matching martyr T-shirts.

17. Martyr cards were commonly printed and handed out by the families of martyrs as mementoes and memorials. Typically, they contained Qur'anic quotations and the name and likeness of the martyr, and often a brief description of the operation he had carried out or the events that had led to his death. In this card for Bashar al-'Amudi, the basmala is followed by the ubiquitous Qur'anic tribute, "And do not think that those who are killed on the path of Allah are dead; nay, they are alive and with their Lord, well provided for" (3:169, "The Family of 'Imran"), while in the rondelle to the left can be found the particulars of the martyr's death. Against a tessellated background of stars formed by pentads, the face of the martyr appears between cutouts of a red-and-black checkered grenade and a rifle with an attached Islamic green banner reading, "There is no god but Allah, and Muhammad is the Messenger of Allah." Embedded among pink roses at the bottom are the silhouettes of mujahidun with guns and an Afghani-style religious figure.

18. In this "certificate for self-sacrifice," Mahmud az-Zaraini, former West Bank commander of Fatah's Black Panther group, announces his martyrdom as if before the fact:

Name: Martyr with a stay of execution
Date of birth: I am as old as the revolution
Occupation: Fida'i ("self-sacrificer")
Summary of above: Certified for self-sacrifice for the homeland

Inscribed at the top of the card is the accolade, "The martyr of Arabitude and the homeland, Mahmud," which is followed by a poem popular long before the intifada:

I will be patient until patience is worn out from my patience
and I will be patient until Allah decrees my condition
and I will be patient until patience knows
that I will bear stoutly that which is more bitter than patience.

The poem plays on the word *subar*, which means both "cactus" and "patience," and is a key term in the nationalist lexicon. In the cutout photograph to the left, Zaraini can be seen pointing to a cactus and, simultaneously, to himself. Behind him is a black panther, his group's totem, which upon his death will be engraved upon his tombstone.

19. In this highly elaborate and somewhat unusual commemorative card, "two martyrs of the Day of Refusal" are presented along with a host of Islamic sanctuaries, some located in the Holy Land and some outside it—the Ka'ba in Mecca, the Mosque of the Prophet in Medina, al-Aqsa Mosque and the Dome of the Rock in Jerusalem, and the Ibrahimi Mosque in Hebron, which is located in the Second Temple Period building that Jews revere as the "Cave of the Machpela," the traditional burial site of Abraham, Isaac, Rebecca, Leah, and Jacob. Following the basmala is a Qur'anic quotation commonly used by both nationalists and Islamists to assert the martyr's immortality: "Among the believers are men who have been true to their covenant with Allah; among them are those who have fulfilled their vow by dying, and others among them are awaiting [their deaths], and have not changed at all" (33:23, "The Confederates"). In the box at the bottom of the card are written the slogans, "You've written with your blood, No to the treacherous Madrid conference," and "We will never forget you, O our beloved . . . The right of revenge is ours."

بسم الله الرحمن الرحيم
من المؤمنين رجال صدقوا ما عاهدوا الله عليه
فمنهم من قضى نحبه ومنهم من ينتظر وما بدلوا تبديلا
صدق الله العظيم
شهدا يوم الرفض
٣٠/١٠/١٩٩٠م
الشهيد سفيان ناصر الدين و الشهيد محمد الرجبي
كتبتم بدمائكم لا لمؤتمر مدريد الخياني ...
لن ننساكم يا أحبابنا ... حق علينا الثأر للرجال
٣٠/١٠/١٩٩٤
حركة المقاومة الاسلامية / حماس

20. The armed men of Fatah and Hamas are often presented as the guardians of Islamic holy sites. In this example, armed men of the Battalions of al-Qassam, now martyrs, are depicted on and around the Ibrahimi Mosque in the West Bank city of Hebron. Written across the sky is the basmala, while the cloud reads, "Date of the martyrdom, 16-4-95."

21. In this card, mujahidun of the Fatah Hawks have been superimposed on and around the Dome of the Rock in Jerusalem. A Palestinian flag flies from the Dome. The emblem above the flag and below each of the hawks features a keffiyah-clad mujahid whose face has been replaced with a white map of historical Palestine.

22. A martyr's children are the focus of this commemorative card for 'Ali Uthman 'Asi, who can be seen in the top right photograph with two of his sons. The older child, who appears to be two or three years old, is dressed in a T-shirt featuring the Dome of the Rock against a map of All Palestine, and holds a rifle much larger than himself, while another child, an infant, sits in the martyr's lap nuzzling the barrel of a pistol. The remainder of the card is dotted with small cutout photographs of the martyr's children, with accompanying legends hugging their contours. Written to the right and left of the martyr and his sons is a legend that, typically, refers to martyrdom in terms of nuptial imagery, *mahr* referring to the "bridal price": "The martyr said it with pride, My homeland is the bride, and its mahr is my martyrdom." Between the top two photographs are words addressed to the martyr's son,

> You will grow up one day, my son,
> and you will embrace the land of our Palestine
> and you will see the Army of Truth all together
> around al-Aqsa, our assembly place

In the bottom photographs, the martyr's sons toy with their father's weapons, while a girl, wearing a dress with blue jeans beneath, stands in the background, holding a pistol. The legend reads, "An eternal vow—You will never be defeated/ Victory is coming when blood flows." The line of writing at the bottom of the card reads, "The sons of the martyr 'Ali Uthman 'Asi, continuing on the way."

الله أكبر
بسم الله الرحمن الرحيم
ولله الحمد
لا إله إلا الله
محمد رسول الله
وستكبر يوماً يا ولدي
وتعانق أرض فلسطينا
وترى جند الحق جميعاً
حول الأقصى مجتمعينا
قراوة بني حسان
أبناء الشهيد علي عثمان عاصي يواصلون الطريق

بسم الله الرحمن الرحيم
من المؤمنين رجال صدقوا ما عاهدوا الله عليه فمنهم
من قضى نحبه ومنهم من ينتظر وما بدلوا تبديلا
صدق الله العظيم
كتائب الشهيد عز الدين القسام
حامي الأقصى
مخيم العروب
الشهيد البطل
رقيب أول
محمد عزيز رشدي
القسام
حركة المقاومة الإسلامية - حماس

Facing page

23. This commemorative card depicts an "officer" of the Qassam Battalions, Muhammad 'Aziz Rushdi, looming above the Dome of the Rock, an assault rifle in each hand. Between the two cutouts is written, "The Battalions of the Martyr 'Izz ad-Din al-Qassam, the Guardian of al-Aqsa."

Above

24. In this poster from a Gaza City mosque, a wounded boy carries a mosque in a pack on his back. Although a follower of Hamas, the artist has been influenced by Sliman Mansur's famous painting *Carry On*. Written beneath the boy in large print is the legend, "Beloved of Allah." To his right can be seen a rendition of the Ship of Salvation inscribed with the motto of Hamas; on his left, a mujahid opens fire in the direction of the Dome of the Rock. The slogan at the top left-hand corner reads, "At your service, Islam of heroism; all of us will sacrifice ourselves in your defense." In the bottom right is the line, "O my son, ride with us and not with the unbelievers."

25. This Gaza poster features three recent martyrs of Hamas, one of them a young boy, all killed within days of one other. "With the loftiest verses of pride and glory," reads the text, "the Islamic Resistance Movement announces its upright martyrs who were awarded the honor of martyrdom in the land of Sheikh Radwan, 'Neighborhood of the Mujahidun.' They insisted on joining the caravan of martyrs."

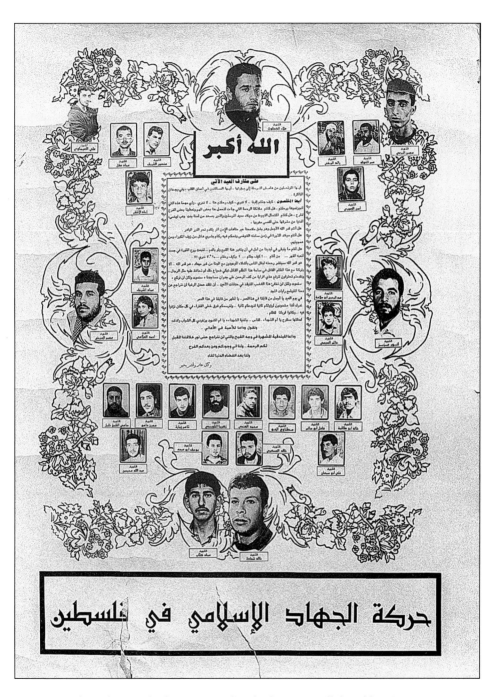

26. In this Islamic Jihad poster, under the banner "Allahu akbar," twenty-nine martyrs of the intifada are presented as angels bringing light into the world: "O you sincere ones," the text reads, "How did you come to us . . . We don't know. How did you leave us . . . We don't know. Were you angels of mercy who came to take away some of our cares and gladden us with joy?"

27. Faces of martyrs superimposed on flowers.

28. Faceless martyr, Gaza City.

29. Following a series of "stabbing operations" carried out against Israeli
civilians, four hundred supporters of the Islamist Movement in the West
Bank and Gaza were temporarily deported by the Israeli government to Marj
az-Zahur in south Lebanon in the winter of 1991. Here in the main hall of
a Hamas-controlled mosque in Gaza City, a Palestinian boy pauses to read a
handwritten communiqué that catalogues the conditions faced by the
deportees and reiterates the movement's opposition to the peace process,
"the suspect deals of the Americans and the Zionists." Addressed to
"the masses of our people in the land of al-Isra' and al-Mir'aj" (meaning
"the Night Journey" and "the Ascension," respectively—references to the
midnight sojourn of Muhammad from Mecca to Jerusalem, and thence to
heaven) and "those arrayed for war on the soil of the beloved homeland,"
the text is entitled "The Marj az-Zahur Exile: Between the Mercilessness
of Winter and the Terrorism of Occupation," and was probably faxed from
one of "the fabled tents" of the deportees to the Gaza Strip. Referencing
"The Tribes of Israel" (Qur'an 17:4), the writers predict that the fate of
Israel will be "at the hands of the Men of Truth and the Detachments of the
Qur'an, and the Raisers of the Banner of Islam."

30. In this hand-painted poster hung in Palestine Mosque, Gaza City, Hamas claims ownership of two recent attacks against "the enemies of Allah and mankind," and reiterates its opposition to talks between the PLO and Israel in visceral terms. Written in large red letters across both panels of text is the slogan, "This is the language that the Jews understand!!"

31. The term "sons of monkeys and pigs" as an epithet for Jews became widespread in Islamist circles as the intifada progressed and is found in this poster from the Gaza Strip. The poster employs graphic images to illustrate Qur'anic verses—donkeys laden with Torah scrolls on their backs, a panting dog saddled with a Torah scroll, a sow and her piglets, and a monkey-businessman, which has been heavily influenced by depictions of Uncle Sam. From top to bottom and right to left, we read:

In the name of Allah, the Compassionate, the Merciful
The Barnyard of the Tribes of Israel

The likeness of those who were given the Torah and then abandoned it
is that of a donkey laden with books (62:5, "Friday")

His likeness is that of a dog; if you set upon him, he pants, and if you
let him alone, he pants (7:176, "The Heights")

And He made them into monkeys and pigs and servants of evil
(5:60, "The Table")

The Islamic Resistance Movement Hamas Palestine
Media Office

32. Photocopies of the identity cards of Israeli soldiers and policemen were sometimes posted in public places in the West Bank and Gaza Strip as definitive evidence supporting a group's claim to a particular armed action. This display in Palestine Mosque, Gaza City, features not only the identity card of the victim as if a trophy—that of an Israeli policeman who was kidnapped and killed by members of the Qassam Battalions—but also the command that authorized his death, a *hadith*, or tradition of the Prophet, transmitted by Bukhari:

> We request from our dear ones and our brothers in Hamas that they make from the title of this announcement a slogan to be written on every wall, and let the slogan at this stage be the hadith of the Messenger of Allah, Allah bless Him and grant Him salvation, 'The Jewish man you have captured, kill him.'

> Truly, it is jihad. Victory or martyrdom.
> And Allahu akbar, and Allah be praised

وهذا قسمنا بالله أن نواصل الطريق، فلا حل إلا بالإسلام، ولا نجاة لنا إلا بالجهاد والعهد أن نواصل المسيرة حتى النصر أو الشهادة.

وأخيراً: نطلب من أحبابنا وإخواننا في حماس، أن يجعلوا من عنوان هذا البيان شعاراً يكتب على كل الجدران، وليكن شعار المرحلة حديث رسول الله صلى الله عليه وسلم:
"من ظفرتم به من رجال يهود، فاقتلوه"

وأنه جهاد نصر او استشهاد
والله أكبر ولله الحمد

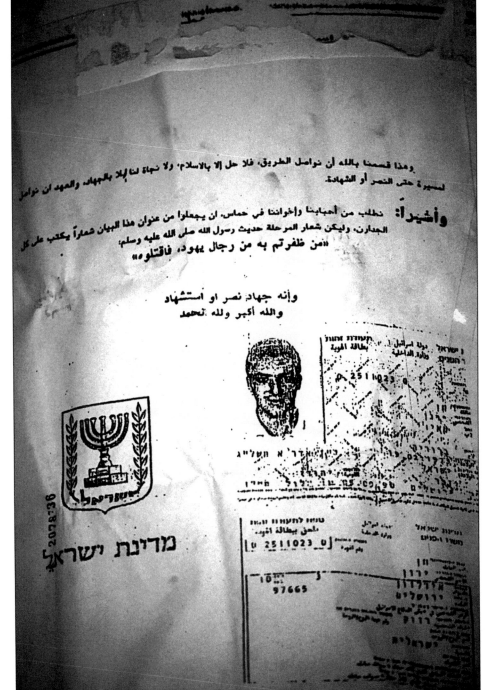

מדינת ישראל

2078:36

33. A Hamas Ninja strangles and stabs an IDF soldier from behind. From right to left, the slogans read, "We will talk to the Zionists by means of our knives and guns," "This is the language that our enemies understand, and we will never talk to them in any other way," and "The debt of the vile Rabin will be paid with soldier and settler blood."

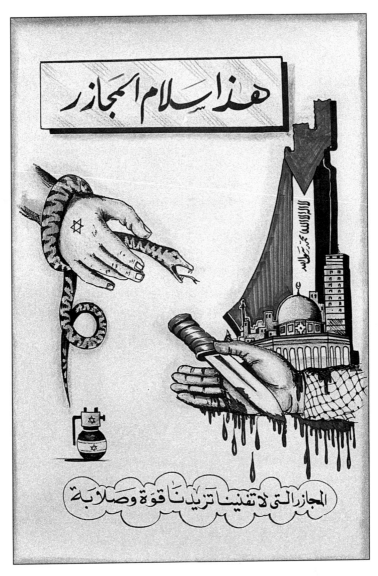

34. With the possibility of peace and a negotiated settlement seeming likely, even imminent, after the signing of the Oslo Accords, Hamas began to agitate strongly against such a solution. In this poster, an Israeli hand ostensibly offered in peace is shown as really proffering poison. The proper response to such a duplicitous offer is implicit in the bloody knife offered in return. In the background is a map of All Palestine inscribed with the shahadatain and a cityscape of Jerusalem featuring the Dome of the Rock and a skyscraper, suggesting the form of a gun. At the top of the poster is written, "This is the peace of the massacre," while the bottom slogan reads, "The massacre that does not destroy us increases our strength and unyieldingness."

35. In this poster from the Gaza Strip, a headless mujahid, capped with crossed rifles and an open Qur'an inscribed with the injunction "And prepare," crushes an Israeli soldier underfoot. The preternaturally large and bare foot is meant to signify insult. In one hand, the mujahid holds prayer beads; in the other, he expands the meaning of the *shahida*, or one-way sign, to indicate that violence is the only way. Written below are the words:

> The negotiator chokes on his words and says,
> "By a tongue of fire or blood, O Battalions"

> I will carry my soul in my palm
> and challenge the pit of destruction
> Either a life that gladdens the friend
> or a death that enrages the enemy

This poem predates the intifada by decades and was used to mourn the death of 'Abd al-Qadir al-Husaini, a major Palestinian Arab military leader from 1931, when he headed the Holy Jihad organization, until his death in the 1948 war. Many intifada texts possess antecedents in the literature of the Palestinian revolts of 1929 and 1936 and the war of 1948, as well as the period when Palestine was a province of the Ottoman Empire.

كتائب الشهيد / عز الدين القسام

غصة المفاوضة صوته فتكلم
بلسانه نار يا كتائب أو دم
× × × × × × ×
سأحمل روحي على راحتي وأمضى بها في مهاوى الردى
فإما حياة تسر الصديق وإما ممات يغيظ العدا

36. In this poster from Gaza, a connection is made between the makeup and American greeting ("hi") of a nationalist student and nationalist ideology, considered by many Islamists to be Western-influenced and invalid. Two Islamist girls dressed demurely in the hijab are discussing a third girl depicted to their left. "Look, my sister, O Um-Salam, she said 'hi' to me," whispers the girl on the right to her friend. "She's full of hot air!" "What really makes me angry," responds the second girl, "is that she said she was going to the university, made-up like that! By Allah, my sister, not on my wedding day, not before and not after, would I paint myself up like that. What a wasted generation. And we say we want a homeland!?!?!"

37. This large mural was painted in 1994 by Fatah adherents in the heart of Gaza City in honor of the return of Yasir Arafat and PLO soldiers and dignitaries. It features many of the major icons of the nationalist uprising— map of historical Palestine, masked Ninja, V-sign, eagle, gun, stone, candle, sun. Inscribed in small letters on the cartouche featured in the middle of the painting is a verse from the *sura*, or chapter, of the Qur'an entitled *al-Fatah*, "We have given you a resplendent victory" (48:1). The word translated here as "victory" is *fatah*, or "opening."

38. With the devolution of authority from Israel to the Palestinian Authority, graffiti and other media in the Gaza Strip were no longer under threat of immediate erasure. They, accordingly, became more elaborate, with more attention paid to lifelike representation, as in this painting of a "giant and lion of al-Qassam," posted on the occasion of 'Eid al-Adha, the Feast of the Sacrifice.

39. This mural was painted by Khalid al-Halabi on the walls of Khan Yunis
Refugee Camp in 1994 as a memorial to a former First Lieutenant of Fatah
in the Gaza Strip, and as a territorial marker for the paramilitary group that
took the activist's name after his martyrdom. The message to the left is a
highly stylized greeting from the group to the Palestinian people on the
advent of 'Eid al-Adha. The artist himself was killed a few months after
finishing the work.

40. In this Hamas poster of an Israeli bus, the target of a suicide bombing, the artist has included such details as the number of the bus route and the name of the transportation company in Hebrew, but other than the massive pools of blood leaking from the bus' battered carcass, he has, somewhat atypically, kept the scene devoid of the carnage resulting from such an action.

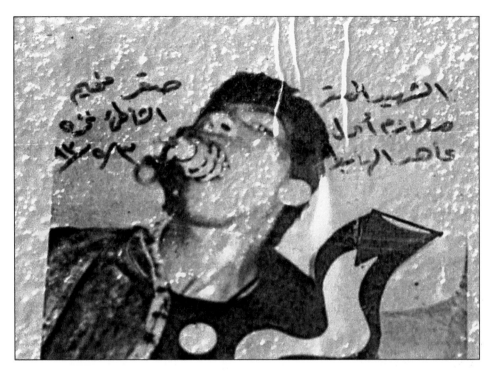

41. In this poster from Shati' Camp, Gaza, a member of the Fatah Hawks poses for the camera before his death, cradling a hand grenade in his mouth like an egg. In an accompanying poster, he posed against a backdrop of graffiti that announced his martyrdom as if it had already taken place.

42. Boys in front of a wall in a public square in Rafah, the Gaza Strip, covered with the names of martyrs of the intifada.

their thoughts, slander their heritage, and defame their ideals after which they could be conquered militarily. And so it was as a preparation for the colonialists' invasion when Allenby [British general and commander-in-chief of the Egyptian Expeditionary Force who captured Jerusalem from the Ottomans during World War I] announced, 'Now end the Crusades.' And General Gouraud stood on the tomb of Salah ad-Din, saying: 'Behold, we have returned, O Salah ad-Din!'" The "ideological invasion" continues today, the covenant continues, "preparing the way for the loss of Palestine."

An event even more dramatic in Arab eyes than Allenby's conquest of Jerusalem took place when the Old City of Jerusalem and its eastern neighborhoods were taken by Israel in the last days of the Six Day War in 1967. Although Moshe Dayan, then Israel's defense minister, afterward turned day-to-day control of al-Aqsa Mosque and the Dome of the Rock over to the Waqf, the Islamic charitable trust, the holy places are, nevertheless, commonly represented in Palestinian media as imperiled, particularly in the media of Hamas, a group that sometimes closes its slogans with the signature, "The Guardians of al-Aqsa." Radical Jewish groups, many based in settlements in the West Bank and Gaza, also consider the site to be endangered. They argue that the Islamic structures now situated on the mount do not belong on a holy Jewish site and, moreover, constitute a major obstacle to the coming of the Messiah; in the mid-eighties, extremists in the Jewish underground actually attempted to blow up the Dome of the Rock but failed.

Many years before, in 1969, the deranged Australian Christian pilgrim Dennis Michael Rohan, perhaps suffering from what doctors in the city liked to call "Jerusalem syndrome,"[18] succeeded in setting fire to a number of structures in al-Aqsa Mosque, including the minbar of Salah ad-Din—an event commonly attributed throughout the Arab world to the Israeli government and even commemorated in government-issued stamps in a number of Arab and Muslim states. During the intifada, the arson was used as a means of delegitimizing peace negotiations between the Israeli government and Fatah-aligned Palestinian negotiators, as in the following message of Hamas, which was posted in the central square of Deir al-Balah Refugee Camp, the Gaza Strip. "No voice rises above the voice of Islam," the graffito reads, "Our al-Aqsa, not your temple. Our al-Aqsa, not your temple. Let's make the anniversary of the burning of al-Aqsa Mosque a day on which to set the land afire under the feet of the Zionist aggressors."

The first part of the message is an Islamist transumption of the well-known Fatah byword penned early in the intifada, "No voice rises above the intifada"; the second, a word-by-word borrowing of the Fatah imperative, "Let's set the land afire under the feet of the Zionist aggressors." A nearby message lays the blame on the United Nations, reading, "8/21 is a day that represents an eternal mark of disgrace on the foreheads of the United Nations and their henchmen, the peace negotiators. The burning of the blessed al-Aqsa Mosque is the proof

and clearest indication of the meaning of the Islamic struggle and the ideological dispute." The rhetoric employed is characteristically Hamas, with terms
commonly used by the nationalists being notably eschewed. *Sira'*, for instance,
translated here as "struggle" with connotations of "to fell to the ground," "to
fight to the bitter end," has been chosen rather than the more common *nidal* or
kifah preferred by the nationalist camp.

In 1996, Palestinian riots broke out again when Israel decided to reopen a
series of preexisting ancient passageways adjacent to the Western Wall as a
tourist attraction. Again, imams called for people to flock to the mount, while
hundreds of Palestinians rioted throughout the West Bank. IDF forces and
Palestinian Authority policemen battled in what was, arguably, the first significant armed fight between them. Approximately thirty-seven Palestinian demonstrators and fifteen Israeli soldiers were killed in the battle.

In September 2000, Ariel Sharon, Likud party member and candidate for
the position of prime minister of Israel, visited the mount. Sharon was widely
loathed by the Palestinians and much of the Arab world as the architect of
Israel's policy of aggressive retaliation for Palestinian attacks as well as Israel's
invasion of Lebanon in 1982, during which nearly a thousand Palestinians[19]
were massacred in the refugee camps of Sabra and Shatilla by Lebanese
Phalangist militiamen, deaths for which Sharon was held indirectly responsible
by an Israeli court of inquiry. Clinton's peace initiative had foundered, and
Arafat had been publicly humiliated after the U.S. president had singled him
out as the primary cause of that failure. Although the decision to resume armed
confrontation had probably already been made,[20] Sharon's visit to haram ash-
sharif, often presented in intifada texts as a "defilement," provided the necessary spark for a new uprising, which quickly became known as "al-Aqsa intifada."

28. Blood, Blood, Blood

The audiocassette *Marj az-Zahur* begins with the words, "Blood, blood, blood,
blood," and thereafter manages to repeat the word some forty times. Everyone
talked about blood during the intifada. It didn't matter whether you were a
nationalist or Islamist. There was blood everywhere. You couldn't ignore it.

Demonstrators were shot every other day and lay in hospital with holes
blown through their bodies, bandages seeping; collaborators were killed, their
bloody, tortured bodies dumped on the street or in front of mosques and the
houses of people who publicly spoke out against collaborator killings so that
everyone could see what happened to traitors. The blood and wounds of martyrs were commonly displayed and photographed. People dipped their hands
in the blood and left handprints on the walls. If a member of the enemy camp
were killed, people sometimes dipped their hands in that too. In song, they
went so far as to drink the blood of the enemy, as in these stanzas from the
audiocassette *Islamic Zajal* 4, which play on the literal meaning of *Hamas* ("zeal"):

The striking of bullets, O my enemy, gives us
power and zeal against those who make of themselves our enemies
By your bullets, you give us drink from the fountain of Kauthar
By your bullets, you give us the key to Paradise

The striking of bullets, O my enemy, gives us
power and zeal against those who make of themselves our enemies
The striking of bullets, O my enemy, gives us
power and zeal against those who make of themselves our enemies

Pour bullets on the people and increase them!
Let the martyrs amongst my people increase!
By the machine-gun, O Muhammad, we'll restore your religion
and we'll drink from the blood of all those who make of themselves our enemies

This kind of rhetoric was not confined to the Islamists. The following message, for example, was posted on a mud-covered wall in Hebron. It references the Palestinian poet Mahmud Darwish's poem "Identity Card" and is signed by Fatah–The Unified National Leadership, a consortium of factions including Fatah, the PFLP, the DFLP, and the Communist Party:

I am Arab
I learned pride before reading books
I am Arab, and when I am hungry,
I eat the flesh of my prey
I am Arab

One thinks of a similar chant for Arafat in which his soldiers are presented as "drinkers of blood":

Abu-'Amar, go, go
Abu-'Amar, go, go
We are with you until victory
We are with you until victory

Abu-'Amar doesn't care
Abu-'Amar doesn't care
Your men are drinkers of blood
Your men are drinkers of blood

The metaphor of ingesting the blood or flesh of the enemy is found in reverse in all those messages in which the hero proffers his own blood as a sacrificial gift, as in the lines from *The Islamic Anthem Festival*, "The child shouts, From my blood, O Jerusalem, I'll give you drink/ And for Jews and Arab traitors, the stone of death!"

Blood was said to come from everywhere. It streamed over walls. It formed oceans. It soaked the land, which was commonly described as "hemorrhaging" like a wound. Streets were washed with blood, "hennaed" with it, as in the lines from the audiocassette *'Ayun Qara*:

O day of al-Aqsa, reality has become mad
As news of the massacre spread, all the people gathered
and the streets of Palestine were hennaed with blood
Blood drains from the wounded
and the martyrs embrace, and pain sings

Mujahidun and revolutionaries were said to pay a "tax of blood and mar-tyrdom." The blood of martyrs was said to light up the way, make henna on the hands of the living, knock on "the gates of freedom," shout "Allahu akbar," flow across the land, cover the land like a libation, and, in perhaps the most common of all intifada figures, "irrigate" the soil of the homeland and the revo-lution unfolding, as in the graffito, "The revolution is a tree irrigated by the blood of the pure."

Variants of the theme of irrigation by blood were virtually infinite, cross-ing over factional lines, as in "My homeland, I irrigate the soil of your borders" (PFLP), or "Palestine is a green tree whose thirst can only be quenched with the blood of the martyrs" (Fatah), or "When the blood of martyrs irrigates/ the land then roses appear" (Hamas), or these stanzas from a song of the PFLP-affiliated al-Qala' Band:

The land, O my comrades, is thirsty; the blood of the martyrs will irrigate it
I listen to the sound of guns, in which the poor seek help

What am I? I am a fida'i

I will fight until the last drop, for the land is calling me
Then make from my body torches and from my love, bombs for the homeland

What am I? I am a fida'i

Blood was presented as a purifying agent, as in the admonition from the Islamic Light Band, "Purify your land—mix its sand with blood." History was written with blood, and it was through blood that Palestine would be liberated, as in the slogans, "Religion and blood are our road to certain victory," "Palestine is the land of heroism and self-sacrifice/ The sole solution is to shed blood," and "By revolution, by blood and by fire, we will return home, O my people." Blood was the means by which victory would be achieved, as in the graffito, "From the Battle of Karama to Beirut and from Beirut to the intifada, the Fatah waterfall of blood continues until victory is assured by the will of Allah." There were water-falls of blood, volcanoes of blood, rivers of blood, seas of blood. Blood was the crucial emulsion in which life itself seemed to be suspended.

It was blood that prevented negotiations, compromise of any sort, as in the Hamas message, "The blood of our martyrs will not be wasted on the negotia-tion table," and the Islamic Jihad graffito, "The blood of the martyrs will re-main a curse on the dirty peace project." Palestinian negotiators were said to talk through their noses while the shabab danced in blood. Unbelievers danced on the blood of the martyrs. Blood was a debt, obligation, and competitive spur, as in the calls to martyrdom, "The debt of our blood is on you" and "Blood demands blood . . . martyr demands martyr." It existed in almost unlimited supply, and was commonly called "cheap," as in the line from a song from the Islamic Light Band, "The blood of our hero-martyr is a spring." Above all, blood was what made things real, as in Muzaffar a-Nawwab's *Night Songs*, which was quoted on the walls, "My homeland taught me that the letters of history are not real without blood."

The zeal was such that some actively invited their own bloodletting. "Flay my bones with a whip; put my neck under the knife," goes the *mawwal* (chanted introduction) of one Hamas anthem, which continues with the lines, "Break, break my bones and shed my blood/ I'm a Muslim, and Allah named me," while another song asserts simply, "We are in love with the color of blood."

29. A Collaborator Breaker Accused of Something Close to Collaboration

The first time we saw the letter before us was at 'Ali's house. A guy had suddenly popped his head through the front door, which was kept perpetually open, and after numerous greetings and a cup of tea, had pulled it from his pocket like a rabbit so unexpected it was. "From the Movement of the Islamic Uprising (Hamas) in Palestine to the family of the detained," the document begins, following the obligatory basmala. "We inform you that your son, the detained 'Abdullah, has exceeded the limits by assaulting members of the Islamic Movement inside prison. For he beat and abused and insulted those following the Islamic way for no reason except that they said, 'Allah is our Lord.'"

The Islamic Resistance Movement, the letter went on to say, was omnipresent and omniscient, capable of ferreting out anyone anywhere. "You should know," it reads, "that the movement of the Islamic uprising in Palestine and the Strip does not and will not allow anyone to attack its sons and will not be silent about them, for the hands of Hamas are long and capable of avenging its sons in every inch of Palestine." If the accused 'Abdullah did not immediately stop his "criminal pursuits," the letter continues, the consequences would be dire: "So we demand of you, O family of the detained, that you inform your son 'Abdullah to cease such criminal pursuits forthwith! Otherwise, we will strike with an iron hand anyone who allows himself to be seduced into assaulting members of the Islamic Movement in or out of prison."

Indeed, if things did not change, the letter asserts, the family would be "the first victim": "And we regret to say that if your son does not turn away from these savage actions, which serve the *mukhabarat* [Arabic for "secret police"], you, the family of the detained, will be the first victim because of the criminal, malicious actions of your son." The letter then closes with another claim of ubiquitous intelligence, "And we inform you that all your movements are known to us in 'Ain 'Arik and Ramallah and Jerusalem and in every place; thus, if this matter is of concern to you, then make haste to restrain your ignorant son from actions that serve the Israeli mukhabarat." "He who warns is excused," reads the final onimous line.

The visitor turned out to be the self-same 'Abdullah of the letter, a journalist whose avowed mission was the "uncovering" of collaborators. His problems with Hamas, he said, had begun in prison, where he'd spent a total of six years, both before and during the intifada. There, he'd turned up a "well-educated preacher" and Hamas leader and set forth the evidence against him in a leaflet. Hamas, in response, accused him of ill will, indeed, of trying to tear down the organization. It was then that his family had received the warning letter, which he, strangely, claimed was actually not the work of Hamas but rather the mukhabarat. And proof of that, he said, was the fact that the mukhabarat had beat him up one morning (so badly that he was in the hospital for five days), and then, amazingly, an Israeli news announcer had reported the beating a mere fifteen minutes later. When 'Abdullah asked the announcer how the station could have received the report in such a short period of time, the announcer replied, "If I told you, I'd lose my job," his voice intimating conspiratorial goings-on.

'Abdullah said that he had learned a great deal from his investigations, and wanted to tell us about them. Collaborators, he said, often killed other collaborators when they were no longer needed and would then claim that the killings had been carried out by some other group. The mukhabarat didn't pick just anybody to be a collaborator; they chose weak people, people who lacked self-confidence, underworld people—"hashish and Mafia" people—and then won them over through promises, threats, or combinations of the two. The Israelis disdained their collaborators, referring to them as "stinkers." Once, he said, an Israeli in the Civil Administration had told him how Hitler had refused to shake hands with one of his Czech collaborators.

The mukhabarat were effective, 'Abdullah said, because they knew the major weakness of the Palestinians—sex. (The topic was normally completely taboo in Palestinian society, but during the intifada, if you were talking about collaborators, you could bring almost anything up.) The mukhabarat, 'Abdullah said, would do things like call people in and photograph them having sex, and then those people would be theirs forever. The possibilities for corruption were endless, but they usually involved alcohol or pornography or sex . . . or all three. The accusation of incest was not uncommon. Once, 'Abdullah said, his voice suggesting, alternately, prurient fascination and moral outrage, a prostitute from Tulkarem had sex with her own brother. And then there was the collaborator from the same city who tied up his mother and raped her as well as his three sisters. Others were guilty of sodomy. Clearly, the Israelis and their collaborators would stop at nothing.

The category of collaborator encompassed not only informers for the Is-raeli authority and people accused of moral misdeed, but also political noncon-formists, backsliders in the faith, drug dealers, social misfits, and ambiguous figures of all varieties. Collaborators were killed on the order of about one every other day in the West Bank and the Gaza Strip during the first intifada, with over a thousand attacks directed against traitors, real and imagined. High holy days were particularly favored for executions.[21] Whereas persons accused of lesser crimes like thievery might simply be beaten in town squares as public spectacles, collaborators were often tortured to death, their mutilated bodies left on the street as warnings.

Women constituted a special subgroup of accused collaborators. All it took to fell a woman, 'Abdullah said, was innuendo—the mere prospect of shame. Stories abounded of women who had innocently gone into the dressing rooms of clothing stores and come out spies, their naked bodies having been recorded by cameras hidden behind one-way mirrors. If the photographs were released to the women's families, there was a good chance that they might even be killed at the hands of their own father or a brother. In actuality, very few col-laborators were women. Nearly all of the 107 women killed by Palestinians as suspected Israeli collaborators from 1988 to 1993, according to one study by the Israeli human rights organization Betselem, were, in reality, victims of "honor killings"—the name given to the killing of women accused of dishonor-ing their families by illegitimate sexual activity or suspect moral behavior. Eighty-one such killings occurred in the Gaza Strip, where they have long been common.

Countless graffiti warned against the dangers and consequences of col-laboration, particularly during the early days of the intifada. More often than not, these messages were not meant so much for actual collaborators as they were for the general population. "We will clean our land from the polluting filth of the collaborators," reads a typical such message. Signed by the Abu-Jihad Brigades of Fatah, the graffito was spray-painted on the outer walls of a local cemetery in Ramallah, while downtown, a group calling itself "The Black Nightingale" posted a threat illustrated with stylized axes, "Especially for the chastisement of collaborators," along with the barb, "Woe to those who erase nationalist graffiti." "For every wall, a window—for every collaborator, a reck-oning," a graffito spray-painted on the front wall of the Christmas Hotel in East Jerusalem during roughly the same time period, expresses the same senti-ment in the form of an apothegm.

Other warnings, in contrast, identified collaborators and suspect persons by name, as in this message we recorded on a wall in Gaza, "To Ahmad Shukri: Your time of dominance will not last long." Occasionally the complete accusa-tion, trial, and sentence of an individual could be found on the walls. In the winter of 1989, for instance, al-Ahli Hospital in Gaza City bore witness to a controversy over the fate of an accused collaborator, Jihad al-Qawasme. The first graffito that was posted stated, "Fatah loathes the attack on Brother Jihad al-Qawasme, and will punish all those who attack innocent people." The organization apparently had a change of heart or received new information, for the original message was crossed out and replaced with "Fatah will have nothing to do with the traitor Jihad al-Qawasme." If an accused collaborator could transform the dispute from one of politics into a family feud, he could perhaps stave off the punishment meted out to traitors. Al-Qawasme apparently tried to do just that, for a few days later, a new graffito appeared that read, "To the collaborator Jihad al-Qawasme. If you portray your beating as a family problem, we will sentence you to death." The UNL also posted this message to any would-be allies of the accused, "We will put anyone who aligns himself with the garbage Jihad al-Qawasme under the telescope of the Revolutionary Security Committee."

Once videotape came to be used during the intifada, Hamas employed it, among other things, to record the movement's interrogations of collaborators and their confessions. In the few excerpts we have been able to watch long enough to understand what is happening—they are unbearable—the accused is often blindfolded with a keffiyah and sits in a chair or on the floor, answering questions. Only rarely does he protest his innocence or argue with his captors.[22] The proceedings always possess an affect of unreality, accentuated by the fact that many have been recorded over old movies, which occasionally break through. (On one, an Egyptian actress can be heard saying in the breathless, supernaturally high-pitched style typical of Egyptian actresses, "Al-beit malakbat!" "The house is a mess!") The feeling of unreality and artifice is further reinforced by the strangely solicitous acts of the interrogators who sometimes offer the accused water, cigarettes, or even pillows, as if he were an esteemed guest rather than a person who has just been kidnapped and probably tortured and is about to have his head blown off. With each of the offerings, the accused, wiping his face repeatedly as if trying to wipe away disbelief along with the sweat, may look confused, even embarrassed.

The story of how the accused says that he became a collaborator is often haphazard, as if he himself did not understand exactly how it had come about, or why. One accused collaborator described meeting someone on the street who struck up a friendship with him and then took care of some or another problem he was having. Another recalled in his written confession that a relative had said to him one day out of the blue that they should go see someone who would be able to take care of his "security," and the man turned out to be an Israeli handler. Another told, matter of factly, of how one day he had been going about his usual business and had come across a couple of Israeli soldiers on the road. The two had been in a car accident and were hurt, and so he took them to Saroka Hospital in Beersheva. The soldiers, it turned out, were bigwigs in the IDF, and a short while later, he received a phone call from one of them—a David Cohen—who asked to meet with him. When he arrived at the "meeting," it turned out to be a big party attended by "very important people" like Moshe Dayan and the president of the Knesset—why, even some Arab leaders were there. David Cohen told the accused that he would like to open a permit office for people who wanted to go to Jordan, and a month or so later, introduced him to a guy named "Gadi," who happened to be a member of the mukhabarat. Thus did he find himself "connected."

Other collaborators, in contrast, presented themselves as powerful figures capable of bringing people down through money or pleasure or sex. On the famous videotape of Ashraf Kahail, for instance, Kahail is shown telling his captors, "Those eight individuals whose names I mentioned—I set out to bring them down, some by money, some by sniffing the breeze and happiness. The captain said, 'If they want money, give it to them; if they want to have fun with Jewish girls, take them to them and catch them.'" Such "felling operations" would sometimes be described in detail by the accused, and, in the end, as a feeling of something like relief or fate filled the room, the accused would be asked what should be done with him, and he would answer, obligingly, that he should be done away with.

30. A Daring Shock of Jet-Black Hair Coyly Peeking Out Beneath Her Veil

Here's a cartoon-style poster that bears witness to the multifarious ways in which "female modesty" was used during the intifada as a rallying symbol for men. Signed by "the Voice of the Islamic Group, the League of Abas Musawi" of Gaza, the poster tries to make a connection between the provocative makeup and American greeting ("hi") of a nationalist student and the political ideology of the nationalist movement as a whole, considered by many Islamists to be Western-influenced and invalid.

In the background can be seen two girls dressed demurely in the hijab ("veil"), a practice mandated by Islamists, who insist that women cover everything but their hands and face. The two are whispering to one other about a third girl to their left. "Look, my sister, O Um-Salam, she said 'hi' to me," one of them remarks to the other. "She's full of hot air!" Her rather pensive companion, in turn, denounces the nationalist girl for wearing makeup before she casts doubt on the nationalist enterprise itself: "What really makes me angry is that she said she was going to the university made-up like that! By Allah, my sister, not on my wedding day, not before and not after, would I paint myself up like that. What a wasted generation. And we say we want a homeland!?!?!"

Although the object of their scorn also wears a headscarf meant to cover her hair and a long dress that hides everything but her hands and feet, a closer look reveals that she is merely affecting the appearance of religiosity. A daring shock of jet-black hair coyly peeks out beneath her flesh-covered scarf; her lips and nails are painted fire-engine red; two bangles dangle from her wrist, which, together with her black robe, form three of the four colors of the Palestinian flag; and, perhaps most provocatively, she has plucked and highlighted her eyebrows into an arch of perpetual sexual surprise that draws even more attention to her Siberian-husky blue eyes. In short, she is *tabarraja*, a term derived from a root meaning "to decorate oneself," but which in Islamist parlance has come to mean an immoral girl or woman.

The artist has not only accentuated the differences between the two religious girls and their suspect counterpart in dress and speech, but he has also made an almost ethnic distinction between them. He has drawn the pious girls with the dark skin and eyes common to the Gaza Strip. With her pale skin and blue eyes, the not-so-religious girl, in contrast, has been made to seem foreign.

In a similar way, a poster that a group of boys brought out to the street for us to photograph in Gaza City presents female adornment as shameful, calling it "nothing more than blind imitation of the enemies of our great religion." Illustrated with a Palestinian flag inscribed with the formula "Allahu akbar" and a masked Ninja brandishing twin swords as if in a Kung Fu movie, the text reads,

> In the name of Allah, the Compassionate, the Merciful
>
> All praise to Allah, Lord of the Worlds, Bringer of Victory to the Faithful, Destroyer of Tyrants, and prayers and peace on the foremost of the messengers, our Prophet Muhammad bin 'Abdullah, Allah bless Him and grant Him salvation, and on His family and His Companions and those who carry the banner of jihad on the path of Allah until the Day of Judgment.
>
> The adorning and unveiling and going out of women with all their finery on display is a disastrous course leading to the pit and a determining factor in the spread of depravity and baseness and is nothing more than blind imitation of the enemies of our great religion. We will watch over our women to prevent them from straying from the teachings of our religion. O people of the blessed intifada, our colossal desire in the Islamic Resistance Movement, Hamas, is that we should put restraints on such unbridled liberty for the sake of our reputation, our honor, and our chastity.
>
> Let the intifada of our heroic people continue until Allah grants us victory or martyrdom. Allahu akbar, and, Allah permitting, victory is ours.
>
> The Islamic Resistance Movement
> Hamas. Palestine

Throughout intifada media, women serve, alternately, as symbols of purity or disgrace, their personal behavior correlated with *'ird*, collective honor, as in the following mawwal from the Hamas-produced audiocassette *Islamic Zajal* 3, which presents the caliph al-Mu'tasim as the savior of female honor and Muslim dignity. Upon hearing a Muslim woman cry out, "O al-Mu'tasim!" after being violated in a Byzantine prison a thousand miles away, the 'Abbasid caliph, it is said, mustered up an army to redeem her honor—a response that is contrasted in the anthem with that of contemporary Arab leaders who, blind to the fact that "the only solution to the problem is blood, knee-deep," do nothing but hold international conferences and send letters of protest to the United Nations:

> O wonderful! We listen in astonishment to wonders and declarations concerning the international conference.
> Even if your conference is held, it won't bring back the rights that we lost many years ago.
> My rights were lost—where will I find them?
> The honor of Islam—where will I find it? . . .
> Where are you, O Salah ad-Din? Where are you, Mu'tasim, to protect it?
> Dictate a message to the heart of the Cross and the Star.[23]
> Muster your army to purify the country.
> Long ago, Mu'tasim sent a letter to that dog of a Greek, saying,
> "The cry of the woman reached me, you filth!"
> But all that the Arabs send are thousands of letters to the United Nations, crammed with statements of protest.
> They say the problem is solved, and a solution has been achieved.
> I say that the problem is not over yet.
> Shame and disgrace on the kings who compromise in order to solve the problem.
> The only solution to the problem is blood, knee-deep.

The same theme appears in a June 1992 Battalions of al-Qassam video featuring 'Abdullah 'Azzam, Kalashnikov in hand. "Jihad is difficult," he begins, speaking in sonorous tones, almost a singsong; "jihad is heavy on the soul. But if there is no alternative, then it is weakness to live as a coward." Appealing to the wounds of victims and the honor of virgins, he then breaks into verse,

> If there is no solution to the problem but to ride it,[24]
> then there is nothing for the compelled to do but ride
> Who is for the victims, consoling the wounds?
> Who is for the virgins, protecting their honor?

"And as ibn al-Mubarak said," he continues, referring to the eighth-century scholar, poet, collector of hadith, mujahid, martyr (he was killed while on a jihad campaign in Iraq), and Muslim *qudwa*, or exemplar, "'How can there be peace of mind,/ How can a Muslim remain calm,/ while Muslim women are at the mercy of the brutal enemy/ Whenever they are afraid of disgrace, they say, Would that I had never been born!'" The lamentation can be compared to Mary's cry of woe recorded in Qur'an 19:23 ("Mary"), which reads, "The birth pangs led her to the trunk of a date palm tree. 'Would that I had died before this,' she said, 'and become a thing forgotten.'" One thinks also of the cry of the unbeliever stuck between life and death on the Day of Judgment (Qur'an 78:40, "The Announcement")—"O would that I were dust!"—discussed by Said Qutb in *In the Shade of the Qur'an.*

Continuing in the same vein, 'Azzam says,

> What value has life
> if we live like a small child under the feet of the unbelievers?
> What value has life
> if we accept to sit with those who remain behind?[25]
> "They preferred to stay with those who remained behind,
> and Allah has sealed their hearts?so they do not understand."

He then goes on to contrast the noble death of the mujahidun with the ignoble death and sure "oblivion" of the *ghaniyat*, a term that means literally "pretty girls" in Palestinian colloquial, but is often used as a euphemism for "prostitutes":

> Killing and fighting have been written for us just as oblivion has been written for prostitutes. It is inevitable that you raise the spear, and it is inevitable that you unsheathe the sword, that you put the index finger[26] on the trigger. And it is inevitable that you die standing on the field [of battle], not under the feet of the lowly and the godless in the depths of the prisons or between the wheels of a car or in a hospital. There is only one death so let it be on the path of Allah.

The antithesis of the ghaniya is, of course, the mother, the primary earthly witness of the mujahid's self-sacrifice and, almost invariably, the address of his last words, as in this graffito, which was posted upon the death of the martyr Khalid Abu-Tariq: "And though three bullets had lodged in his pure body, he dragged himself from the house on top of which he was standing and went to his mother, and said to her, 'O my mother, I have been martyred. I witness that there is no god but Allah, and Muhammad is the Messenger of Allah.'" Here, as throughout intifada media, the mother's generative power is commonly transumed into the machinery of war, as in messages like, "As long as mothers are bearing babies, then the intifada will continue," "My mother gave birth to me to struggle—Fatah gave me the weapon to hold," and "My mother bore me to die, and Hamas taught me perseverance." She is said to have suckled the hero with "the milk of pride." Alternately, her bosom is said to be filled with Molotovs. In still other messages, she is displaced entirely either by the youth's faction, as in the message, "Fatah is my mother, and the machine-gun is my father," or Palestine itself, as in this graffito, which we recorded in the Jerusalem neighborhood of Beit Hanina:

> I forgot my name
> I forgot my address
> I came to you, O Mother of All, and carved my name on my machine-gun—
> Fatah man, revolutionary, fida'i, Palestinian

When at last her son is martyred, she is said to be overjoyed to hear the news and emits a *zaghrada* (a high-pitched wailing sound made by women on happy occasions such as the entrance of a bride and groom at their wedding), sometimes even expressing the wish that all her sons will thus be taken.

31. Monkeys and Pigs and Servants of Evil

This photograph always excites in us the urge to run. We can see him now, charging out the door, a big man with a big beard. He's wild-eyed, raring to go, as if he's been waiting for this moment for a long time. He demands to know what it is exactly we think we're doing. We quickly snap some shots of the poster in front of us while our guide, a Hamasawi, talks to the angry man. (It's clearly not the early days of the intifada when people cried out, "Welcome, welcome!" and pulled us in for a cup of hot tea and conversation.) The angry man soon softens up a bit—in fact, feels downright obliged to explicate "The Barnyard of the Tribes of Israel" in detail.

Although a product of "the media office" of Hamas, the poster uses graphic and, accordingly, forbidden images to illustrate Qur'anic verses. The "barnyard," as the man points out, is full of animals bearing the primary symbol of Judaism and the state of Israel, the Magen David. There's a monkey businessman, a sow and her piglets, a dog and some donkeys carrying Torah scrolls on their backs, along with three Qur'anic citations. The first reads, "The likeness of those who were given the Torah and then abandoned it is that of a donkey laden with books," a verse derived from the chapter of the Qur'an entitled "Friday" (62:5); the second, "His likeness is that of a dog; if you set upon him, he pants, and if you let him alone, he pants," which is taken from "The Heights" (7:176); and the third, "And He made them into monkeys and pigs and Servants of evil," which is drawn from "The Table" (5:60).

To call someone an animal or talk about him or her as if an animal constitutes a particularly grave offense in Arabic. During the intifada, Israelis and Jews were commonly described in the media of nationalists and Islamists alike as animals—octopuses, dragons, monkeys, and so forth. Israeli leaders were favorite targets, with then Israeli Prime Minister Yitzhak Shamir depicted as a donkey (a play on his name, "donkey" in Arabic being *himar*); Yitzhak Rabin, then minister of defense, appearing as a monkey; and Ariel Sharon, then minister of trade and industry as an elephant. It was not until 1991 or so, around the rise of the Qassam Battalions, however, that we began to notice the more sinister phrase *ibna al-qird wa al-khanazir*, or "sons of monkeys and pigs," being used as an epithet for Jews. It soon became something of a convention for the Islamist groups.

Some of Fatah's strike forces, especially those in the Gaza Strip, adopted the epithet as well, as can be seen in the following excerpt from a communiqué that was released in Gaza in 1992 in response to a Hamas leaflet attacking the nationalist group for, among other things, disparaging Islam:

> Fatah set out for peace consciously and with an understanding of the plans of the enemy. Fatah knows well that it is negotiating with the Jews and knows who the Jews are—the descendants of monkeys and pigs.

Fatah understands that the journey is long and hedged with thorns and will continue for years. [Fatah] also understands the Arab and Islamic situation, and it will continue to raise the rifle in one hand and the olive branch in the other till "Allah may end the matter that has been accomplished." (Qur'an 8:42, "The Spoils of War")

The phrase "sons of monkeys and pigs" has a peculiar feel to it. Indeed, whenever it appears, one senses the intrusion of . . . let's call it "the beast"—a realm not entirely human, as in this excerpt from a videotape of the Battalions of the Martyr 'Izz ad-Din al-Qassam, in which the group takes credit for killing fifteen Palestinian collaborators and wounding four more. "According to the reckoning of the sons of monkeys and pigs," we are told, "the group has killed four Gaza policemen and wounded two others, including Major General Yossi Avni, leader of the Gaza police, and also two of the mukhabarat in Sheikh al-Ajlin." Even the victims of suicide bombings are described in Hamas media as monkeys and pigs, as in the following quotation in which the organization claims responsibility for the Beit Lid bombing in January 1995, "The Islamic Movement gives its condolences to the hero of the attack, which led to the killing of twenty pigs and the injuring of sixty monkeys."

The phrase was also popular among members of the rival Islamist group, the Islamic Jihad, as can be seen in the following leaflet in which the Jihad offers Yasir Arafat "three dead pigs stained with their own blood" as a "gift." The leaflet was hand-drawn, photocopied, and then distributed surreptitiously hours after the group ambushed an Israeli patrol near Kfar Darom on the eve of the return of the PLO chairman to the Gaza Strip in June 1994. Although it celebrates an attack that was carried out in the same manner as any number of such operations over the years, its timing was a clear challenge to the PLO and a personal insult to Arafat, who had recently signed documents outlawing such operations.

In the name of Allah, the Compassionate, the Merciful

The Islamic Jihad Movement in Palestine, QSM Brigade,[27] announces its responsibility for the Kafr Darom operation, which left three dead pigs stained with their blood.

And we in the QSM Brigade give this operation to Yasir Arafat as a gift on the occasion of his return to Gaza-Jericho.

And we offer our gift to Abu-'Amar with sincere devotion.

The Islamic Jihad Movement
30/6/94

Hamas also made frequent use of the term *gift* in its media, a rare example of irony in Palestinian Islamist literature, as in the following graffito put up in Deir al-Balah under the signature of the military wing of the movement. "The Battalions of 'Izz ad-Din al-Qassam," the message reads, "present this first gift to the government of Rabin by killing two Jews in a citrus factory in Nahal

Oz"—a reference to an operation in which two Israelis were stabbed to death in front of their Palestinian employees in a warehouse on the border between Gaza and Israel.

32. The Mad Dogs of Language

The Hamas videotape *The Promise* opens with four vignettes—barbed wire illuminated by blinding rays of light, a herd of goats with bells around their necks jingling like a bell choir, a flock of sheep flocking, a group of dogs savagely attacking one another.

The meaning of the scenes is unclear, and no interpretation offered. While the sun is commonly used in intifada media to represent the inescapability of truth, the herd of goats and the flock of sheep belong ostensibly to the realm of the pastoral, even if the affect of these particular shots is not especially in the bonny glenn. It is the dogs that are unforgettable—they resemble wolves, and bite each other viciously on the neck as they chase each other round and round, madness and fury with nowhere to go.

When they finally disappear, the viewer breathes a sigh of relief. A second later, the screen reads, "The International Company for Art Production presents *The Promise*," the characters of which are rendered in an elongated, swordlike script. A song follows, its words choreographed to iconic shots of the intifada—burning tires and billowing black smoke, masked shabab flinging stones with slingshots, a Palestinian flag waving in the wind, Islamist banners featuring crossed swords and the slogan, "And prepare for them." The filmmaker has even thrown into the mix a waving Israeli flag and an ultra-Orthodox Jew in long black robe and forelocks swaying back and forth in prayer. There's also a globe spinning round and round, bringing to mind the triumphalist phrase with which Hamas likes to end its documents—"Palestine . . . and all the world."

The song is actually not a song, but an anthem with a beat hypnotic and rousing at once. There are no musical instruments involved, this being Hamas—only human voices. The men, what sounds like a small army of men, issue their call for martyrs as though they themselves already inhabited the next world. "Revolutionaries! Revolutionaries!" they sing in smooth masculine harmony, stretching out the last syllable of *thiwar* ("revolutionaries") till it hums and vibrates as if on its own effortlessly, the last unit of sound warbling in perpetuity or as long as breath will last:

> O winds of Paradise, blow
> O river of martyrs, flow
> Islam is calling, who will answer?
> O righteous people, get up!

Revolutionaries! Revolutionaries!

You can meet us on the roads of al-Aqsa
The horses of pride are wandering with us
The blood of martyrs makes henna on our hands
Paradise needs men

Revolutionaries! Revolutionaries!

A picture of al-Aqsa Mosque then fills the screen, while the voice of Sheikh Hamid al-Beitawi, a preacher and one of the December 1992 Hamas deportees, can be heard in the background delivering the Friday sermon. His voice is overpowering, urgent and beseeching, and makes the hearer feel that something horrible is imminent. You can't escape from such a voice. As the screen reads, "O al-Mu'tasim," a reference to the ninth-century caliph, we hear the sheikh saying, his voice sharp and rising, "We implore all Muslims to rise up to help us. We are in trouble. O our brothers in the Islamic world. The usurpers, the tyrants, are tyrannizing us. They are violating the holy places, the holiness of the blessed al-Aqsa Mosque." Thus begins a film whose unifying theme is violation and its avengement.

The video cuts to a recent Hamas martyr, whom we initially see in a hospital bed, shrouded in a banner inscribed with the *shahadatain*, the credo of Islam, "There is no god but Allah, and Muhammad is the Messenger of Allah." Someone has placed a large Qur'an near his head. He appears to be alive but in a coma. A middle-aged woman sits beside his bed. She could be his mother, but as she speaks, it becomes clear that she is his grandmother. She describes how the youth had been shot in the eye while throwing stones and then beaten in the face with guns.

The video begins to skip about, one rapid-fire image succeeding the next, spliced between segments of interview with the grandmother. A scene entitled "Nablus during the Curfew" displays a completely empty city, which is followed by more footage of the grandmother pointing to the entrance wound of the bullet that felled her grandson. A little girl veiled in white sings about the son of al-Mu'tasim to scenes of an infant being rocked in a wooden cradle. The grandmother tells us that ever since her grandson was little, "he was always throwing stones at the Jews." She was always reminding him "that his father had a big family and that he should help him, but he always said, 'I want martyrdom, I want martyrdom, I want to be in the life everlasting.'" The father appears at this point and says that he is proud of his son because he possessed a better degree than himself—a reference perhaps to the "degree" of martyrdom, then the video cuts again to a bearded young man appears suddenly onscreen and, speaking presumably of the Israelis, says, "At the beginning, they allowed everybody to work and to tell their opinion and allowed religious freedom, but when the street people began turning to Islam, and people began to understand Islam as a way of life, they began bothering people. They do more than destroy mosques."

The scenes continue, almost without mercy—old men, schoolgirls, arrests, destroyed buildings, injured people, medical logs, Islamist leaders. A man in a white lab coat, presumably a doctor, leads the viewer to a wall covered with photographs of youth who've been injured in clashes and confrontations with soldiers and settlers, or who perhaps were just in the wrong place at the wrong time. "These shabab," he says, gesturing toward the photos, "are around eighteen. This picture of a martyr—he was married, and his wife had twins after he was martyred." He moves on to the next photo. "This youth," he says, "was shot in the head, and this one, the Jews threw a hand grenade at his house, so he lost both his legs." He moves on to the next. "This child," he says, "is thirteen years old; he was admitted to the hospital three months ago. The students had left school. One of them threw stones at the car of a settler. Another settler began shouting and shot this child in the neck from the back. Now he is completely paralyzed. Also, he is living by a respiration machine."

Following this horrifying sequence of the injured and dead, Sheikh Hamid al-Beitawi appears again. This time he speaks as though addressing Israelis directly. "Your criminal bullets," he says, "will only increase our insistence and steadiness. The Muslims say and sing,"

> Kill me, rend me
> drown me in my blood
>
> You will never live in my land
> You will never fly in my sky
>
> Kill me, rend me,
> drown me in my blood
>
> You will never live in my land
> You will never fly in my sky
>
> O swords of Allah, rise up from sleepiness to light
> Teach the usurpers a lesson and send them to their destruction
>
> O swords of Allah, rise up from sleepiness to light
> Teach the usurpers a lesson and send them to their destruction

The song is remarkable, masochistic one minute, the next calling for the divine destruction of the enemy, sheep and wolf virtually in the same breath. It is followed by a former prisoner's description of his interrogation in an Israeli prison:

I entered Corridor Seven after half an hour, and prayed to Allah. Praise the Lord, I called Allah, and then they called me to be interrogated. I said,

O Allah Who changes hearts and sight, let our heart be steadied by our religion. O Allah, I want that you should shut their throats and save me from
their evil. I was reading verses of the Qur'an. I was sure that Allah would be
with me, no matter what the result. Thank Allah, the interrogation of the first
day was for nothing. On the second day, they took me to be interrogated and
put me under the sun for a long time. The interrogation on the second day
was harder—there was a lot of beating.

The prisoner's testimony is followed by interviews with a number of Hamas
leaders, including Sheikh Mahmud az-Zahar. He no longer wears Western attire, as he did when we met with him in his office at the beginning of the
intifada, but rather an Islamic robe. Sitting in front of a depiction of the Dome
of the Rock, he takes note of some of the many "positive effects of the intifada,"
which, he says, include more women wearing Islamic dress and fewer "shameless weddings," by which he means weddings featuring music and dance. The
camera cuts again to Sheikh al-Beitawi, who is delivering a sermon in an unnamed mosque, or perhaps continuing the one shown at the video's beginning,
for the topic, again, is the caliph al-Mu'tasim:

O people and leaders of the Islamic world, did you not hear, did you not read
in history, of one of the Romans who tried to attack the honor of a Muslim
woman, and she shouted for help from Caliph al-Mu'tasim? Our mothers,
wives, and daughters are shouting, O Islam! Palestine is Islamic, and the duty
of all Muslims is to rise up to rescue Palestine. O people and leaders of the
Islamic world who stand looking, the day will come when you will say, 'I wish
I had been killed the day when the white bull was killed.'

The reference is to the well-known fable of the hungry lion and the three
bulls, according to which a hungry lion spies in the distance three bulls—one
black, one red, one white. He welcomes the bulls into his presence, allowing
them to graze before him. Time passes, and becoming hungry, the lion takes
the red bull and the black bull aside and tells them that the white bull, being
white, might attract dangerous predators and that he will have to go. And so
the hungry lion eats the white bull, and the red bull and the black bull do
nothing. Time passes, and the lion's hunger once again grows too strong to
ignore. This time, he takes the black bull aside, and informs him that the red
bull, being red, might attract dangerous predators. Thus it is that the red bull is
eaten as well, and the black bull does nothing. A few days later, the lion is
hungry again. As his teeth sink into the black bull's neck, the black bull cries
out, "Truly, I was eaten the day the white bull was eaten."
    The fable, a warning against Arab complacency and plea for action, is fol-
lowed by a song that promises the return of Khaibar, often used in intifada
media as a call for slaughter:

Khaibar, Khaibar, O Jews, the Army of Muhammad will return
Khaibar, Khaibar, O Jews, the Army of Muhammad will return

By the intifada, by the intifada
By the intifada, by the intifada

The intifada will continue until the land returns free
The intifada will continue until the land returns free

Intifada, intifada
Intifada, intifada

O son of high-minded Jerusalem, its flame is Islamic
O son of high-minded Jerusalem, its flame is Islamic
O son of high-minded Jerusalem, its flame is Islamic
O son of high-minded Jerusalem, its flame is Islamic
O son of high-minded Jerusalem, its flame is Islamic

Set it on fire with the light of the Qur'an and march forward in all countries
Set it on fire with the light of the Qur'an and march forward in all countries

By the intifada

In light of the initial spectacle of the dogs, it might seem that what is being represented in the rest of the video is not only violation and vengeance but also the wrenching of speech from speechlessness, the deliverance of men from "pure instinct"—the gift of religion—but the rhetoric and reality are so blood-soaked that the process seems aborted or incomplete. Perhaps, the mad dogs represent not instinct but rather "infidel wolves," meant to remind the viewer of the dangers of defilement. Or perhaps, unbeknownst to them, they serve as the "natural" analogues of a language and reality so violent that they bite their own tails as they go round and round in infinite repetition. For sure, by the end of the first part of *The Promise*, one hardly knows what to make of the disconcerting mixture of pity and rage, victimage and triumphalism. One sits there, speechless and resourceless, before this extended discourse of the weak and the wounded.

33. A Notice of the End of the World

Here's a notice of the End of the World that one of us snapped in the main hall of a Hamas-controlled mosque in Gaza City, while the other sat in the car, the faces of a dozen curious people pressed against the glass.

Entitled "The Marj az-Zahur Exile: Between the Mercilessness of Winter and the Terrorism of Occupation," the document is addressed to "the masses of our people in the land of al-Isra' and al-Mi'raj," and to "those arrayed for war on the soil of the beloved homeland" (al-Isra', "the Night Journey," and al-Mi'raj, "the Ascension," referring to the midnight sojourn of Muhammad from Mecca to Jerusalem, and thence to heaven), and was probably faxed from one of the fabled tents of the Hamas deportees in southern Lebanon. It catalogues the conditions faced by "the deported brothers," reiterates the movement's opposition to the peace process, "the suspect deals of the Americans and the Zionists," and predicts that the fate of Israel will be "at the hands of the men of truth and the detachments of the Qur'an, and the raisers of the banner of Islam." "The Noble Qur'an informs us of the good news," the writers assert, alluding to a section of the Qur'an in which it is written that "the Israelites" will be permitted by God to spread corruption (*fasad*) in the land twice and will then be attacked and defeated by an adversary sent by God.

It is the term *fasad* that alerts us to the fact that we are here in the realm of Last Things. Fasad is a key eschatological concept of the Islamists, as is its cognate *ifsad*, "the spreading of corruption"—or, according to some, "one who spreads corruption." It is a characteristic attributed both to the Dajjal, the king of the unbelievers, and to the Jews, as in the Hamas leaflet "Who will control your purchase, O my country?" where we read, "The Israelis! . . . Who are they? *The Israelis are a motley blend of peoples . . . united by Western maltreatment by virtue of their Jewishness! They are one of the errors of the West and one of its sins . . . who spread corruption throughout the land."

The theme of the Jews as corrupted corrupters appeared early on in the intifada, and can be found in Hamas' covenant, where it is written, "And there is absolutely no war that has occurred here or there but their fingers have been in it. 'As often as they light a fire for war, Allah extinguishes it. Their effort is for corruption in the land, and Allah does not love corrupters'"—a quotation from Qur'an 5:64 ("The Table"). Indeed, according to the authors of the covenant, the Jews have been behind every war and almost every revolution (excluding their own)—"the French Revolution and the Communist Revolution and much of that which we have heard and are hearing about revolutions here and there," for the goal of the Jews is "to destroy societies and further the devices of Zionism." This goal is achieved through "destructive spying organizations" like "the Masons and the Rotary Clubs and the Lions and the B'nai B'rith and others." In addition, the League of Nations, the United Nations, and the Security Council are all, according to the covenant, creations inspired by the Jews so that they can control the world.

Jewish fasad is also a major theme in the eschatological writings of Sheikh Bassam Jarrar, one of the Hamas deportees. In his audiotaped *tafsir*, or exegesis, of surat al-Isra' (alternately known as "surat Bani Isra'il"), he attempts to explicate what he calls a hitherto now "unknown prophecy," which he explains elsewhere "was previously a prophecy in the Torah"—a book that, although corrupted, nevertheless, "stands in need of interpretation or symbolic analysis even on the numerical level." The Qur'anic verse to which he refers is brief, reading, "We decreed, O Bani Isra'il, that you spread fasad in the land twice." Jarrar's exegesis is long, and begins with the elaboration, "[Allah] said that the Bani Isra'il would enter Palestine and would erect in it a state, and then would bring forth great corruption, then Allah would bring forth a nation and would eliminate this state, and the Jews would be dispersed; then a second and last state would be erected and would vanish forever and would never be resurrected after that vanishing." In his 1990 book *The Wonders of 19: Between the Inattentiveness of the Muslims and the Errors of the Falsifiers*, he actually goes so far as to proffer a date on which Palestinians can expect the state of Israel finally to be done away with—2022.

Jarrar is not the only Islamist leader who believes that surat al-Isra' holds the secret to the destruction of the Jewish state. Among others, Sheikh As'ad at-Tamimi, author of *The Disappearance of the State of Israel Is a Qur'anic Inevitability*, presents the same sura as evidence that the Israeli state is doomed. "And you are living today a promise of Allah," he writes, "promised by the tongue of His Prophet and by the verses of al-Isra', which bring you news of it, and by the verses of 'The Table,' which I elucidate in my book on how the state of the Jews will disappear."

In intifada media, we find the notion of fasad tied not only to ideas about the disappearance of Israel, but also used in a more general way to indicate an upside-down era, the time of the so-called lesser signs of the End of the World. The "days of fasad" (*yom fasidi*) were commonly said to be characterized by skyscrapers, sexual promiscuity, usury, and the disobedience of children—and these signs, many warned, should be taken as calls to repent before it was too late, for the end would come about so suddenly that it would be like "a man being shot or a bottle exploding in one's hands," as Sheikh Akrima Sabri described it to us when we met with him in 1994, the year in which he was appointed Supreme Mufti of Jerusalem by Yasir Arafat. In this capacity, he quickly became famous for his fiery sermons in which he spoke of Jews as "the sons of monkeys and pigs," called Britain and France "infidel nations," and asserted that Allah Himself would "paint the White House black."

Numerous religious leaders, including Sabri, made an explicit homology during the intifada between the rules of *tauba*, or repentance, for Palestinian collaborators and the rules of repentance that would obtain during the Last Days. Just as each human being must return to God of his own free will before the time of the Greater Signs of the coming end, so must the Palestinian collaborator return of his own free will to the national fold before he is found out and hunted down. In the following excerpt, Sheikh at-Tamimi issues a call for the repentance of such collaborators, connecting them with the eschatological Gharqad Tree, and then goes on to draw a parallel between America and "the

people of 'Ad," a people mentioned in the Qur'an destroyed for their over-
weening pride and disobedience to God, whose punishment, like that of the
collaborator, was not limited to this world but extended infinitely into the next:

> And the Gharqad is two Gharqads: It is a tree planted in Palestine as well
> as those who act as proxies of the Jews at summit conferences and their inter-
> nal helpers and spies and collaborators and those who protect Jews and work
> with Jews, and [sell] their land and their honor and spy on the umma. I call on
> them to repent and to return to reason and good sense, for the gate of repen-
> tance is open to those who wish to repent. If not, [their fate will be] shame in
> this life and the torment of Allah in the Hereafter.
>
> When the Muslims faced their greatest calamity and the Messenger stood
> on the day [of the Battle] of the Trench in the raid of the confederates, he
> brought good news to his umma of the victory that would follow their siege,
> and brought good news to his umma of the opening of Persia and Rome and
> Yemen. And after that, he brought them good news of the opening of
> Constantinople and other places. And all of that which he promised came to
> pass, and we have been promised the disappearance of the state of Israel . . . .
> Listen to the word of Allah threatening America as he threatened the people
> of 'Ad,
>
> And as for 'Ad, they were big with pride in the land, without right, and
> said, "Who is stronger than us in might?" Did they not see that Allah who
> created them was stronger than they in might? But they refused to believe
> our signs. And we sent upon them a screaming wind in ill-omened days that
> we might make them taste the torment of disgrace in the life of this world;
> but the torment of the Hereafter is more disgraceful, and they shall not be
> helped. (Qur'an 41:15, "Ha Mim")

At first glance, the ideas of clerics like Jarrar, Sabri, and at-Tamimi might
seem dense and esoteric, but by the end of the first intifada, they had gained
enormous popularity. The title of at-Tamimi's book—*The Disappearance of the
State of Israel Is a Qur'anic Inevitability*—became a major slogan and was spray-
painted on walls throughout the West Bank and Gaza. Cooks in Jericho, taxi
drivers in Rafah, and video salesmen in Ramallah could all tell you something
about the end-time ideas of Jarrar. Indeed, great interest was shown in all things
apocalyptic, which served to endow the figures and events of the uprising with
teleological purpose and sacred import. At the same time, however, the turn
toward the End, we could say, showed the intifada under severe threat, its truth
revealed only in ecstatic obliteration—precisely the logic of the suicide bomber
who would save his world by blowing it up.

PART THREE

■

A Death on the Path of God

34. The Green Line

In 1993, we moved from Jerusalem to Cambridge, Massachusetts. We may have left Israel and the occupied territories, but in no way had we left the conflict behind. The august halls of Harvard's Center for Middle Eastern Studies were as politicized as the stony streets of Jerusalem and the sandy alleys of Deir al-Balah, even if the rhetoric was more refined.

And, of course, there was still the archive, that vast compendium of suffering and misery, which we had dutifully schlepped from Jerusalem and which now took up most of our guest room. The large canvases created a violent dreamscape above the bed, exploded buses oozing blood and body parts, while beneath peeked cardboard boxes crammed with martyr cards and photographs of gaping wounds. If they had seemed odd in Jerusalem, they were downright sinister in Boston. It was as though a demented decorator had raided the set of a horror movie and the files of the city morgue, and then set about rendering the space in modern abattoir.

Stark as the materials were, we had long since become inured to their horror. It was only when we looked at them through others' eyes that we were able to see them differently. On a visit to the Harvard Divinity School, we had occasion to pull out one of our portfolios to share with the acting dean of one of the school's centers. We were, if we remember correctly, inquiring about possible research positions.

The Divinity School is a bucolic place. The brochure for the center described the gentle life enjoyed there—"many students play musical instruments;

it is not uncommon for us to have musical evenings together in the foyer." After a few moments of browsing through our portfolio, the dean came across the photograph of an exhumed corpse, outlined in fluorescent orange—blackish-green skin, mouth twisted in a rotting smile. Behind the bloated body crouched two guys holding a banner extolling one of the Palestinian factions.

Who was he? It was hard to tell. His could have been the tortured body of a collaborator exhibited as a trophy. On the other hand, he could have been a companion of the two youths behind him who had been killed by the IDF and was now on display as an uncorrupted martyr. In any event, the picture was a triumphant image that had once graced the wall of a West Bank mosque. And to our jaded eyes, it was an interesting document.

"It's interesting," we explained to the dean with some excitement; "the body has been converted into a banner or talisman—a corpse turned into both sign and symbol." It was not interesting, however, to the eyes of the acting dean. "Are these your pictures?" he asked, aghast. It was not until we looked into his eyes and read the horror there that we fully understood the question. The man believed we had taken the picture. Perhaps, we had even been participants in this ghastly ritual, whatever it was. What kind of monsters were we? Needless to say, the acting dean did not offer us positions at the Harvard Divinity School.

We removed the photo from the portfolio—what had we been thinking?—but the growing realization that we'd become crypt-keepers did not stop us from our task. When we returned to Gaza, we got in touch with Ra'id, a guy we'd started working with several years before after a few too many stones had missed our heads by too few inches. Ra'id was interested in getting into the powdered milk business, but, in the meantime, made money, a fair amount of it actually, by taking people around the Strip in his car, a beat-up red Mazda that for some time had been on its last leg. The car, despite its derelict condition, was one of the major reasons that journalists and others resorted to Ra'id's services—you'd have to be a little crazy to drive your own car into the Strip. If you took a rental car into Gaza and something happened to it, that was your problem; the insurance companies wouldn't give you a dime toward the damages.

Ra'id said he had some materials for us, so we took a taxi down from Jerusalem to the Erez checkpoint and traipsed across the Green Line to our usual meeting place behind a gas station. A stray dog the color of sand had found safety there in the no-man's land, and she trotted back and forth across the dunes with seeming purpose, her swollen teats sweeping the ground. Further on, we could see Ra'id circling the Mazda, now and then planting a nice little kick in its wheels.

35. The Fixer

Ra'id was well over six feet tall and razor thin. He had wavy black hair and an angular, almost hatchetlike face. The intense, almost manic concentration that was his usual mode could at the right moment give way to a nervous melancholy. Like his idol Said Qutb, Ra'id had lived for a time in America and spoke glowingly of his years there—particularly his time in California. After a couple of years, he had come back home for a family crisis and found that he was unable to renew his visa.

Driving the Mazda down the mean streets of Gaza, he would wax nostalgic about his glory days of freedom, which found symbolic expression in the blue expanse of Highway 101, the mythic highway hugging the western coast of the United States. "How about that Highway 101!" he would exclaim out of the blue, slapping our knees in exaltation, as we chugged down the road bordering the Gaza coast punctuated by red peppers growing like so many exclamation points, the clutch of the Mazda growling in protest.

Some memories were darker. He had at times felt put upon in America due to his Islamist orientation. At times, he had even lied about his true feelings in order to fit in. His manager at Dunkin' Donuts had once asked him about Iran in a challenging tone, as if to say, "Are you with us or against us?" "Hey man," Ra'id had replied, "I had to leave myself in order to be free." The memory of that encounter still rankled. Even back then, Ra'id had been committed to the Islamist enterprise and at one time had shepherded 'Abdullah 'Azzam on his fund-raising swings through Muslim communities in the mid-West.

Trapped now like an angry fly in a bottle, he careened through the Strip, not halfheartedly trying to run over the gaggles of children who followed foreigners wherever they went, screaming and shouting and jumping on their cars, some making obscene throat-slitting gestures through the windows with their little fingers. Passing one of the joint Israel-Palestinian patrols then still operational in the Strip, he became furious. "Look at those motherfucking queers!" he screamed, referring to the Israelis. "I'd like to put my foot up their motherfucking ass!" GRR CHUCK CHUCK went the car, dispelling with each sick grunt any fantasy we might have had of using it as a possible getaway car.

Ra'id had arranged a meeting for us with a sheikh affiliated with Hamas who taught at the Islamic University, but now it seemed that the sheikh was not home. Ra'id was furious and insulted. "Bastard sonofabitch," he said, continuing a manner of speaking he considered appropriate for Americans; "it's not proper for a Muslim to act that way. He has responsibilities." Ra'id then felt that he had to find something worthwhile for us to do. There had been a battle in Rafah, he said, between "the motherfucking PA" and Hamas. He wanted to take us there. "Those goddamn motherfuckers are worse than the motherfucking Jews!" he exclaimed, as we roared past a row of beautiful old eucalyptus trees, RRRRR GRR CHUCK CHUCK.

Ra'id was not always so half mad. Sometimes, he'd suddenly become quietly pious and excuse himself to pray. Or he'd confide in us a secret, forbidden thought. He'd been thinking of buying a boat, he once told us. It cost eight thousand dollars, and when his newborn daughter was a little older, he was going to take her out on it and let her swim to her heart's content—in a bikini, no less! He didn't care what anyone said. The more you heard him talk about it, the clearer it became that the boat was Ra'id's fantasy island, his own little USA, floating in the Gazan sea.

"There's where Yusuf lives," we said, as we passed near his house. We had once brought Ra'id and Yusuf together in typically disastrous fashion. The two had distrusted each other from the start. With his obvious Hamas markers, Ra'id was looked upon askance by Yusuf and his nationalist-oriented friends and family. Ra'id, in turn, disdained the obvious impiety of Yusuf and his crowd. We had once tried a not dissimilar introduction between 'Ali and our friend Muhammad from the Arab village of Umm al-Fahm in Israel. The two had sat glumly on the couch, staring at the floor, resisting all our attempts to jumpstart a conversation.

We soon arrived in Rafah, one of the largest and most desperate parts of the Strip. The city is a sort of poster locale for all that is most hopeless about the plight of the refugees of 1948. One hundred fifty thousand people, descendants of families who fled their homes in what is now coastal Israel, live in politically mandated stasis in thousands of cinderblock shanties. We drove around until we came to an open area. The battle had occurred here at this spot, Ra'id said. There was little now to see—tire tracks on the muddy ground, pockmarks in the wall that Ra'id said were bullet holes, not much else. He thought we were disappointed, which, in turn, disappointed him.

Mobs of bored, hyper-excited children chased after Ra'id's car. "Little shitheads," he shrieked, slamming on the brakes so that some of the children collided with the back of the car. "Let's grab some and throw them in my trunk, then we can take them somewhere and beat the crap out of them!"

Luckily, we did not put Ra'id's plan into action. Instead, we roared back onto the highway toward Gaza City. Ra'id had an inspiration. He wanted to try to find a Palestinian miracle worker who, he said, could dispel evil jinn. The man was famous, he said, and had been featured in many newspapers. Arriving at the doctor's office, we found that he was indeed famous. He had clippings tacked all over his front door, many of them from Israeli newspapers, with his name highlighted in fluorescent yellow for those who might be unfamiliar with Hebrew.

As dusk fell, we headed back to Jerusalem with the twenty or thirty rolls of film we'd shot during the course of the day, headaches from the hot sugar overdose—constant swigs of blood-temperature Kinley orange soda and coffee masbuta ("just right")—and the several dozen posters and videotapes we'd just acquired, hoping we wouldn't be stopped at the border.

Last time we'd been down, we'd been with Yusuf and had run into an impromptu roadblock manned by a PA policeman who had ordered the driver to get out of his taxi and open the trunk almost as if he'd known about the Hamas propaganda in our possession. The PA had just taken control of the

Strip from the IDF, and Hamas tapes were considered suspect, if not contraband. As we exited the taxi to talk with the official, newly transplanted from Tunisia or Iraq or Yemen, Yusuf smiled anxiously from the backseat—no one yet knew what these guys were about.

The policeman asked us to open our "luggage"—giant black garbage bags of dirty laundry into which we'd thrown a bunch of Hamas videos and long rolls of posters so tightly wound and bandaged with duct tape that the policeman quickly tired of trying to pry them open and told us to open them instead. We tugged and pulled at the tubes with grunts and sighs of exasperation for some time until, finally, the man grew tired of it all and waved us through the checkpoint with a disgusted "Go!" The three of us sat in the back seat, grinning madly with relief, as the taxi driver sped down the highway like a bat out of hell, dodging carts and donkeys, women balancing massive bags of UN flour on their heads, and men laden with straw and pink plastic jugs, while a documentary about the Challenger shuttle disaster blared from the radio. "Is it true?" Yusuf asked, referring to the shuttle. "Of course," we replied, perhaps for a moment doubting it ourselves among the palms of Gaza.

This time around, Ra'id had started driving us to Erez when a report came over the radio that the border had been unexpectedly closed due to a visit by a U.S. dignitary. Ra'id pulled to the side of the road and flagged down a taxi for us. We waved goodbye, and, once again, set out for the border, the taxi driver proceeding with some trepidation, as though he did not know what lay ahead. Suddenly, he pulled to the side of the road. This was as far as he could take us, he was sorry to say. We would have to find some other way of getting to the border.

We gathered our belongings from the back seat and trunk, hurriedly stringing cameras around our necks and stuffing videos under our clothes. The posters we would have to carry—they were simply too big to hide or camouflage. It was swiftly getting dark, and hundreds of Palestinian workers were trudging homeward through air thick with yellow dust and premonition. We set out for the border, walking in the opposite direction from the workers. Every twenty yards or so, a PA soldier would stop us, request to see our identification, and execute a brief interrogation. No one seemed to find it exceedingly odd that we were bulging in unexpected places and carrying rolls almost as long as ourselves.

36. Ghosts with Guns

First, there had been the endless cups of Coke, then the meal of *maqluba*, or "upside down"—a heavy dish of rice, chicken, and cauliflower—and then had come the endless cups of tea along with the smoke from too many cigarettes with nowhere to go but through the room's lone window. By the end, we couldn't have moved if we had to. 'Ali popped one of the Hamas tapes we'd just picked up in Gaza into the VCR. Written on the jacket of the tape in red ink was the title *The Giants of al-Qassam*—*imlaq*, the Arabic term for "giant," evoking an atavistic, demigodlike image. The machine whizzed and whirred, the Egyptian belly dancers disappeared in a final flash of sea-blue sequins, and the face of a suicide bomber flickered across the screen.

The picture was grainy, of exceptionally bad quality even by Gazan standards, the tape probably having been recorded over dozens of times. The boy who immediately appeared in front of us looked like a ghost with a gun. In fact, he was already dead, parts of the recording having been made but a few hours before his death.

We've called him a boy, but he must be somewhere in his early twenties. There's something of the *puer aeternus* about him. For sure, he doesn't seem to belong among the thug types that dominate early Hamas videos—the stocky, testosterone-shot he-men striking ludicrous poses with their legs planted far apart, pelvises jutted forward, guns pointing heavenward—but rather to a type with which we would soon become familiar—the "sensitive terrorist," let's call him. He doesn't look as though he could cut somebody's head off with a knife. He has curly brown hair and brown eyes, jerks his eyebrows up and down like Groucho Marx when he talks—resembles Woody Allen, if Woody Allen could look so happy.

He says he wants nothing less than Paradise, and intends to take as many Israelis with him as possible. He's happy, too happy, slightly embarrassed by his happiness, as he and the other guys in his group—"Force Three," as they call themselves—prepare for their final act, a "martyrdom operation" against an Israeli bus capable of "carrying nearly eighty-five Israeli citizens." This operation, we are told, will be carried out "for the sake of raising the banner of 'There is no god but Allah, and Muhammad is the Messenger of Allah'" and as a "message to the members of the Palestinian delegation who are negotiating empty-handed." If Israel refuses to meet their demands and release Sheikh Yasin and a few other unnamed prisoners, the mission, they say, will come to an end with Force Three in Paradise and the people they blow up in Hell.

Watching this kind of stuff should feel more creepy than it does, but during the course of several years, we've become accustomed to a lot of things we'd earlier have found macabre.

These guys knew they're going to die. Life in the meantime has become unbearable. They just want to get it over with. At the same time, we get the feeling that life has never seemed better to them—so intense, so exuberant, so full of meaning. Perhaps that's why they keep on smiling—they just can't believe they're about to become Martyrs, about to take their place in the roster of great men. Who would ever have believed it? they must be thinking. Won't the people they grew up with be just a little jealous?—they shouldn't have underestimated me!—and won't their mothers be surprised, so proud and so broken. They've never gotten so much attention in their lives.

It's not like they've put themselves forward, they want you to know—rather, the movement, the "Call," has chosen them. Indeed, as the group's trainer, Muhammad 'Aziz Rushdi, tells us later in the video, Allah Himself has chosen them for their fate, just as He chooses all "the shabab of the military apparatus":

> And I say to the shabab of the military apparatus that Allah, Mighty and Majestic, has chosen you, so be among those held in good opinion by the one who chose you, and act for the sake of the pleasure of Allah, Mighty and Majestic, and don't be contentious, and multiply your good deeds and worship and rely on Allah, Mighty and Majestic, and do not rely on your own strength.

At the same time that Rushdi presents the Giants as chosen, he takes great pains to emphasize that "military action is only one part of the Islamic Resistance Movement," "one action among many actions." It's not meant for everyone. In fact, he points out, if everyone participated in these actions, there would be only "mujahid shabab and military shabab."

Listening to Rushdi speak, one would be excused for thinking that people were lining up for the opportunity to blow themselves up. And, according to Hamas, they were. The organization would later say it had to turn people away—guys were knocking their doors down, guys who, all the experts and psychoanalysts assured us, were completely normal young men—nothing pathological about them. In fact, as the years went by, Hamas grew fond of saying that it would take only "normal" people—you couldn't be depressed or suicidal or crazy, or they wouldn't have anything to do with you. Your motives had to be pure, your soul unblemished, your eyes fixed on Heaven.

37. The Last Words of Mahir ("Hamza") Abu-Surur

The first of the three Giants to offer up his last will and testament is Mahir Abu-Surur—a guy with many names. Sometimes, he's called "Mahir"; sometimes "Hamza," his nickname; sometimes "Abu-ash-Shahid," or "Father of the Martyr." This last one he has chosen for himself, and it is his favorite. Watching him, you think to yourself, Here's a guy who thinks of his death as something like a trophy, a guy who thinks he's acquiring a head start on Heaven by jumping the gun on the End of the World.

In fact, he begins his last testament by directly connecting the two events. "It is the day of encounter," he says—an allusion to his coming appointment in Paradise and a not uncommon reference to the Last Day. "It is tomorrow," he continues, gazing at the eye of the camera, his eyebrows jerking wildly up and down. "Thursday, insha'Allah, is the day of leaving . . . leaving this world."

Leaving this world had long been Abu-Surur's goal. Indeed, people said that Abu-Surur constantly tortured his mother by telling her that he didn't like the *dunya* (Arabic for "this world," a word often contrasted with *al-akhira*, the world to come) and couldn't wait for the Last Days—a sentiment echoed next on the video when he quotes surat al-Isra' 17:51—"Say, it may be that it will be soon," a verse often interpreted as a refutation against those skeptical of the possibility of resurrection:

> It is the day of meeting the Lord of the Worlds and approaching and bearing witness to the Messenger, May the prayers of Allah be upon Him and upon the Companions, all of them, and upon the martyrs and all the saints and all the mujahidun of Palestine and every part of the world . . . and upon the mujahidun of 'Izz ad-Din al-Qassam, in particular.
>
> To all of these, we will, insha'Allah, present our spirits and make our blood cheap for the sake of Allah and out of love for this homeland and for the sake of the freedom and honor of this people in order that Palestine remain Islamic, and Hamas remain a torch lighting the road of all the perplexed and all the tormented and the oppressed, and Palestine be liberated.
>
> "And they ask you when. Say, it may be that it will be soon." Tomorrow, insha'Allah, will be the day when the storm rages against the occupying usurper, the day on which we will raise the value of all life . . . [trails off]

Abu-Surur isn't being strange here. Lots of people felt obliged to talk about the Last Days during the intifada. Some, like Abu-Surur, explicitly connected their own deaths with end-time events.

He soon turns his attention to the operation itself, and as he and Muhammad Rushdi rally back and forth, one begins to sense a certain one-upmanship at work. At times, Rushdi seems ill-prepared and unrehearsed; in contrast, Abu-Surur comes across as having thought about what he would say for a long time:

ABU-SURUR: We expect that our blood will flow cheaply in the service of our homeland, with the help of Allah the one and only, insha'Allah. We rely on Allah, Lord of the Worlds, and not on the weapons we are carrying. The weapon is a tool, and the objective is, insha'Allah, what it is aimed at.

RUSHDI: For the Islamic Movement and . . . for the Battalions . . . did they provide such resources, insha'Allah?

ABU-SURUR: We thank Allah that they have provided us with considerable resources, but, as I said, we depend on Allah, Lord of the Worlds—"And you smote not when you smote, but Allah smote" [Qur'an 8:17, "The Spoils"]. "All power belongs to Allah" [Qur'an 2:125, "The Cow"]. We are all setting out, insha'Allah, on our operation, and what will be, insha'Allah, is a gift from Allah, be it martyrdom or . . .

RUSHDI: Insha'Allah, Lord of the Worlds. The greatest expectation is that they be martyred?

ABU-SURUR: Of course, the greatest expectation is martyrdom, and this is what we have been aiming for since we were knee high to a grasshopper [lit., "since our fingernails were soft"].

RUSHDI: Knee high to a grasshopper, insha'Allah. And we'll give the enemy a taste of agony, won't we?

ABU-SURUR: Insha'Allah.

RUSHDI: A word to the Cubs of Hamas [the Hamas-affiliated boys' group] and the shabab of the Battalions in the prisons . . .

ABU-SURUR: I charge them, insha'Allah, before they pick up a rifle, to carry 'aqida in their hearts, as well as faith, for if they carry 'aqida and Islam in their hearts, they will be able to carry the rifle. Islam and faith without 'aqida and without action doesn't exist.

Our slogan will always, insha'Allah, be—'aqida next to the rifle and the rifle next to 'aqida. This is our slogan, insha'Allah. And to all of those who also choose honorable martyrdom with their heads held high . . .

RUSHDI: For all must die.

ABU-SURUR: Yes, all . . .

Abu-Surur here elaborates the concept of 'aqida, a term derived from a verb meaning "to tie or knot," and defined as "faith, doctrine, practice" or "creed, dogma, conviction, or ideology." The term appears throughout Islamist discourse, as in the graffito, "I will continue to cling to the rope of my 'aqida and die in order that my religion live." Abu-Surur tells the viewer that what is needed is both 'aqida and the rifle, faith and armed action. Not that the two are equal. They aren't. 'Aqida must precede the rifle, he says, not the other way around.

Strangely, it is only at the end of the interview that Rushdi asks Abu-Surur his name. For a moment, Abu-Surur, the guy of many names, the guy never short of words, is speechless.

"My name," he says, and pauses. "Your brother in Allah, Hamza Abu-Surur." And then, before giving his nom de guerre, he laughs. Why does he laugh? Is it because all of this information is well known, or because he no longer effectively exists and finds it strange to have a name at all?

38. The Smile of the Martyr

We have said that Abu-Surur smiles almost nonstop. It's a strange smile—a proud, ain't-I-lucky kind of smile. Why is he so happy? Why, he is on his way to meet the Prophet, by Allah, let it be soon! He and the others plan on getting to Heaven by boarding an Israeli bus, and then blowing themselves up, along with everybody around them. What's not to smile about?

If the script Abu-Surur puts forth on videotape is well known, completely expected, and appropriate—it's a martyr's script recited by a martyr-to-be—his smile, on the other hand, seems slightly out of place. It's a bit too self-satisfied, verges on a smirk, and can be found in no other of the martyr videos produced by Hamas that we've seen. One has only to watch Abu-Surur for a moment to see the way in which he fondles his words, caresses them in his mouth before releasing them, to note a hedonic relation to language and death—language in the face of death. One gets the impression that words never felt so wondrous to him as now, so full of consequence and meaning, so self-fulfilling, so pleasurable, so lush and exciting. When he speaks, it's as though he's eating something delicious. Now that he's treating himself as if he were already dead, he feels more real than ever.

He epitomizes "the happy death" touted in countless slogans of the intifada, as in the Hamas messages, "I will die smiling in order that my religion live," "Death has become sweet, become sweet/ Revolution against the strangers," and "O Muslim, say 'Allahu akbar!' with joy, and let's march forward, carrying our coffins." The idea was popular among nationalists as well, as can be seen in slogans like "How sweet is death for the sake of the homeland," "Mother, I am happy, happy to die for freedom," and "What is more beautiful than to die alone in order that a million might live?"

The idea that you had to prepare for self-sacrifice, rehearse your death lovingly as many times as possible—indeed, think of it in terms of happiness—was commonplace during the uprising. Media often seemed to serve precisely this function, vivifying death with the notion of happiness. The "natural" or "accidental" death was something ignoble to be avoided at all cost—an idea aptly expressed in the PFLP imperative, "Beware of natural death. Don't die except in a shower of bullets."

You could turn nowhere during the intifada without encountering a call to death. The land called—"Palestine is a green tree whose thirst can only be quenched with the blood of the martyrs," and "When the land calls us, we sacrifice ourselves proudly." Cities called—Jerusalem . . . Haifa . . . Jaffa . . . Mecca. Stones called—"From Jerusalem the stone cries, No to the conference! No to the conference!" Blood called—"The blood of the martyrs is calling us." Truth called—"The call of truth summoned its sons . . . so respond to the voice of the summons. Purify your land, purify it . . . dye its sand with blood." Religion called—"Islam called, the Qur'an called: Who will answer the call?" Paradise was said to hunger for more inhabitants—"Paradise wants men!" Death itself was capable of issuing its own invitations—"Till death, our hearts are with [Palestine] . . . Because of it, death has become a sport for us. And if death calls us to protect it . . . we will run to meet death." Abu-Surur and company grew up with such notions. Anyone who wanted to be a hero spoke in these terms.

At the same time that Abu-Surur's smile epitomizes the happy-death formula, it also seems to undermine the unspoken rule that one is to speak the formula but not exhibit it. What we mean is that Hamza Abu-Surur seems to be enjoying himself too much; his smile is extravagant, suggests a secret that flies in the face of the anti-secret of the intifada—the anti-secret of every revolution as a mass movement. It verges on laughter, a derisory force.

Abu-Surur probably doesn't mean to smile in the way he does, doesn't mean to smirk. The idea might even mortify him. Nevertheless, in the gap between what he says he's about and what his smile says he's about, we glimpse something subversive. The smile constantly breaks through his speech, and we don't know its meaning.

If we look again at his opening speech, for instance, we seem to have the perfect martyrological formula as sanctioned by Hamas. The speech is filled with extravagant invocations and greetings to the dead and the expressed hope of joining them in Paradise. There is a statement of purpose; the requisite eschatological motifs; the ritual lexicon of "homeland," "freedom," "honor," "Palestine," "Islamic," and "liberation"; the sacrificial imperative encapsulated in the proxy phrase "for the sake of"; the Qur'anic imprimatur; the frequent repetition of the formula *insha'Allah*. Abu-Surur's smile, on the other hand, introduces a different element into the picture, throwing into question precisely what these rituals can be said to arrest—individual quirkiness, solecism, the risks involved in making a "giant" of a mere human.

Hamza Abu-Surur smiled all the time, everyone said, even when he was sad—a habit, or quirk, that to some suggested a secret. "He had something in his heart that he wouldn't tell anyone," his brother told us when we met with him in 1996. Abu-Surur himself suggests such a masking in "Dreams," a poem he wrote when he was around thirteen years old—"I see the smile on my lips/ With sadness wreathed/ I see it as a counterfeit 'Ahhh' . . ./ forlorn, designating meaning." He seems much like the girl in another of his poems, "My Sad Beloved," the dyadic structure and content of which seem to mirror his own search for a remedy against a type of sadness that much to his relief, one imagines, turns out not to be a constitutional defect but rather the direct result of the occupation:

> O beautiful flower,
> I saw you—sad
> A strange look
> A wounded heart
> With an innocent smile
> and imprisoned laugh
> In her eyes I beheld
> a buried tear
> In her palms I felt
> the innocence of childhood
> I pondered her
> I loved her
> and she became my lover, my beautiful flower
> I came close to clasp her in my arms
> to feel the tender warmth in her chest
> to sip the scent of her cheek
> and so reduce the burden of her sadness
> and suddenly
> I recognized the secret of her sadness

It is the barbed wire
surrounding the tower of my beloved
tightening the siege
Yet she remained
like a steadfast rock
Her eyes almost began to tear
but the Son of Dahaisha screamed
The Son of the Strip rose up
Don't let your tears fall!
You will never be left under siege
You will never be left thirsty
That's not our way, not in our blood
That is not our blood
Our hearts shall be your bridge
and we will rip down the barbed wire
We will rip down the barbed wire
The End

At the poem's close, Abu-Surur has signed his name in such a rococo manner that it resembles a *tughra*, or royal seal.

39. A Still Blue River

A still blue river winds its way through the American West. A boy stands before the scene for his portrait. He must have chosen the backdrop from many selections typically available in a Palestinian studio—Arabian palms, bright blowups of daisies and poppies, Swiss Alps, ice cream dreams in the desert. He is dressed in blue jeans, very blue, and a white tie. A keffiyah is draped around his neck. He wears a rust-colored sports jacket made of crushed velour, or perhaps suede—very seventies. The jacket is way too big for him. It makes his shoulders preternaturally long and angular; the sleeves almost obscure his hands. He sports a black pork-pie hat that covers his dark, curly hair. He tips it for the eye of the camera without the slightest hint of irony or humor. He's deadly serious.

We have seven such photographs, seven hints of the "before" of Abu-Surur. In one, he tweaks the branch of a palm; in another, he stands in front of an unfinished fountain, staring upward, showing only his profile. Yet another features a white room, bare but for some books, a flying eagle transfixed to the wall, and a poster of a brown-haired girl resting her face in chubby little girl hands, gazing upward. Two yellow daisies dangle above her head, incongruously. And there is Abu-Surur standing to the right of the cherub. He is dressed in black pants and a black shirt with bold white ornamental patches on the shoulders and chest. He leans against a table, avoiding the eye of the camera; there is a faraway look in his eyes—sad, melodramatic, self-conscious, wistful.

In another photo, he poses in front of the family home in 'Aida refugee camp, just behind Rachel's Tomb on the road to Bethlehem. You can see just a hint of the rutted dirt track that runs between the walls of the cinderblock houses that converge, narrower and narrower, until, right at the Abu-Surur house, it becomes too tight for a car to pass through. In the photo, Abu-Surur is standing with one hand on the front gate, the other on his hip. He has on sunglasses and looks off into the distance with a feigned nonchalance, like he belonged elsewhere, was imagining himself elsewhere.

Looking at the photo, you remember your visits to that house—the elaborate gate covered in grapevines, the long flight of stairs up to the front door, the painted wrought iron, bare dirt courtyard, sickly fruit trees, rose-patterned demitasse cups, gold couches, the mother's feeble memories of her son when he was a child—"I don't remember much. He played in the mud. He was calm."

The aunt had more distinct memories. Hamza, she said, would be sent to the store for something, and would return with nothing, having filled his belly with candy. He substituted *t*'s for *k*'s, saying *tursi* instead of *kursi* and *aish bidit* instead of *aish bidik*. He liked to tell jokes, his brother said, but they did not always get the desired response. "We're not laughing with you," people would say to him; "we're laughing at you," and then they'd laugh some more.

Here are two shots taken clearly after Hamza had become a member of the *mutaradun*, the "hunted." He wears the beard of the Muslim Brothers—it's dark and slightly patchy. In one, he poses with a little girl and smiles; in the other, he wears a red, white, and blue tennis sweatband (headbands were his trademark, it seems) and stares outward, blankly. There is a whiff of fear that exudes from this last photo, the kind of blank concentration one sometimes sees in the dead and the dying.

The last photo we have of Abu-Surur was taken directly after he'd killed Haim Nachmani, an Israeli General Security Service agent with whom he'd collaborated—or, some say, pretended to collaborate. In the photo, an axe hangs on the wall in the background, like a sign, and two of his fingers are bandaged. He is clean-shaven, dressed in a green jacket and a blue-and-white keffiyah, with another kefiyyah, in nationalist red-and-white, wrapped around his neck. In his right hand, he displays Nachmani's black pistol, his most prized possession.

By all accounts, Mahir Abu-Surur, who was called "Hamza" by everyone who knew him, was something of a dandy. He liked to dress up and wear cologne. Nothing, people said, was more important to him, and he would allow no one to accompany him on his buying sprees. He was shiny and reflective, like the white suit he bought for himself when he was seventeen. No one could forget the way he had strutted around town in that suit, asking everybody who saw him, "Am I not handsome? Don't I look like a bridegroom?"

"You do look handsome," the aunt had told him, "and with a bride you'd look even nicer." For his dream, they say, had always been to be a bridegroom. When he was in kindergarten, he had asked his teacher to marry him. He had once asked a visitor from 'Amman for the hand of her daughter, but the woman, even though she was a relative, didn't like the idea of her daughter living in a refugee camp. Another time, they say, a relative came to visit, and brought his daughter along with him, and Hamza said that when she grew up, he would marry her. But it was only talk. The girl was very young.

Hamza spent all his time dressing to the nines, but he was also religious. He started praying when he was seven years old, according to his mother, and he never skipped a prayer. He read Qur'an and even memorized some of it like a *hafiz*, who knew the entire book by heart. He went to the mosque often, and on Tuesdays and Thursdays, he fasted. During Ramadan, he prayed the *tarawiyah* prayer. He forbade certain songs as haram, forbidden and shameful.

He watched Hamas videos all the time, listened to the apologist Ahmad Didat, and read religious books like *Christ (Peace Be upon Him) in Islam*, *What the Bible Says about Muhammad (Peace Be upon Him)*, and *What Is His Name? His Name? His Name? His Name? His Name?*—to cite but three that his uncle pulled off the shelf for us once when we were visiting. He particularly liked the work of Sa'id Hawwa, Ahmad Hamid ar-Rashid, and Fathi Yaqan.

Sometimes, they say, Abu-Surur would turn on the television and see someone who'd been martyred, and he would say, "O Lord, make me like you!" Then he would do *wadhu*, wash his body, and say, "I declare there is no god except Allah, and Muhammad is the Messenger of Allah." He would often say, "O Lord, what world is this?" and he would wish for shahada, for martyrdom. If anything happened on the street, he would say, "This world is not worth it. Work for the better one. Insha'Allah, this world will pass." If his mother protested this kind of talk, if she said anything back to him at all, he would reply, "Don't talk—just wish me luck, ya hajja," the term referring to a woman who has made the hajj to Mecca. The mother was old and tired, and thought her son was just talking.

Abu-Surur drove her crazy, they say, with his talk of Paradise. He'd say to her, pointblank, "I'm going to Paradise," and she'd reply, "Just go away." He talked about the hur al-'ain all the time—"their impossible beauty," in the words of his uncle, who despite being his uncle, was of the same age. Their fingers looked like the sun, he said, and you could see their bones and even under their bones, for the virgins of Paradise were transparent. He would sit for long periods of time, just imagining what they must look like. He liked to imagine even the water they drank as they drank it.

The mother and aunt scolded Hamza because he didn't work and hung out with the shabab all day long, throwing stones at the soldiers and giving chase. One time, the soldiers followed him all the way to the house and left a bullet hole in the screen above the couch as a reminder that they'd been there. If the aunt asked him why he was doing all this—he was going to get himself killed—he would just start laughing like it was all a joke. She didn't understand him, she had to admit.

When he was in high school, the IDF arrested him and put him in prison for three months in the Negev desert in southern Israel along with hundreds of other shabab. By the time he was released, he was a changed man. He wouldn't eat. Sometimes, he would sit in the house doing nothing, just sitting. The aunt couldn't understand it. "Maybe they hit him in the head," she said, referring to the soldiers; "maybe they hurt his mind." She wanted to take her nephew to the doctor.

Abu-Surur enrolled at Bethlehem University, but he left after a month or two because of "the politics." Besides, he'd made up his mind to study hairdressing. In June 1992, he finally got his wish when he received a hairdressing diploma from the Duri and Gidi Hairstyling School in Jerusalem. It so happened that our next-door neighbor in Jerusalem used to work in Gidi's salon, and he told us where we could find Gidi. The salon sits on Ben-Hillel Street just off the midrechov, the most popular street in west Jerusalem. The area is crammed with dozens of cafes, pizza joints, clubs, and the best hummus in town. Since the intifada, it has generally been unfrequented by Palestinians, although in later years, it would become a prime site for suicide bombers, given the fact that hundreds of people could be killed or injured in a very small space. As might be expected, Gidi had no desire to speak to anyone about the suicide bomber who used to work in his place of business.

We glanced around carefully before leaving. It wasn't difficult to imagine Abu-Surur in this milieu. In the long expanse of mirrors stretching the entire length of the salon, he must have caught sight of himself dozens of times during the course of a day—that's one handsome son-of-a-gun right there, you imagine him thinking to himself. You imagine him dressed spiffily as he tidies up his workstation, tossing combs into the bright blue jar of Barbicide in the corner, sweeping up the still-damp clumps of hair that have fallen silently to the floor.

You imagine him washing the enemy's hair, his hands covered in thick, foamy suds of apple pectin shampoo, tiny flyaway bubbles of iridescence drifting upward now and then like motes on a beam. He clips the wet hair with scissors as sharp as a butcher's knife—the hair makes a slight squeaking sound, so slight as to be almost inaudible. He's a pretty good stylist. He likes to chat a bit with his clients, stopping what he's doing now and then to glance at them in the mirror, scissors in hand. He knows what they're looking for, what they want—complete and utter transformation. When at last he whirls them around with a little flair and proffers them the mirror, they all want to believe it's somebody else they're looking at.

40. The Killing of Haim Nachmani

On the day that Hamza Abu-Surur killed the Shin Bet guy, one of his brothers recalls that he walked into the living room, where Hamza was sitting on the couch—the very couch we are sitting on right now, we are told—with his head on the armrest. He was "sleeping with his eyes open." The brother said to him, "See ya later. Have a nice dream," and that was the last he saw of him.

Later that same day, Hamza's aunt recalls, she had stood with him on the stairs leading to the front door, and said to him, "Why are you doing this? What do you think you're doing? Enough! Why are you so confused? Why can't we just talk? What will you do when they're shooting rockets and you're throwing rocks?"

He replied, "It's up to Allah. Everything will be all right." Fifteen minutes later, a friend called, and he left. And that was the last she saw of him.

With that phone call, Abu-Surur was off to kill his Shin Bet handler, a guy who worked under the name "'Afif." (Many agents of the Israeli counterintelligence and internal security service possess Arabic nicknames.) The agent often dropped by the salon Abu-Surur had recently opened in Mukhayyam al-'Aza in the house of a woman who had taken a great liking to him, even going so far as to offer him space for his salon in her own home.

"Why won't you cut the soldiers' hair?" 'Afif would say to Abu-Surur, teasing him. Who knows where the two first met—perhaps in the camp, perhaps when Abu-Surur was in prison several years earlier, perhaps when he worked in Duri and Gidi's salon in Jerusalem. They were just a few years apart in age.

It can't have helped business, the Shin Bet guy dropping by like that all the time. In fact, Abu-Surur's brother told us when we met with him that everybody thought Abu-Surur was a collaborator. Suhail al-Hindi, Muhammad al-Hindi's brother, insists that this was not the case in *Abu-Zaid, Muhammad al-Hindi: From His Birth to His Martyrdom* (no author, date, or place of publication listed), the hagiography he wrote after his brother's death. Abu-Surur, he says, only pretended to agree to the demands of his Israeli captors so that they would release him from prison. When the Israelis did let him go, al-Hindi says, Abu-Surur went straight to the Qassam leaders Muhammad Rushdi and Khalid ad-Dazir to ask them what he should do. The next time 'Afif came by his barbershop, Abu-Surur agreed to meet with him.

At their first meeting, Abu-Surur requested that he be given cash and also that he be trained in the use of weapons. Immediately afterward, al-Hindi tells us, he again contacted the leadership of the Battalions, and the organization worked out a plan for him, enlisting the help of two of Hamza's relatives, his cousins Mahmud Abu-Surur and Nasir Abu-Surur—a claim that contradicts Israeli reports contending that Abu-Surur acted on his own accord and not on orders from Hamas,[1] as well as what one of Abu-Surur's brothers told us when we met with him. According to the brother, Abu-Surur had confided in his cousins about some of the things the Shin Bet agent had been asking him to do (sleeping with his cousins was on the list), and, together, they had made a pact to kill Nachmani.

According to Suhail al-Hindi, the three did not wait long to carry out the plan. Abu-Surur and Nachmani had begun to meet in a safe house in Jerusalem, and one day, Abu-Surur took the bus there, while, so as to avoid suspicion, the cousins drove. Nachmani welcomed Hamza at the door, and began stroking his shoulder, saying, "Ahlan, Mahir," "Welcome," when all of a sudden, Suhail writes,

> Mahir drew the holy dagger and stabbed him seven times all over his filthy body, and even so, the pig remained alive for he was a big man, and in that moment, the pig was able to reach his pistol, which had fallen on the ground, and get off two shots, and just then [Mahir's] two cousins entered the house. One of them grabbed a hammer and began striking the head of the pig Haim Nachmani. And Mahir began slashing his neck with his knife until he had cut the head from the body. And after it was over, Mahir went to the bathroom and washed his face and his clothes and so did his cousin, given they were drenched in the blood of that impure pig; then the three of them left the house.

Hamza Abu-Surur and his cousins walked away from the scene with Nachmani's pistol and briefcase, which was said to be full of intelligence documents; and as they were leaving, al-Hindi writes, an Israeli passerby eyed them suspiciously, so Abu-Surur began to speak with his cousins in Hebrew about some problems he was having at work, and how tired he was. The Israeli continued walking down the street, and soon discovered Nachmani, his beheaded body slouched in the doorway.

The Battalions dedicated the act to "the Lions of Hamas in Marj az-Zahur," the Hamas deportees in southern Lebanon; and Abu-Surur, al-Hindi writes, became a full-fledged member of the Battalions and "the most wanted man in the West Bank." He came back home to visit one last time, dressed as a woman. The soldiers came for him, dressed as Arabs.

41. The Last Words of Salah Mustafa ʻUthman

"What are you doing in the Bank, O Abu-Hamza?" Rushdi asks Salah Mustafa ʻUthman, the second guy to be interviewed on *The Giants*, referring to him by his nom de guerre. (ʻUthman, it seems, was so enamored with Hamza Abu-Surur and the story of his killing of Haim Nachmani that he took Abu-Surur's name as his own. Indeed, "Abu-Hamza," one could say, claims a certain begetting power.)

Under the circumstances, the question seems a kind of wink, as though they're all there to attend a party or visit buddies, and ʻUthman responds with a conspiratorial chuckle. "Allah, Praise Him and raise Him on high, brought us to this land in order that we should be murabitun on every handbreadth of the land of Palestine," he says, using the term for those who fight according to Qurʼanic prescriptions.

"Allah preserve you all," says Rushdi.

"And you," replies 'Uthman.

Rushdi then inquires about the "errand," as he euphemistically calls the suicide operation that is to take place the next day:

RUSHDI: Tomorrow, you have an errand—our brother Abu ash-Shahid has told us about it—and, insha'Allah, we know that you will participate. So tell us about the resources and the movement and its enemy and their strength and the plan.

'UTHMAN: By Allah, insha'Allah, tomorrow I am determined to set out on an errand.

RUSHDI: Allah permitting.

'UTHMAN: Allah permitting. We ask Allah to bestow upon us one of the two beautiful things—either martyrdom or victory.

RUSHDI: And the plan is . . .

'UTHMAN: The plan is the road to . . .

RUSHDI: To kidnap Israelis. And if they don't meet the demands?

'UTHMAN: If they don't meet the demands, naturally, we're going to destroy the bus.

One gets the impression that 'Uthman has forgotten some of his lines, or is executing them in an incorrect manner, for Rushdi interrupts him often, completes his sentences for him, prods him gently along in a voice adults usually reserve for children. A lot of the interruptions and interpolations consist of religious formulae such as "insha'Allah"—fillers meant, one supposes, to ritualize the event as well as to remind both the Giants and those watching them that God is the ultimate director of this play.

When Rushdi asks him to say "a word to [his] brothers," 'Uthman can only murmur. "Say it," Rushdi quietly urges. "I pray to Allah that He fortify us and them to be in the right," 'Uthman says, before Rushdi interjects another "insha'Allah"—less an interruption, one feels, than an encouragement. "And that He will admit us into the spaciousness of His Paradise, and that there will be a meeting with the Lord of the Believers there when we are with the Prophets and the Righteous and the Martyrs." Like Abu-Surur before him, 'Uthman presents the afterworld in terms of a "meeting" with God in Paradise. In contrast, the enemy, he says, will "descend to Hell":

'UTHMAN: The operation, insha'Allah, will, of course, be in a place . . .

RUSHDI: The right place, insha'Allah?

OTHER VOICE: Allah permitting . . .

'UTHMAN: The place will be Jerusalem.

RUSHDI: Inside . . . inside the depths of Israel, as they say?

'UTHMAN: Yes.

RUSHDI: Yes.

'UTHMAN: We're going to enter the bus in disguise . . .

RUSHDI: Allah permitting, yes?

'UTHMAN: Insha'Allah. We'll board the bus; we'll take out packages of explosives; there will be enough to blow up the entire bus. There will be a great quantity of explosives, insha'Allah. We'll also have many weapons—a machinegun and pistols and hand grenades and a great quantity of ammunition. And, naturally, if the enemies don't comply, insha'Allah, we will ascend to Paradise, and they will descend to Hell.

[The camera pans over the Giants' weapons.]

RUSHDI: To Hell?

'UTHMAN: Yes.

RUSHDI: May Allah preserve you, insha'Allah, Lord of the Worlds. May our Lord grant you success.

The last words of 'Uthman are markedly different from those of Abu-Surur. This is partly due to the kinds of questions that Rushdi directs at him and, one presumes, partly due to differences in personality. Those differences are clear even in the military maneuvers that initiate each Giant's allotted section. Whereas Abu-Surur jumps and skittles around the olive trees and dry-rock walls in the grove where they are filming, dressed in jungle camouflage, imitating every action movie he's ever seen, 'Uthman executes his maneuvers calmly in street clothes. Whereas Abu-Surur glances nervously over his shoulders, left and right, as he's interviewed, 'Uthman's eyes rarely stray from the camera. Abu-Surur's presentation is highly dramatic and stylized; 'Uthman's affect, in contrast, is largely controlled, with only a glimpse of something like inner panic breaking through now and then. Whereas Abu-Surur talks avidly about the Last Days and meeting "the Lord of the Worlds," as if trying simultaneously to dramatize and ease his way into the next world, to prefamiliarize himself with it, 'Uthman plods his way through an entanglement of formulae, whose sequence must be executed just so.

42. A Happy Man

We were back in Deir al-Balah again, staying with Yusuf and Faradis, his wife. It was good to be back, but Yusuf was depressed. The heady days of the intifada were over, and he and his friends spent hours in pointless and sometimes heated discussion over who had lost the battle. It was Arafat's corruption, the unrealistic program of the Popular Front, Hamas' fanaticism. The Americans. The Soviets. The British. The betrayal of the Jordanians and the Egyptians. The list was endless with partners and meddlers, enemies and allies, alike held up and examined in despairing detail. The conversation would go on until it dissolved in mock anger, and then the anger would become real, and everyone would be shouting. Finally, Muhammad would pull out his 'oud and sing, *Ya laili, ya 'aini,* "O night, O my eyes," the oud strings humming and thrumming like jinns lost in the Gazan night, and people would calm down a bit.

Ra'id had promised to secure us an interview with Salah 'Uthman, who, it turned out, had survived the Giants' operation and, for unknown reason, had been released by the Israelis. Perhaps they thought he was going to die; perhaps he had given them information during his detention, and release was his reward; perhaps his injuries had made it clear that he would no longer be a threat. We later interviewed an Israeli officer in the West Bank military headquarters near Ramallah and when we brought up 'Uthman's name, he informed us in a tone that conveyed he was privy to secret information that 'Uthman was residing in Ramallah. It was unclear why he gave us false information or if he himself had been misled.

That night at Yusuf's, the dream returned. We are riding in a Jerusalem-Gaza shared taxi. We have just passed the Erez checkpoint. A few kilometers later, we pass rows of car-repair shops, their Hebrew signs designed to lure Israeli customers with cheap service still there, but now incongruous. The shops have been closed by order of the strike committees, their steel doors slathered with coat upon coat of competing messages and slogans. Now, we are passing the soccer field that Gazans call "the swimming pool," already a swamp after the recent rains and destined to become a dirty grey lake for the duration of the oncoming winter, and then the Mosque of as-Said Hashim, the Prophet Muhammad's grandfather, who was said to have died in Gaza. Finally, we approach the butcher shops, which are exempt from closure. They hardly need signs. All have their wares hanging prominently in the open—fat-tailed sheep, young goats arrayed in rows, skinned bulls slit down the middle hanging from hooks embedded behind their Achilles tendons. On all of them, blue-veined testicles bear witness to the fact that they are tender males. Flies are kept away with white gauze sheets draped loosely around the carcasses. Gazans rarely buy an entire joint; rather, the shopper designates how much meat is wanted, whereupon the butcher slices off the desired quantity with a long steel knife, flensing the carcass until the bones show whitely through the flesh and the ribs stick out like "quills upon the fretful porpentine." In the dream, the flayed cattle look like so many corpses wrapped in shrouds.

We alight from the taxi, and Yusuf is there. He is anxious to show us something. He brings us down to the Gates of Gaza, the absurd plastic structure reading "Gaza Welcomes You" in Arabic, erected by Israel in more optimistic, or perhaps self-deluded, times. In the dream, the gates have large hooks embedded in the plastic, and on each hook is a flayed steer wrapped in white linen. As we near the gates, Yusuf pulls aside the cloth, not with his usual dramatic flourish but conspiratorially, as if revealing a secret. "See, my friend, look!" he whispers. We do and, behold, these are not steers, but rather men, martyrs recently felled in confrontation with Israeli troops. "Yes, my friend, this is our life," says Yusuf, sadly. And we realize that he is happy. Happy and proud to show us these corpses.

The sun was the color of sulfur by the time we met up with Ra'id the next day and headed off to meet 'Uthman. The 'Uthman family home was set in an alley branching off one of the main roads that run through Jabalya Camp, and as we pulled up to the house in a borrowed Peugeot, Ra'id's Mazda having finally succumbed to engine rot, Ra'id said, "Look, it will not be good to be too conspicuous. The PA does not even know that he is here."

A blue iron door opened into a small sandy courtyard and then into a receiving room, empty, save for woven plastic mats on the floor and half a dozen straw-stuffed bolsters lined up against the wall. 'Uthman was lying on a pallet, propped up on a few of the pillows.

At first, he looked very much as he did on *The Giants*, but it soon became clear that he was profoundly damaged. The bullet that injured him went through the center of his head, entering near one temple and exiting through the other. The entrance and exit points were still clearly visible. His body shook with spasms and tremors that began in his legs and worked their way upward through his body. Uncontrollable vocalizations punctuated his speech, sometimes sounding like moans, at other times like angry growls. His eyes bugged out of their sockets in an alarming fashion. At times, each eye would roll independently of the other, chameleonlike. He spoke in a dull, husky voice, very slowly, with many pauses and vocalizations between thoughts. Sometimes, his speech was clear; more often, it was thick and punctuated by stammers and stutters as if a lightening storm had erupted in his head.

Despite the supposed secrecy of our visit, the room was mobbed with people—friends, relatives, people from the neighborhood.

"I was one of those children," 'Uthman began, "I mean, Allah bless our master Muhammad . . . I mean, who went from home to school and then school to home. I didn't go out to the street to play, only once in a while; therefore, I kept my heart clean."

The extent of his incapacity took us aback.

Ra'id, perhaps sensing hesitation as incomprehension, leaned in close and whispered, "Cleaner than other kids who enjoyed themselves."

'Uthman continued. "I mean," he said, "I was very good at school, at my studies. I mean, all my life all I cared about was my studies. I have been praying since I was in the fifth grade . . . "

Ra'id leaned in again, and said, "Which is like around ten years old."

"I always wanted to go to the mosque," 'Uthman said, "but Satan always came to me and told me . . . he raised objections to going." A teacher, however, had continued to encourage him to go to the mosque, and one day when 'Uthman came home from school, he decided to perform the *wudu'*, the ritual washing before prayers, and go to the mosque. And since that time, he had prayed five times a day.

"I began raising myself," he said, "because, you know, I didn't know anything at all about, you know, the movements in the field. I didn't know anything about Fatah or the Muslim [Brothers] or . . . because until then, all my life was dedicated to my studies. I asked . . . in a book . . . I'd heard of the book called *The Torments of the Tomb*. I wanted to read it, and Allah had destined it for me, because the one I asked was 'Imad 'Aql. I asked him about the book, and he told me, 'I have it.'"

"Was 'Imad 'Aql just a friend, or was he already known as a leader?" we asked.

"No," Ra'id burst in, "'Imad 'Aql was known only during the intifada." He turned to 'Uthman. "So," he said, "Imad 'Aql, what was he? A friend? Or . . . ? And all of these events took place before the intifada?" It was as though something had suddenly ticked him off.

"Yeah," said 'Uthman, answering only the last question.

"What year?" Ra'id inquired.

"In '86 . . . '87," 'Uthman replied.

"How old was 'Imad 'Aql? Was he younger?" asked Ra'id.

"No, 'Imad 'Aql, he was five . . .," said 'Uthman, his speech breaking down into long, drawn-out syllables.

"You were born in which year?" asked Ra'id, undeterred.

'Uthman paused, as if he couldn't remember exactly. "In . . . '71."

"And 'Imad?" asked Ra'id.

"'67," said 'Uthman. "But 'Imad was raised in an Islamic way since he was small."

'Uthman's father entered the room. He was a stocky man, bearded and wearing the white robe and skullcap that signify a pious man. He seemed surprised to see the crowd in the room. Ra'id jumped up to talk with him. The father looked at us dubiously but offered us tea nonetheless.

'Uthman continued his story where he had left off as though Ra'id had not interrupted him. "'Imad said, 'I have the book—come and get it.' And since that day we have been very good friends, and we have been together all the time. I go to see him every day; if I don't, he comes to me."

He spoke as though 'Imad 'Aql were alive, as though he had not been dead for years.

"What was it about the book that was so important to you?" we asked.

"The basics of religion," one of the watchers, a cousin, said, answering for him.

"From the standpoint of politics," Ra'id added.

'Uthman said, "I read . . . I read *The Torments of the Tomb*, and I raised myself. I raise myself . . . by this book." His speech was breaking up again.

"You know, it puts fear in the heart," Ra'id said to us.

"Have you read it"? we asked Ra'id. "Is it a powerful book?"

"Different people have different aspects to them," said Ra'id. "Some people . . . they . . . want to go to heaven; some people they are scared of Hell-fire; some people, they just love Allah, and they don't care if they . . . you know what I mean?"

"So, this book is more Hell-fire . . . ?"

"It's a scary book," said Ra'id. "It scares you about what is going to come next, so you don't have to go through . . . so you can correct yourself."

'Uthman continued, "I and 'Imad and all the shabab, Allah bless our master Muhammad, and, you know, we were reading the Qur'an . . . I and he and reading, I and he, he . . . you know . . . we were praying." He was stuttering violently. It was as though he were being attacked. He recovered but was exhausted. Beads of sweat dotted his forehead. No one seemed to notice.

"Is he OK?" we asked. "Should we go on?"

"Yes, yes, go on," they said. This was just how it was to talk with Salah.

"When and how did you come to the decision not just to fight the soldiers in the street but to become a mujahid fi sabil Allah?

"Allah bless our master Muhammad, man is created of *fitra*," said 'Uthman, "and his fitra is from Islam."

Ra'id leaned in again. "Allah created people from fitra. Do you know what fitra is?" he asked.

"Mud?" we asked, thinking of the section of Hamas' mithaq in which it is stated, "Man is an exceedingly wondrous creation made from a handful of mud and a puff of breath . . ."

"No, no, no," Ra'id said. "That is *tin*. Fitra is like they could create you with the good intention inside of you, and then you could destroy it by your wrongdoings."

"Free will?" we ventured.

"Right, but always if you just keep yourself with the fitra, you will choose the right way." Ra'id thought that was close enough. But we still hadn't gotten it right. Fitra, as we were soon reminded when we got home and looked the word up, is the notion that man is created with a pure nature oriented toward God. That nature is changeable, however, and if one is raised improperly, it can be turned toward something less desirable. It is in this sense that many of the pious do not speak of converts to Islam, but rather of reverts, in that they consider themselves to be bringing the prodigal back to their natural condition.

"And I told you my fitra was correct in the beginning," 'Uthman continued; "nothing took me off the right path. I was going from school to home and from home to school. I never stayed with anyone or any group that tried my intentions or my heart.

"As for, you know, the thing that pushed me, that guided me to take this dangerous road, that thing is the same thing that changed the condition of Bilal the Ethiopian from a slave to a respected master. And 'Omar from an evil unbeliever to the most just of men. It is Islam that makes man. Islam raises man in courage, in justice, in bravery, in fairness."

"In the video, you say that you want to fight on the path of God and to be martyred on the path of God. What did you mean?"

"The push was the noble verse that says, 'So he fulfilled the need to fight for Allah's promise, to fight them, to kill and be killed, and then Allah, Exalt Him and praise Him, will give them the reward.'"

"When you and Hamza Abu-Surur and Muhammad al-Hindi made the video, you seemed torn between happiness and excitement. Could you tell us what was going through your mind at the time?"

"On the night before our operation, we had that feeling when you first get married, on the night of the wedding, so excited."

This provoked mirth from the observers; some even made ribald asides.

"Weren't you scared?" someone in the room asked.

"No, no," replied 'Uthman. "That feeling comes from the fact that soon you will see the Gardens of Heaven; you will see the Prophet and your friends who died before. We were so excited, and we were full of happiness. In that moment, we lived a sort of higher faith. It's a feeling like you are in the sky, like you are flying up to the sky, and the dunya gets smaller and smaller and smaller. This feeling gives you all the happiness."

As 'Uthman slipped into this persona, the persona of the imam, his speech improved as did his tics. The watchers got excited and began to vie for more time in the conversation. Out of the hubbub, one of 'Uthman's cousins joined in. "You feel pride," he said—al-'izz wa-al-karama. "When you stay and do nothing, it is just like you're crippled and hung with chains. This is how you lose these chains."

"In your video, and in other videos as well," we said, "people talk about how they have seen the dunya, and the dunya is found wanting. Could you explain this?"

Another of the onlookers broke in. "I'm going to bring it as an equation," he said; "the dunya can never extend beyond seventy or eighty years."

"And life is a mixture of joy and sadness next to each other," added Ra'id.

"And," continued the cousin, "because there are two opposing lives in the Hereafter—eternal life in the Fire and eternal life in Paradise. Forever. In Heaven, in the eternal Paradise of pleasure, it's like what the Messenger, Allah bless Him and grant Him salvation, said, 'The pleasure that the eye cannot behold and the ear cannot hear and the heart cannot fathom.' Allah has given us so many gifts that our minds cannot comprehend them. It's like a car that can travel a hundred kilometers but cannot go beyond that—you cannot picture what is beyond that."

"It is like someone who lives in Beach Camp or Jabalya who doesn't know what's going on in America," added Ra'id, scoring a point or two against people in the room who had never stepped foot outside Gaza.

"Naturally," said the cousin, "Hellfire and the Torments of the Tomb—this is what you must fear; you can't imagine the enormity of the suffering. But there is something that is greater than Hell-fire and Heaven itself. Now, I will make an illustration for you. If President Clinton sent an invitation to you . . . the most powerful president in the world, right? . . . Before you went to him, you would dress in your finest clothes; you would clear your mind; you would consider it a great honor that the president invited you. But in Heaven, you'll see our Lord, creator of the whole universe."

Clearly, Ra'id and the cousin could have gone on trying to outdo each other for some time. We tried to steer the conversation back toward 'Uthman again. "Is that how you felt?" we asked.

"Exactly," said 'Uthman. "You know, I . . . Without Islam, I don't have the power." He stopped abruptly, losing his train of thought.

"What did you talk about with each other the night before the action?"

"About what we were going to see," 'Uthman said. He meant what they were going to see in heaven.

Ra'id broke in again. "Did you go out with the intention of never returning?" he asked, slightly accusingly.

"Absolutely, not even 1 percent!" 'Uthman exclaimed. He meant that he had not thought that there was even a 1 percent chance that he would survive.

"What did you talk about?" we asked again.

"Allah bless our master Muhammad, for example, I would say, 'O Lord, make me a martyr before 'Imad 'Aql.' And Muhammad al-Hindi would say, 'O Lord, make me a martyr before you and before 'Imad 'Aql.'"

"And Hamza Abu-Surur?"

"Allah bless our master Muhammad, he would say . . . Allah bless our master Muhammad, you know, Hamza, he would say, 'Seventy virgins are enough for me. I'll give you and Muhammad two.'"

Ra'id leaned in and said, soberly, "The sheikh gets seventy-two."

43. A Happy Man (continued)

"Picture . . . picture a man who wants to die," 'Uthman said when we asked him if he'd been scared.

It was strange, hearing him say something like that. We'd expected the language of martyrdom, but not language that verged on the suicidal.

"To be martyred," the father intervened, for the first time correcting his son.

"Or wants to be martyred," said 'Uthman, "wants to leave the dunya."

The father turned to us. "How many times do you die?" he said. "If Allah wants it, that's it—good-bye."

"But how would he feel about never seeing his father again, or at least not for many years?" we said to Ra'id, referring to Salah.

"Well," said Ra'id, "this is a matter of 'aqida. The dead see us, but we don't see the dead."

"But his father would have been very sad if he died," we said. "Did he think about that?"

"How long would we be separated?" said 'Uthman. "Twenty years, forty years, but after that we are going to see them, if Allah wills it. And we're going to see seventy of our family. The martyr brings seventy of his family and friends."

"No matter what," explained Ra'id. "Not only have I paid my tax, I paid for others, you know. So I'll see them. I'll bring them to heaven, and I'll see them forever."

"If you had seen your son before the action, the operation," we said to the father, "would you have said, Don't do it. I'm scared for you?"

"We spoke to him a lot, but he didn't listen," the father said.

The comment roused 'Uthman. For the first time, real emotion registered on his face, and he looked as though he were trying to raise himself from the pillows.

"How many?!" he cried, challenging his father.

The father leaned in and said to his son, "It's over." Then to us, he said, "It was his own will."

'Uthman, however, was still worked up. "Allah bless our master Muhammad," he said, "jihad, jihad . . . the Jews in this situation, in defending our land . . . their jihad is a jihad. A fard al-'ain. Under a fard al-'ain, the slave may go out against the will of his master, the son may go out against the will of his father, and the wife against the will of her husband."

Someone else in the room repeated the words by heart with 'Uthman. We recognized them from the mithaq of Hamas.

"Allah bless our master Muhammad, my father does not have the power to stop me or not stop me," said 'Uthman. "You know, Allah bless our master Muhammad, obeying the father is an obligation on us, but if your jihad is against . . . So, you know, the situation is that my father . . . then it would be *shirk* [the sin of attributing partners to God] with Allah, Praise Him, even if he wants it— it is not an obligation on me, nor . . . to obey mother." He began again and again, stuttering wildly.

"On the videos," we said, "they say that being hunted fi sabil Allah is an experience like no other. What does this mean?"

"We began to feel more happiness than when we were safe," said 'Uthman, "because we began to feel that we knew we were worshipping Allah the best we could."

"On the videos, you say that your friendship was also at a different level when you were hunted."

"How do you feel toward yourself?" asked 'Uthman. "Your feeling for your brother is more precious than what you feel for yourself. I'll tell you this story. Allah bless our master Muhammad, I, you know, began as the *amir* [leader] of the group for the operations, but when, Allah bless our master Muhammad, I became hunted, you know, I realized that Muhammad was better than me, you know, better than me at managing the group. I kept after him for two days to become the leader of the group, and finally he accepted. When we were, you know, going around in the mountains, we were, you know, competing to see who would be in front, where there was the most danger, in front of his friends."

"Was it always the three of you?"

Most of the time, 'Uthman replied, but at one point, Rushdi had spent ten days with them in their cave near Hebron. Later, Hamas' chief bomb maker Yahya Ayyash came and stayed with them also.

"Can you tell us more about your two friends who were martyred?" we asked.

"Allah bless our master Muhammad, he was an umma [unto himself]," 'Uthman said, referring to al-Hindi. "You know," he said, "Muhammad al-Hindi prayed and was silent. And silence is proof that he was thinking. Thinking was not difficult for him. He thought, you know, and wouldn't say anything until he had thought it over a million times."

Suddenly, he began to talk about their life in the caves. Sometimes, he said, they would have to spend as many as three days excavating a cave, making it big enough to hold three or four mattresses. "You know," he said, "Allah bless our master Muhammad, one of the caves had a door like a well, taller than the height of a man, then a narrow space you had to squeeze through, and, finally, a big room. Allah bless our master Muhammad, we had to, you know, take turns guarding. One about every twenty-four hours. One would guard, and the other two sleep. At night, we would go out. We'd train and hike and go up."

Not infrequently, the caves were located in archaeological zones, where local people liked to dig in the old tombs for artifacts even though it was forbidden to do so. The guys would have to be particularly careful then, he said, because people would come and dig until one or two in the morning, which was the time when the guys took their baths and washed their clothes.

"Living in a cave," we remarked, "is almost like being in a tomb. When you were there, did you think back to the book you'd read?" We were referring to *The Torments of the Tomb*, the book 'Uthman credits with having set him on the path of martyrdom.

"We thought of the tomb," 'Uthman replied, "but we were happy in the tomb. Allah bless our master Muhammad, either the tomb becomes a Paradise, one of the gardens of Paradise, or it becomes one of the pits of Hell. You know, it encouraged us to carry on during this time. We were encouraged to action and possibilities in that way so that our tombs would be a Paradise for us—you know, Praise Allah, just as Allah made them to draw out power for man in the tomb so that he knows his place is in Paradise and not in Hell."

We inquired again about Hamza Abu-Surur, feeling that 'Uthman was avoiding speaking of him.

"Allah bless our master Muhammad," 'Uthman said, "Hamza, Allah bless our master Muhammad, had been living alone in the cave for three months before we came. Picture a person spoiled by his mother, the youngest child of his mother. . . . Picture, you know, the pain of this child."

We showed 'Uthman a photograph of Abu-Surur that his family had given us. Something about the picture reminded him of the tomb robbers who had once stumbled upon Abu-Surur in one of his caves. There were more than ten of them, he said. Abu-Surur could see them, but they couldn't see him, and when they got close enough, Abu-Surur pulled out his pistol and demanded to see their identification, and told them not to say anything to anybody about what they'd seen. And then he left and searched for a new cave.

It seemed the perfect fantasy for Abu-Surur, something he'd always dreamed of—seeing people who couldn't see him. We thought of his poetry. We thought of the scene in *The Giants* where he jumps around the olive grove with his gun, moving as though if he moved in just the right way, he would be invisible.

Once 'Uthman began to talk about Abu-Surur, people in the room became agitated. The father, in particular, clearly thought it was time for us to leave. Ra'id began to talk to the father, trying to allay his anxiety.

"On the operation itself," we continued, "the one during which your friends were martyred, how did you feel? What was inside of you?"

"During this time," 'Uthman said, "we always used to ask our leaders to prepare a martyrdom operation for us. And Yahya Ayyash came to prepare a car bomb for one of us. And the leadership kept telling us to be patient, you know, patience, not now, you know, Allah bless our master Muhammad, and Muhammad 'Aziz came once . . ."

The father interrupted, asking if anyone would like some tea, or maybe juice. A conversation ensued over the choice, and 'Uthman once again lost his train of thought.

"Allah bless our master Muhammad," he began again, "you know, Muhammad al-Hindi was in a place near Muhammad 'Aziz and Mahir Abu-Surur, and Abu-'Aziz came to us, saying, 'You're now going to be with the Messenger of Allah and 'Umar and Abu-Bakr the Truthsayer and the martyrs.' You know, we were to be gathered with the martyrs, so we were overjoyed. We were . . ."

"Released from suffering," said someone else in the room, completing the sentence for him.

'Uthman repeated the phrase—*qarb al-faraj*. "Released from suffering. And Muhammad 'Aziz wanted to come with us, but his responsibilities forbade him from doing that. And then he was martyred . . ." His voice trailed off.

"We were sent out from the Strip and the Bank while it was under closure," he continued, "and we were in Hebron, then notification came that there was a bus that was to be seized, a bus that had been observed carrying government employees. And if it were kidnapped, insha'Allah, they would answer their demands . . . and if they didn't answer our demands . . . the bus would be blown up, with us in it."

The father interrupted again, but by then everyone in the room was carried away by the story and in no mood to stop it.

"So I went to Jerusalem," 'Uthman said. "We wanted to spend the night in Jerusalem. On the night of the action, we went from Hebron to Jerusalem. And we woke up there and washed, and we prayed two rak'atain, Praise be to Allah."

"Is this a special prayer for one who is to face martyrdom?"

"With the intention of leaving life, you know . . . and we were fasting," said 'Uthman. "And we arrived at the bus stop. We waited twenty-five minutes on the route of bus twenty-five. I was disguised as a student, wearing the clothes of a university student. I was carrying a bag."

"A Jewish student? With a kippah?"

"No, no. Just the cut of my hair . . . cut like a Jew, and dark glasses. I was wearing a shirt and cowboy pants," he said, referring to blue jeans, "and carrying a bag full of explosives. Muhammad al-Hindi was disguised as a businessman. His character, you know, is silent, and he is pale, and he doesn't have a beard. He was wearing a shirt and tie, and had a briefcase with explosives in it. And Mahir Abu-Surur was dressed like a Russian soldier returning to his base and carrying a big bag."

"At that moment, when you were standing there, waiting for the bus, did you for a moment feel any doubt? Did you say to yourself, 'Maybe I shouldn't do this'?"

"No," he said, "we wanted it to take place as soon as possible. The bus was late. We didn't say a word to one another. Finally, the bus came. I bought a ticket and got on at the back. Muhammad al-Hindi and Mahir Abu-Surur got on after everybody else so that they would be by the driver. The bus was carrying about eighty . . ." His voice began breaking up again. He managed to gather himself together and continue.

"And Muhammad al-Hindi, Allah bless our master Muhammad, we told him, 'You sit there. If we are martyred, you blow up the bus. Or in case you hear an explosion behind you, blow up the bus immediately.' So, Allah bless our master Muhammad, when the bus started moving, Hamza announced that it was hijacked."

"In Hebrew?"

"Yeah," said 'Uthman. "He took out his M-16—if you didn't know better, you would think he is a Jew; he is fair like them. So he raised the M-16 and said, 'This is a hijacking.' I pulled out a pistol and said, 'Allahu akbar!' and fired into the air. Then the driver pulled the bus right up onto the island between the two lanes, on the island directly across from a government building, and that government building was the Jerusalem police headquarters . . . I was saying . . . What was I saying? The bus stopped, Allah bless our master Muhammad . . . Had I got to where we got into a clash with the people or the police?"

"So, why didn't you blow up the bus?" asked Ra'id, ignoring the question.

"Allah bless our master Muhammad, I said, I'll tell you something. There I fell ill. I was wounded . . . I was wounded and fell to the ground, you know . . ."

"And what?" Ra'id persisted. "You got into a clash right away?"

"He was shot right away!" said the father, coming to his son's defense.

"Allah bless our master Muhammad," said 'Uthman, "I didn't see the situation because the pistol was gone; the pistol was taken from me, and I was shot." He began to stutter. "I was on the point of pulling the pin. I didn't have the strength. I passed out. The bullet went from here to here," he said, pointing out the entrance and exit wounds on his head.

"What happened next?" we asked.

"I heard on the news, I heard on the news that they found five empty clips in the bus. Mahir Abu-Surur had six clips, six magazines. It is my analysis that it didn't explode because the detonator broke . . . that was with Muhammad . . . Mahir that he shot." He was stuttering violently.

"I have told you why the bus didn't explode. Then Muhammad al-Hindi kidnapped . . . he withdrew . . . a lady soldier . . . and they withdrew. During the withdrawal, they were throwing grenades. But there was a checkpoint between Jerusalem and Bethlehem—it's called the 'Gilo checkpoint.' The helicopter was following them . . ."

Apparently, the news of our visit had spread, for the little room kept filling with onlookers, who watched us suspiciously. Ra'id tried to calm them while 'Uthman, now affecting the language of an explosives expert, an engineer, continued his story.

"In my analysis," he said, referring to the bomb, "the reason it didn't produce was due to the high explosive mixture in the detonator. The novelty for the user . . . and there is no one who knows how to use it yet in the Muslim Brotherhood. Allah bless our master Muhammad, no one knows how except one or two people . . . I mean here in Palestine. And, you know, look, with just a little crystal of it, you can make an explosion that will knock down half a house—or a whole house!"

"May it be used soon!" exclaimed Ra'id, momentarily back on the side of 'Uthman.

"Yeah!" said 'Uthman. "They sent out a martyr-shabb two weeks later on the same bus." He couldn't seem to remember exactly what he wanted to say next. "Speaking of why the bus didn't explode . . . revenge for the burning of Muhammad."

"Muhammad who blew up a bus?" asked Ra'id.

"Allah bless our master Muhammad," 'Uthman managed to utter. He could barely speak.

Ra'id pressed on. "Whose operation?" he asked. "The operation of Sliman . . ."

"No!" exclaimed 'Uthman, suddenly in control again. "No, no, no," he said, clicking his tongue in disapproval. "Before that, there was another unsuccessful action when the bomb didn't go off. He got on at the first stop, then he got off at the second stop, and said to them, 'It didn't explode.' So they examined the battery, but it worked. They examined the filament, a tungsten wire . . . they found that it had reacted with the explosive and melted, so it didn't explode. After that, they fixed it, and in the next operation, it worked."

"What did you think when you woke up and realized that you were not a shahid?" we asked.

"Allah bless our master Muhammad, someone told me . . . I forgot everything that day. I couldn't move my legs or hands. I couldn't say anything except two words . . . And they brought the mukhabarat to me, and there was a heavy guard—policemen and Border Guards—at my head twenty-four hours a day and policemen at the door of the room. Muhammad al-Hindi's i.d. card was burned, so they wanted to find out about him. They said, 'You, Mahir, and who else?' I, you know, wasn't able to speak. Wasn't possible.

"Then . . . you know . . . one of them said to me, 'We will make you better . . . we'll make you feel good . . . we will help you to walk and to move . . . just talk.' He kept coming to me. Finally, in the end, he said, 'We're going to take you to a military hospital, and you will die a slow death.'

"They took me to a military hospital in July, in the most intense heat, to a hospital in Be'er Sheba. The heat was fierce, and when we arrived, they put me in a room half the size of this one. Its doors were of metal, and they would open by electricity.

"They put me in front of a window. They put my upper body in the sun and my lower body in the shade. And Praise Allah, our Lord sent a cool breeze blowing, and I slept. I slept so deeply they thought I had passed out. So they put me in the shade, and then I felt so bad that I really fainted.

"Allah bless our master Muhammad, I was thinking about the noble verse, 'You may hate something that is a boon for you, and you may love something, and it is an evil for you, and Allah knows all while you do not.'" 'Uthman was revisiting a theme found in 'Abdullah 'Azzam's *Join the Caravan*. It was an idea Abu-Surur had also been fond of.

"Actually," he continued, "this was a boon for me. I said to you that before my being hunted, I prayed that I would be martyred and not be put in prison.

Allah answered my prayer, and he made me like this, twisted by the Jews like this."

"Like a dead body," said Ra'id.

"A professor at 'Ein Kerem declared me clinically dead," 'Uthman continued, unfazed by Ra'id's comment. "So, you know, Allah, May He be praised and exalted, wanted this boon for me, so, you know, he made me like this. I was brought to Shifa Hospital, and, Allah bless our master Muhammad, I am getting better."

After awhile, we managed to turn the subject back to Hamza Abu-Surur—we had many questions in need of answers. Abu-Surur, 'Uthman said, had first been arrested when he threw a Molotov for Hamas, and was tortured by the mukhabarat. In the middle of the interrogation, he was offered the choice of collaborating or staying in prison. They wanted him to penetrate the highest levels of Hamas. We'll give you a day to think it over, they said, and put him in a cell. In the end, he agreed to work for them, but, secretly, he planned either on becoming hunted or leaving for the outside. This is how Abu-Surur got out of prison immediately, 'Uthman said. After he was released, he told his brothers in Hamas what he had done, and they also gave him a choice—either he could go back to prison for two years or continue to work with the mukhabarat until he was able to kill his handler.

"You know," said 'Uthman, speaking of the operation in which Haim Nachmani had been killed, "the noble leader of this operation was Muhammad 'Aziz. He planned the operation, he and Khalid ad-Dazir. Khalid ad-Dazir was the connection between Mahir and Muhammad 'Aziz." It was ad-Dazir who took care of all the steps. In the meantime, Nachmani was instructing Abu-Surur on how to gather information and was trusting him more and more. Nachmani even gave Abu-Surur and his cousin a stolen car.

One day, said 'Uthman, Abu-Surur went to the door of the apartment and rang the bell. When Nachmani opened the door and said, "Ahlan!" Abu-Surur said, "Here's your Ahlan!" and jumped him. "He stabbed him about seven times," said 'Uthman, "and after he stabbed him, he took his pistol . . . he took his pistol and shot him. At that moment, his cousin came. Mahir cut off the hand that held the pistol and, with his other hand, he slit his throat while his cousin held the head."

"In the video, Hamza had a knife and a gun. Was this the same knife and gun?" we asked.

"It is Nachmani's pistol, but the *shibariya* belonged to Hatim al-Muhtasib," 'Uthman said, referring to a dagger whose blade is shorter than that of a khanjar. "He said, 'I entrust it to you. Take it in trust that you will use it only to slit the throat of a collaborator or a Jew.'"

"So did he bring that knife and gun on the operation?" we asked.

"No," replied 'Uthman, "the operation demanded only explosives and weapons, you know."

"So what did he do with the knife and the gun?"

"He gave them to Muhammad 'Aziz," said 'Uthman.

"What is your hope for the future, now that you have been through all of this?"

"I was married, Allah bless our master Muhammad," 'Uthman replied, "and . . . I started studying . . . computer programming. And, insha'Allah, there will be given to me a new 'Imad soon, insha'Allah." He was referring to the fact that he was planning on naming his unborn son after his friend, the martyr 'Imad 'Aql. He began to stutter madly. "And I want," he continued, "Allah bless our master Muhammad, you know . . . and I am trying to straighten out my body . . . you know the condition."

"Do you feel different about the dunya?"

"The essentials haven't changed. You know, Allah bless our master Muhammad, the Muslim and the believer know that . . . Allah bless our master Muhammad, knows this and knows that he must put sin behind him. The desire of man is to worship Allah. And, you know, those who know this—it doesn't matter if they can walk or if they are in a wheelchair. And the worship of Allah to the greatest extent possible . . . if he worships Allah, May He be Praised, then he is worshipping."

"You know, "he said, "I am not able to make jihad any more. But I pray, and I fast. I treat people well. That's enough. I accept that which Allah has apportioned. And I am happy." He paused. "You know," he said, his face covered with the sweat of his assertions, "sometimes the feeling comes over me that I am the happiest man on the face of the earth."

44. The Last Words of Muhammad Hasan al-Hindi

We're watching the video again. A third guy steps in front of the camera, the camera goes blank, then blinks on again. Muhammad al-Hindi introduces himself to the viewer by his full proper name, the only one of the Giants to do so. When asked his age, he replies in the usual fashion, "Twenty-one years have passed, and my jihadi age is since early childhood, and the time I have been hunted is three and a half months."

His mission, he tells us, is to set out on "a martyrdom operation against an Israeli bus" if Israel refuses to meet the Giants' demand that it release a number of detainees. Interestingly, he cites the names of prisoners who belong not to Hamas but rather to Fatah and the Islamic Jihad. He adds that the group will broadcast five or so names on Radio Jerusalem—a station that, he takes care to note, is controlled by Ahmad Jibril's leftist Popular Front for the Liberation of Palestine-General Command. If Israel does not release the detainees, then the

Giants, he says, will pursue their plan of blowing up an Israeli bus and themselves with it—an operation that he says will come to an end with "the ascension of the three [Giants] to Paradise, Allah permitting, and the rest of the bus in the Fire."

"Allah, Mighty and Majestic, permitting," Rushdi responds, and al-Hindi joins in the refrain. (As the video goes on, one increasingly gets the impression that a great deal of pleasure is derived through the repetition of these formulae, or even that there is some sort of competition as to who can toss them first into the mix.)

"How do you feel given that it is certain that tomorrow will be the day of martyrdom?" Rushdi asks.

"Tomorrow, Allah permitting," al-Hindi replies, "will be the day of martyrdom, if Allah the Most High wills it, and it is a feeling not felt by any but the believing man, a feeling of trusting in Allah, and it is certain that victory is from Allah and that martyrdom is from Allah, Praise Him and raise Him on high. [The believing man] loves martyrdom, and he loves Paradise, and tomorrow, Allah permitting, we will meet the Beloved Muhammad and his Companions."

Al-Hindi then sends greetings to the members of the Battalions who welcomed him and the other Giants in the West Bank and, oddly, greets Rushdi in the third person by his nom de guerre—Abu-'Aziz. Before al-Hindi joined up with Abu-Surur and 'Uthman, he had belonged to a group named after the two martyrs Hatim al-Muhtasib and Ya'qub Mutau'a, and he next sends them greetings as well as "our hero-martyr, the hero of the suicide operations, 'Amir Thawabta, who ascended on high on 21/10/1990" (he died while preparing an explosive charge on French Hill in Jerusalem). Al-Hindi had probably known some or all of these youth before they had martyred themselves, and, no doubt, like Abu-Surur, thought of himself as their avenger. After Mutau'a had been martyred, Abu-Surur, according to his cousin, had gone so far as to go to Mutau'a's mother and tell her, "I will kill everybody who killed your son."

Upon Rushdi's request, al-Hindi offers a special word to the Cubs of Hamas, the youngsters in the movement, before reiterating a theme we have already seen several times on *The Giants*—military action is not for everyone:

AL-HINDI: I direct a good word to our extraordinary Cubs, whom, Allah permitting, the near future awaits, for such is our call, my beloved.

RUSHDI: Are you in favor of the entirety of the shabab of Hamas turning toward military action?

AL-HINDI: No. Tell them the Messenger, Allah bless Him and grant Him salvation, said, "All of you are on the brink of a chasm . . ." For, as we know, the movement has a number of wings, and each man must remain in his place until the Call assigns [a task] to him, and he is obligated to fulfill it, and everyone will be rewarded. Naturally, the military apparatus, or the Call, chooses the appropriate man at the appropriate place. The Call, as you know, chooses, and the selection takes place outside the occupied land.

Ad-da'wa, "the call," is a key concept in the Islamist lexicon. The major task of the Muslim activist in most Islamic societies, as the Muslim Brotherhood has traditionally seen it, is to lay the groundwork for a future Islamic structure through a combination of education, agitation, and persuasion, all of which can fall under the rubric of *da'wa*. The term is often used to mean a call to action, thus the "call to prayer" and the "call to jihad." The importance of such "spurring on," as 'Abdullah 'Azzam calls it in *Jihad sha'b Muslim* (The Jihad of a Muslim People),[2] cannot be underestimated. Playing on the meaning of the word *Hamas*, 'Azzam writes that there are "two linked commands that cannot be separated relating to the obligation of jihad and they are: fighting and spurring on. Because fighting is dependent on zeal [*hamas*] and kindling emotion and provoking resolve and awakening ambitions and boiling blood."[3] In addition to its meaning as "call to action," *ad-da'wa* can also be used to signify the Muslim Brotherhood as an organization, as in "the Call," and this is the meaning al-Hindi seems to mean here. For reasons that are unclear, he is at pains to indicate that the leadership of the military wing of Hamas is located outside the West Bank and Gaza rather than inside it:

RUSHDI: This is the leadership of the Movement?

AL-HINDI: Yes, the leadership of the Movement located outside.

RUSHDI: The Battalions is an apparatus detached from Hamas and not related . . . ?

AL-HINDI: The Battalions of Qassam is a wing, as we know, of the Islamic Resistance Movement, which is a wing of . . .

RUSHDI: The international movement of the [Muslim] Brotherhood . . .

AL-HINDI: The international movement of the Brotherhood. But every apparatus is separated from the other, and, as you know, the leadership of the military apparatus is located outside.

RUSHDI: Insha'Allah, they will bring honor upon themselves, Allah, Mighty and Majestic, permitting.

AL-HINDI: What Allah wills is above everything.

Rushdi asks al-Hindi if he would like to offer a word to someone named "Abu-Suhaib."

"Yes," al-Hindi replies, "we convey the warmest greetings and most pleasant salutations to our brother Abu-Suhaib."

It is only when Rushdi responds a second later with the words "Insha'Allah, he is with his Lord in Paradise" that we realize that Abu-Suhaib, although addressed by al-Hindi as if alive and well, is actually dead.

"And, insha'Allah, Lord of the Worlds," al-Hindi says, "our meeting will be in Paradise. As the poet says, 'Don't mourn, O my brothers—I am a martyr who has faced my ordeal/ Our time of death is fixed—we will meet in Paradise.'"

The interview draws to a close when Rushdi asks al-Hindi if he would like "to make a comment . . . given that only hours remain before we part."

Al-Hindi replies, "Allah permitting, we will depart for Paradise."

"Allah permitting," Rushdi says.

"We direct a word to the families," says al-Hindi, "and we say to them, We request that the mourning ceremony be a wedding party so that there will be a celebration in Paradise and a celebration in the dunya, Allah permitting."

Only here at the end does al-Hindi depart from the general sobriety that has thus far characterized his last will-and-testament. He would like for his death to be the occasion for a "wedding party," he says. He will be the "bridegroom." The women, he imagines, will ululate. Sweets will be passed around. His mother will be addressed by the honorific *Im-shahid*, "Mother of the Martyr"; his father, *Abu-shahid*, "Father of the Martyr"; and when they think of his death, his body blown to smithereens, bits and pieces of it pulled down from trees and scraped off the sidewalk and collected in plastic bags by the ultra-Orthodox Jewish Zaka, they will express pride, happiness, and joy.

45. Intimate of Heart

Suhail al-Hindi's description of his younger brother's birth in the martyr book he wrote for him after his death is classic Joseph Campbell:

> In Jabalya Camp, in a small ramshackle house, its roof held down with cinder-blocks, on a dark and stormy night at the end of winter, on the last hour of that night, the first of March of the year one thousand nine hundred and seventy three, over the sound of thunder and lightning and the cry of the muezzin calling "Allahu akbar!" broke the voice of Muhammad of al-Qassam, shouting out his first cry.
>
> That day he was born for revenge . . . revenge for me and my country and my people and the honor of my umma. Revenge for Majdal [the name of the Arab town where the Israeli city of Ashkelon now stands] from which my parents were forced to flee, despite their passionate love of its soil, despite their sweat and blood, despite their huge love of its soil. Yes, he will take revenge, he will take revenge, he will take revenge, Allah permitting. And at the moment of this cry, the soldiers of Zion were breaking into houses, searching for cells of fida'yun belonging to the Liberation Army or other groups, as was their wont during that long period in the history of Palestine.
>
> At the moment they entered, upon hearing the voice of Muhammad of al-Qassam, they looked into the face of the newborn and asked his mother, "What is his name?" and she replied in the voice of revenge, "Muhammad!"

The book continues in this mode, the descriptions becoming increasingly baroque. One gets the feeling that the reader has been spared no detail. Here, for instance, is the description of Muhammad al-Hindi as a young man: "His white skin was tinged with pink; his two eyes were set wide apart, and his tongue lent a beautiful sharpness to the letter 'r,' beautiful to the soul"—"expressive" features to which are attributed an almost supernatural power for inspiring ardor for jihad. We are told almost nothing else of the young Muhammad until he reaches his third year at High School "G," where he is said to be "the favorite of his teachers." That year the intifada broke out, and Muhammad "led his classmates in attacking the Jews," and "with their holy stones and their blessed slingshots," they inflicted "numerous injuries" on the Israeli soldiers, whom Muhammad was convinced were afraid of him and the Battalions.

After the attack, Suhail writes, Muhammad was more determined than ever "to fight the Jews and to inflict harm on their spurious pride and their lying heroic mythology." He entered college "in a mood of gentle happiness," for he was "the possessor of a noble soul and a lofty mind," and became "one of the torches of the intifada in Jabalya" and a founder of the Islamic Bloc.

It was only with the help of some of the "armed dogs" of the Shin Bet, Palestinians who had been "brought down into the stinking mud of betrayal," that Muhammad was one day arrested and sentenced to fifteen months' detention in the desert prison Ansar 2. There, despite suffering a high fever and being subjected to "bodily and mental torture," he continually praised the name of Allah and called people to Allah and quoted from the Qur'an and chanted "joyous anthems of truth," and refused to confess to having done anything. The Hamas leadership inside the prison (prisons being organized according to factional lines during the intifada) was greatly impressed with Muhammad and chose him to serve as an interrogator for the security apparatus of the movement inside the prison.

It was in prison that Muhammad met a youth who would change his life forever. Suhail al-Hindi's writing being unamenable to paraphrase or synopsis, we quote in full the section of the book in which he discusses his brother's friendship with Yasir an-Nimruti, a relation he defines in terms of 'aqida (literally, "knitting together"). Although unattributed by Suhail al-Hindi, the section has been derived in large part from Said Qutb's commentary in *In the Shade of the Qur'an* on Qur'an 15:47 ("The Rock")—"And we shall pluck that which is of malice from their chests; [they will be] as brothers on raised couches [in Paradise], face to face":

> And their spirits embraced, and their hearts condensed. Yes, he loved Yasir, and Yasir loved him. Truly, this 'aqida was wondrous in effect. Truly, when hearts mingle, they are changed into a mixture of love and intimacy and affection of the heart, which softens the harshness and smoothes the edges and moistens the dryness, connecting them with a firm, profound, tender connection. Hence, the glance of an eye and the stroke of a hand and the girdling of the limbs and the beating of the heart become chants of familiarity and devotion and support, kindness and consideration. Its secret is not known except to those whose hearts are united, and its taste is not known except by these hearts.

And this 'aqida cries out with joy the call of the love in Allah, and plays on its strings the melody of purity and reunion with Him, and consequently, it was answered. That miracle whose secret is known only to Allah came to pass. "The Messenger of Allah, Peace upon Him, said, 'There are those among the servants of Allah who are neither prophets nor martyrs, whom the prophets and martyrs will deem fortunate on the Day of Judgment because of their place in relation to Allah.' They said, 'O Messenger of Allah, tell us about them.' He said, 'They are people who love one another by the spirit of Allah among them more than those who share the womb. They don't occupy themselves with amassing wealth. By Allah, their faces are of light, and they have light. They will not fear when men fear, and they will not be grieved when men grieve.'

"Abu-Da'ud came forward, and He [the Prophet], May Allah bless Him and grant Him salvation, said, 'Truly, the Muslim, when he meets his brother and when he grasps him by his hand, the sins of the two of them fall away like the leaves from a dry tree in a violent wind, and the sins of the two of them are forgiven even if they be like the froth of the ocean.'" Related by at-Tabarani.

And the two giants promised each other to move forward on the path of raising the banner of Heaven, the banner of aiding truth, and they vowed to take up arms and the rifle to scourge the Jews and their collaborators.

Yasir an-Nimruti was the first of the two to "move forward" and die as a martyr, and when he "went to meet his Lord," he was wearing a pair of "sports boots" that Muhammad had bought for him with his own money, as it is written in the hadith relayed by Abu-Da'ud, quoted by Suhail al-Hindi, "Allah will afflict the one who has not raided, or provided for a raider, or helped the family of one, with a calamity before the Day of Resurrection."

After "graduating" from prison, Muhammad enrolled in the department of mathematics at al-Azhar University in Gaza and, there, quickly became a leader in the Islamist movement, raising the slogan, "Islam is the answer!" at a time when "others were calling for worldly programs such as secularism and leftism and nationalism, which have no basis in godliness," Suhail al-Hindi writes. At the university, Muhammad stood up to the administration, spoke out against the peace process, and protested the administration's support for the nationalist groups. The administration threatened him, but in the end, Muhammad sent its messengers away shamefaced—a confrontation Suhail recounts with great relish.

It was during his university years that Muhammad became head of the da'wa office in Jabalya Camp, with responsibility for secondary school students. "Such was the heart of this Qur'anic man," Suhail writes, "that his chief concern came to be the sowing of the meaning of martyrdom on the path of Allah in the hearts of youth; his chief concern came to be his Call, which his Lord contracted to help prepare him for sacrifice on the path of the realization of its goals." And so, he says, he "made a contract with his Lord to aid it and to offer sacrifice on behalf of the realization of its goals." Besides his work with students, Muhammad would often go out on the streets on his own, and argue with the neighbors about "the nature of goodness." He tried to convince them that there was "a vast and cunning international conspiracy" at work and that "taking up weapons and fighting the Jews" was their only choice. He called upon them to join the Muslim Brothers—whom he liked to refer to as "the Riders of the Heavenly Call."

46. Al-Hindi and Abu-Surur Meet

Reading Suhail al-Hindi's account of his brother's life, one gets the impression of a young man at once angry and idealistic, pious and judgmental, emotional and hardhearted, a youth who held himself to exacting religious standards—and everyone else as well. He particularly despised "those who dress in the *jilbab* [a robe often worn by the devout] and carry prayer beads and stand in the first row while at the same time their hearts and tongues drip hatred on the sons of the Islamic Movement and the shabab of the mosques," writes Suhail. He was constantly admonishing people to be better than they were. Once, Suhail recalls, he rebuked a youth who had just turned thirty with the words, "Review your faith, O my brother, for you have passed thirty years and have not met Allah as a martyr."

Muhammad doubted himself, Suhail offers, because he had not yet martyred himself, despite the double death vow he had made with his friend Yasir an-Nimruti. "I still remember your calling the people beseechingly," he writes, as if speaking directly to Muhammad, "until tears ran down your cheeks such was the fervor with which you plead with your Lord, May He be exalted, to bless you with martyrdom and join you with your brothers who proceeded you, for they attained martyrdom, while you were doubting your faith because you had not joined them."

So, it seems that Muhammad was always thinking of his martyrdom. It was just a question of when. Who knows how long he might have waited had he not been arrested following the kidnapping and killing of IDF officer Nissim Toledano and sentenced to eighteen days in prison. He had sworn to God never to return to prison—"Why not fulfill his oath to his comrade of the road, Abu-Muadh, Yasir an-Nimruti," Suhail writes, "and so meet Allah on the field of honor as a martyr in the land of the olives in the city of Gaza?" And so, Muhammad requested to be enlisted in the Battalions, but was refused by its leadership. Frustrated by the refusal, he finally announced, "No one in the world will be able to stop me from meeting Allah as a worthy martyr whose wonders are mentioned in the verses of Allah and the ahadith of the Messenger of Allah, May Allah bless Him and grant Him salvation." And the leadership relented, and let him in.

Muhammad had heard on the news about a guy named Mahir Abu-Surur who had cut off the head of a Shin Bet agent with his "holy knife," and Muhammad "loved Mahir when first he heard of him," Suhail writes, and "so strong was his love that he wrote a play to show how Mahir was able to save himself from this Jewish pig, and the role of Mahir was played by Muhammad." The play, Suhail tells us, was held in the Mosque of the Rightly Guided Caliphs in Jabalya Camp, and the people who saw it, he says, are still talking about it to this day.

It was in this same mosque that Muhammad, a short while later, spent lailat al-Qadr, "the Night of Power," "in fervent devotion to Allah." On this night, the Qur'an was first revealed to Muhammad; and according to the Qur'an (97:1–5, "Fate"), it is better than a thousand months. The gates of Heaven are wide open, and angels descend to the earth, saluting those who are worshipping Allah as they go. Those who are lucky, it is said, have direct access to God. It is a night of destiny, and Muhammad al-Hindi believed he knew his already.

A few days before, he had taken his university fees—fees that his father had obtained with great difficulty because of financial troubles—and spent them on "something more exalted than the university, more exalted than the life of this ephemeral world—jihad and battle." He had gone to the "merchants of the white weapons" (the phrase referring to knives, daggers, and axes as opposed to firearms) and had bought from them a dagger and a set of knives and other things for battle, "remembering always the words of the Most High, 'Prepare for them that which you are able in steeds and forces, to strike terror into the hearts of the enemies of Allah and your enemies'" (Qur'an 8:60, "The Spoils").

And when dawn arrived at the close of the Night of Power, Suhail writes, Muhammad took the weapons he had bought and "felled three of the sons of pigs and monkeys," and then fearing that he would be arrested, decided never to return home again, "despite the effect that this action might have on the health of his mother, especially due to the fact that she was stricken with heart disease, and she was extremely attached to him." He had "never in his life, not even once, said 'no' to her." Before he left never to return, one of Muhammad's brothers requested that he stay home and complete his studies at the university, rebuking him with the words, "Is it thus the Muslim Brothers have taught you?"

Three days after Muhammad left home, the leaders of the Battalions sent him and Salah 'Uthman to the West Bank. They were each supplied with a pistol and the promise of more suitable weapons once they got to their destination. Upon arriving "at the gates of Hebron," the brother writes, the two came across "valuable quarry"—a couple of Israelis who worked for the taxation department. Al-Hindi and 'Uthman stopped their car, and began firing "bullets of Qassamite fury" at the two, seriously wounding one of them, before taking off. They were followed and overtaken by other Israelis, but miraculously escaped when a car of the same color and model as their own happened to drive by. The car contained three thieves, and it was the thieves who were arrested instead of al-Hindi and 'Uthman.

When the two finally arrived in Hebron, Suhail writes, "Muhammad finally met the one whom he had loved without ever seeing—he met Mahir Abu-

43. Sheikh 'Abdullah 'Azzam, a Palestinian from the village of Silat al-Hartiya near Jenin, the West Bank, was one of the first Arab fighters to join the ranks of the mujahidun in Afghanistan fighting the Soviets; he soon became an influential figure in Palestinian Islamist circles and throughout the wider Islamic world. He is believed by some to have founded al-Qa'ida together with his protégé, 'Usama bin Laden. In this still from a Battalions of al-Qassam videotape, he is shown, weapon in hand, arguing for death "on the path of Allah," a reference to jihad. "Killing and fighting have been written for us," he says, addressing the camera directly, "just as oblivion has been written for prostitutes. It is inevitable that you raise the spear, and it is inevitable that you unsheathe the sword, that you put the index finger on the trigger. And it is inevitable that you die standing on the field [of battle], not under the feet of the lowly and the godless in the depths of the prisons or between the wheels of a car or in a hospital. There is only one death so let it be on the path of Allah."

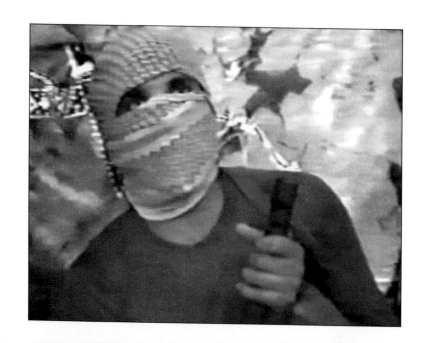

Facing page

44. Intifada videotapes are generally of very poor quality, many having been recorded over pirated versions of movies like *Hulk Hogan Suburban Commando* and *Terminator 2*, themselves often the copies of copies of copies. In this still from an early videotape of the Battalions of al-Qassam, we see a grainy, ghostlike image of a mujahid, masked in a keffiyah and holding his weapon.

45. A weapons training exercise in a grove in the Gaza Strip featured on an early Battalions videotape

Above

46. In this still from a Fatah videotape, a member of the organization accused of stealing under the guise of nationalism has been tied to a rack in a public square in Nablus, the West Bank, and is about to be beaten by masked men in front of a crowd of onlookers. The action was recorded as a warning to others as well as an assertion of factional power.

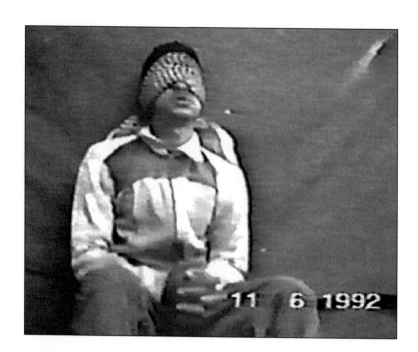

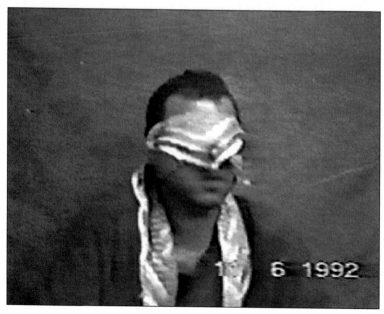

Facing page

47–48. The category of collaborator encompassed not only informers for the Israeli authority and people accused of moral misdeed, but also political nonconformists, backsliders in the faith, drug dealers, social misfits, and ambiguous figures of all varieties. Collaborators were killed on the order of about one every other day in the West Bank and the Gaza Strip during the intifada, with over a thousand attacks directed against traitors, real and imagined. The interrogation of those accused of collaboration was often filmed and released on video. These tapes make up an important subgenre of intifada videos. Typically, they feature, as here, the accused masked and alone against a plain backdrop.

Above

49. Hamas videos often feature long sections in which mujahidun discuss their weapons while assembling and disassembling them. Here, in a safe house somewhere in the Gaza Strip, a weapons expert offers his charges a lesson in "hunting."

50–55. Many of the commemorative celebrations held in honor of the martyrs of Hamas and the Islamic Jihad feature children cast in the role of holy fighters. Sometimes, a child is brought onstage, as here, and posed with a weapon to show that a future martyr is standing by to pick up the torch of his fallen predecessor.

56–57. A crowd of children wearing matching uniforms with caps reading "Allahu akbar" brandish Qur'ans and placards at a funerary march featured on the Hamas videotape *The Lion of Palestine*. The children are later brought forward to offer congratulations to the family of a Hamas member who has been killed in a "martyrdom operation."

58. Shadi 'Eid, 18, delivers his last words before carrying out a so-called stabbing operation. Stabbing operations preceded suicide bombings and involved sending young men from the territories into Israel to stab as many people as possible before they were shot and killed. Although the scene was filmed largely as though the youth were alone in an empty room, with the viewer his only witness, in this shot, we catch a brief glimpse of a sheikh witnessing the would-be martyr's last testimony.

59–62. In these clips from the video dedicated to Shadi 'Eid, the martyr's father extols his son's actions before a crowd in Gaza City. Later, he is carried triumphantly on the shoulders of the crowd, while the martyr's grandfather presents a picture of his grandson to the cheering crowd. Finally, young relatives of the martyr carrying guns and long daggers are posed and paraded before the crowd.

63. A young man wearing a photograph of Shadi 'Eid on his chest moves through the crowd at the martyr's *hafal at-ta'bin*, or commemorative celebration, in Gaza City.

64–65. A number of Hamas videotapes feature plays by Hamas-affiliated theater groups. The acting is broad, loud, and earthy, played for laughs in the style of local soap operas and family dramas. The content, in contrast, is serious. In this still, also from the videotape devoted to Shadi ʿEid, members of the Qassam Battalions work their way up a chain of weak and contemptible collaborators, killing each one in turn. Finally, they confront the chief collaborator and kill him as he cowers before their feet, helpless despite his Israeli protectors.

66. *The Islamic University Festival* features a reenactment of the kidnapping and killing of an Israeli soldier that had recently taken place. Dressed as religious Jews, Hamas members are shown in this still pretending to drive the car that was used to pick up the hitchhiking soldier. By play's end, the kidnappers are laughing as the terrified soldier screams for his mother as they beat and, finally, kill him.

67. Martyr videos often make use of special-effects technology built into video cameras. In this elaborate example, an animation loop, a disembodied arm repeatedly stabs an Israeli soldier with a dagger, like a machine gone mad. The arm is formed from the word "Hamas," while bloody letters above spell out "Allahu akbar."

68. By the end of the intifada, martyr videos sometimes even included coming attractions, as can be seen in this still, which features a mujahid in a tree aiming his gun straight at the viewer and the advertisement, "Coming, the commemorative celebration of the martyr Osama Hmaid."

Oh, my exalted martyr, you are my example

69. Martyr videos had a profound effect on Palestinian society as a whole. The content of what began as an underground medium particular to the armed wing of Hamas had by the end of the intifada found wide acceptance in mainstream Palestinian media.

I'll turn into a suicide warrior in battledress!

70. In these stills from an episode of the *Children's Clubhouse* (13 February 1998), a popular PA-sponsored television show, the hostess sports a Western-style haircut and is dressed in attire Islamists would deem entirely inappropriate—low-cut shirt, pants, and men's wear-inspired jacket.

I have drenched with all my blood

71. Her young charges perform songs whose lexicon has been taken directly from Hamas, all against a backdrop of Mickey, Minnie, and Donald.

72–77. The last minutes of the Hamas video *The Giants of al-Qassam* feature the martyrs-to-be posing with their weapons before they set out on a suicide operation in the Jerusalem neighborhood of French Hill. The posing session soon morphs into a weapons dance with the figures moving trancelike back and forth in front of the camera.

78–80. The trainer's soliloquy.

81–83.

Rushdi: I notice a weapon in your hands that is striking in its modernity. We don't know where you got it or where you bought it because this type is unknown on the market now.

Abu-Surur: By Allah, it is new . . .

Rushdi: Mahir . . .

Abu-Surur: It was booty from the mukhabarat officer, Haim Nachmani. I wanted my friends to have such booty, so that I would be a partner with them, share with them from the outside, and they were sharing from the inside, but fate decreed that they be inside, as I said . . . that . . . it was booty, difficult booty to acquire.

Rushdi: Booty for you or for the Muslims?

Abu-Surur: By Allah, it's booty for the Muslims! In Islam, everything—our lives, ourselves, and everything we do—belongs to Allah and to the Muslims, for without Allah and Islam, it would not be possible for us to exist.

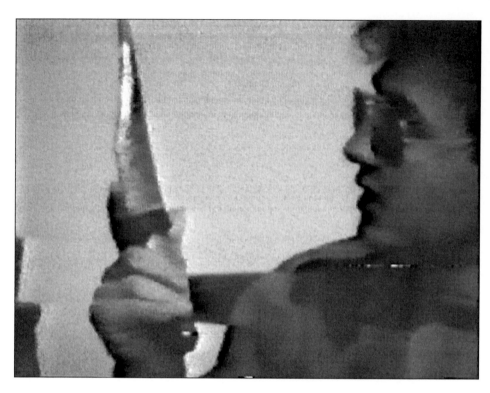

84-85.

Rushdi: Is there something he gave to you to remember him—a gift or something or . . . ?

Abu-Surur: By Allah, there is a very dear gift—a dagger. And he bequeathed me this gift so that I could cut off the head of a Jew or a collaborator. If, Allah permitting, I remain alive long enough, then I will be able to fulfill the vow.

Surur, conqueror of the Shabak [the Shin Bet] and executioner of the mukhabarat agent Haim Nachmani." Muhammad was "able to talk with him about this matter," and when the two were martyred together at last, "their two pure spirits were able to rise together, witnessing to the earth and the sky on behalf of that love, which is of Allah and which is honorable and pleasurable to the Lord of the Worlds, for the Mustafa [a reference to the Prophet Muhammad], Peace be upon Him, said, "Those who love one another for my glory will sit in pulpits of light, and the prophets and martyrs will deem them fortunate."

"Yes," writes Suhail, completely carried away, "this is the love you two shared, and this martyrdom is your martyrdom, O men!" And Muhammad told Abu-Surur "the story of his love for him—even that he had played his part in the killing of Nachmani, so that their hearts could embrace and cry out in one resounding voice—What god could be greater than You who unites hearts and souls even before bodies meet?"

47. Circle and Vow, The Trainer's Soliloquy

On the video, the Giants have formed a tight circle on the ground. Al-Hindi holds a miniature Qur'an in the middle of the group, his arm stiff and uncertain. Abu-Surur and 'Uthman grip their pistols, which they do not seem to notice are pointed ominously at the head of al-Hindi. Dressed in a red-and-white keffiyah, Abu-Surur leads the group in a collective vow, with 'Uthman and al-Hindi solemnly repeating the words after him:

ABU-SURUR: We swear by Allah the Almighty . . .

AL-HINDI and 'UTHMAN: We swear by Allah the Almighty . . .

ABU-SURUR: To depart tomorrow.

AL-HINDI and 'UTHMAN: To depart tomorrow.

ABU-SURUR: Forward!

AL-HINDI and 'UTHMAN: Forward!

ABU-SURUR: To the fulfillment of our demands . . .

AL-HINDI and 'UTHMAN: To the fulfillment of our demands . . .

ABU-SURUR: Or to martyrdom, Allah permitting.

AL-HINDI and 'UTHMAN: Or to martyrdom, Allah permitting.

It had been Rushdi's idea—the vow. He'd first heard it, his brother told us, on an Islamist audiocassette to which he liked to listen. "In Islam, you know," the brother said, "it's a horrible thing to run away." In fact, he said, there is a verse in the Qur'an that says that anyone who runs away in the middle of battle will go straight to Hell. Rushdi, he said, had meant for the vow to make the Giants brave, so that they wouldn't run away.

After Abu-Surur and the guys have finished making their vow, a voice breaks in from the side. "For the sake of raising the banner of 'There is no god but Allah,'" the unseen person says, and the Giants repeat the words in a ragged chorus, before making an addition of their own, "Muhammad is the Messenger of Allah, jihad or martyrdom." "May Allah bless you," says the disembodied voice from the sidelines.

The Giants rise from the circle and, for a moment, seem unsure as to what they should do next. 'Uthman stuffs his pistol back in his pants, and the three stand in a line, with Abu-Surur in the lead. Al-Hindi throws his arm over 'Uthman's shoulder, leaning against him—a buddy gesture. 'Uthman follows suit, throwing his arm over the shoulder of Abu-Surur. He and al-Hindi make the *shahida*, the one-way sign, with their index fingers for the camera, while Abu-Surur holds Nachmani's sleek black pistol high in the air, and smiles and closes his eyes as if in a trance. Looking at Abu-Surur, 'Uthman grins, as if slightly embarassed, as if to say, There he goes again. He catches himself, glances around. No one else is smiling. He stops.

A figure suddenly enters the picture from the sidelines. Hitherto now, we've known Rushdi only by his voice. And it's the voice of someone who tells other people what to do, and they do it—an Oz-like voice, the owner of which you don't ever expect to see. Now, looking at him for the first time, you see that he's gaunt, a little bit older than his charges, quite a bit taller, dressed completely in black. Abu-Surur and the others are delighted to be seen with him and smile madly, as if they've been waiting for this moment forever. They're electrified by his presence. He shakes each of their hands in turn, each Giant holding his hand with both of their own for as long as possible. Al-Hindi doesn't seem to want to let go at all, and so, still holding his hand, Rushdi squats down on the ground with the three, forming again a tight ring of men. They exchange a ritual greeting.

"How is the operation going?" Rushdi asks. "Insha'Allah, it will be to-morrow?"

"Insha'Allah, Lord of the Worlds," the Giants respond.

The section of the tape that follows is fuzzy, the camera having been placed too far away from the subjects. As it's moved closer to Rushdi, the volume increases, and the trainer can be heard saying, "Naturally, you will depart this world for Paradise, and will go to be with Abu-Bakr and 'Umar and 'Uthman and 'Ali"—a reference to the first, second, third, and fourth caliphs, respectively. He wishes the Giants victory, before his voice begins to fade away again.

"Insha'Allah, Lord of the Worlds," the guys answer in a droning murmur.

A fifth and unknown person—perhaps the cameraman—cuts in with a question. "By Allah," he says, "excuse me, my brother Abu-'Aziz [Rushdi's nom de guerre for this operation], what is your opinion on tomorrow's operation and your comment on the situation?"

The Giants listen to every word of Rushdi's lengthy answer as if their lives depended on it. At points, Rushdi starts and stops as if unsure as to what he wants to say, or how he should put it:

> Allah, Mighty and Majestic, says, "Kill them where you find them." The plan tomorrow—Allah, Mighty and Majestic, permitting—is to kidnap a Zionist bus, Allah permitting, in order to exchange . . . although the concept is not simple . . . it seems certain that Israel will never agree to the demands. But we want to make it clear to the world that the true killer is Israel because our demands are legitimate. . . . So what are they doing to a defenseless, totally paralyzed sheikh, holding him in isolation for four, going on five, years? And he really suffers. If there were legitimacy and international legality—as they claim to be democratic—they would have to release him without resorting to these methods.

Rushdi next turns to the negotiations then taking place between the PLO and Israel in Madrid:

> Moreover, we want to make clear to our revolutionary brothers [i.e., in Fatah] that in order for negotiation to take place, there must be a balance of power, because the weaker party in negotiations is always inferior and must always make concessions. So we would like to send this message to the members of the Palestinian delegation who are negotiating empty-handed, as was made clear by the results of the ninth round, or the tenth, which resulted in zero.
>
> And this zero is because they are weak. We would like to make clear to them that there is an alternative to negotiating, endorsed by the Battalions of 'Izz ad-Din al-Qassam, and, thanks be to Allah, Lord of the Worlds, we have laid out this plan, Allah permitting, and supplied the resources, and, insha'Allah, tomorrow, by the grace of Allah, Mighty and Majestic, we will bring the plan to its fullest completion, insha'Allah, Lord of the Worlds.

"Insha'Allah," echoes the fifth voice from the sidelines while 'Uthman can be seen in the background, compulsively rubbing his pistol across his mouth and nose.

Rushdi directs a smile toward the Giants, and wishes them success, "given that tomorrow, insha'Allah—and this is for sure—they will be transported from dwelling in this world to dwelling in the world to come, Allah, Mighty and Majestic, permitting." The Giants, he says, are going to make the enemy, Allah permitting, "drink from the same glass as they made the most noble of all noble men drink, for Israel is continuing its policies—destroying houses, arresting children and old men and shabab. And it continues to liquidate the shabab, and we, the hunted, know that a decision has been made in Israel—its name is, you know, the death certificate or the death sentence with a stay of execution."

They are all marked men, in other words. In fact, he wants to makes clear, everybody alive is marked for death, and death will come to all of them whether in the form of being trampled by a donkey, struck down by a heart attack, hit by a car, falling off the roof of one's house, or being killed by a collaborator:

> And we want to offer a lesson to our brothers, whether they belong to other organizations or to the shabab of Hamas—a lesson that we are writing with our blood in order to make this road clear. And the truth, O brother, as everybody knows, is that there is the one . . . you know, who falls off his donkey and dies, and there is—May Allah postpone it—the one whose donkey tramples him, and he dies, and there is the one who is hit by a car and dies, and there is the one who dies by heart attack, and there is the one who falls off the roof of his house, and there is . . . the one whom—I take refuge in Allah—a collaborator kills, and he dies, but what a difference there is between one death and another, and like Dr. 'Abdullah 'Azzam said, "Truly, there is only one death, so let it be on the path of Allah."
>
> And we have observed this ephemeral dunya, and we have found that it doesn't amount to anything. We wish to meet the Messenger, Allah bless Him and grant Him salvation, and the Companions. We ask Allah, Lord of the Great Throne, that he gather us with them at His noble fountain, and that we be given drink from His fountain, after which we will never thirst again, Allah, Mighty and Majestic, permitting . . .

"Allah, Mighty and Majestic, permitting," the Giants say in chorus.

Yes, Rushdi continues, all this world is ephemeral—it is nothing but "pleasurable deception." People cling to "family and children and home and work and clothing," but on the Day of Resurrection, the judgment awaiting all mankind, "everybody arrives naked, with their foreskins intact, just as their mothers bore them. And a man leaves behind his father and his sister and his brother and his friends and his squadron that has protected him. He leaves behind everybody . . . those on earth who have sheltered him . . . he leaves behind everybody for the sake of his salvation, for his soul, for a man must act for the sake of his soul and for the sake of his salvation in the Hereafter."

The major themes of Rushdi's soliloquy are well known to students of apocalyptic texts. Of utmost importance is the salvation of one's soul. The here-and-now is illusory. People cleave to things that comfort and seem to protect them, but, in fact, they are hanging above the abyss by the sheerest of threads. The real world is not here but elsewhere. Only death stands in the way of reaching that world.

Rushdi next turns back to the subject of family, as though he wanted to make sure that his charges will not be deterred from their mission by earthly ties of love and kinship, the very memory of which, he assures them, will be obliterated at the end of time, when the only thing that will matter is if one is carrying his "book" in his right hand or his left. The *mizan* refers to the weighing scale on which one's deeds will be weighed by God on the Day of Judgment, as it is written in the Qur'an (7:8–9, "The Elevated Places") that those whose good deeds are heavy will prosper while those whose good deeds weigh lightly will suffer.

> For everybody knows that the man leaves behind his mother and that our master Moses left his brother, saying, "O Lord, my self, my self." And we all know the hadith of the Messenger where 'Aisha questioned him and cried, while [his head] was on her lap, and he was speaking to her, and he said, "Why are you crying?" And she said, "I was thinking of the Hereafter. Will our families remember us on the Day of Resurrection?" And the Messenger, Allah bless Him and grant Him salvation, said to her, "By the One who [holds] my soul in His hands, in three ranks . . ." [see Qur'an 56:7, "The Event"].
>
> As for the meaning of the hadith, the lover will not remember his beloved nor will the relative remember his relative. At the mizan, will he see that his mizan is made heavy or light? And when he stands there holding the pages, will he see the pages in his right hand or his left? [See Qur'an 56:8–9, "The Event."] For O, what a difference there is between one who has brought his book in his right hand and [one who has brought] his book in his left hand! We ask Allah the Almighty, Lord of the Great Throne, that we be among the people of the right, insha'Allah, Lord of the Worlds.

That here at the end, Rushdi chooses to emphasize the ultimate solitariness that awaits every human being seems a bit odd, given the fact that the Giants are headed inexorably toward a death they seem to see as the ultimate seal of their love for and dedication to one another. It is a death Rushdi has trained them for, and he offers hope that their deaths will be swift, employing the "royal we," as though he, too, were about to join them. "As the time draws near," he says, "until it is seen whether [one is going] to Hell or Heaven, we ask Allah that we be among those who pass over the earth quickly like a knock or a lightning bolt or like a blink of an eye, insha'Allah, Lord of the Worlds." These are words, one would be forgiven for thinking, that might make someone who was about to die envision a quite opposite possibility.

The long lesson ends with the introduction of another oath of sorts. Quoting Qur'an 6:162–63 ("The Cattle"), Rushdi says,

> "Say: Truly, my prayer and my sacrifice and my living and my dying belong to Allah, Lord of the Worlds. He has no partner. And by that I am commanded. And I am the first of the Muslims. We promise Allah the Almighty, Lord of the Mighty Throne, that we will follow our road to the end, under the shadow of our Islam, under the shadow of the Islamic Resistance Movement, Hamas, and the leadership of the crippled Sheikh Ahmad Yasin, until our goals are realized either through victory and intensification ["winning completely," as Hans Wehr tells us] or martyrdom and the meeting with the beloved ones [i.e., the Prophets and Companions] and meeting with Allah, Mighty and Majestic, May He be pleased with us.

"Insha'Allah," the Giants say together, and the screen goes blank.

48. A Tourist in the Dunya

The family home of Muhammad Rushdi is located in al-'Arub, a little village not far from Bethlehem in the midst of small, round mountains. We went there, bringing with us a small entourage—the former bodyguard of a prominent West Bank nationalist leader, whom we'll here call Ramsey, and his cousin, Yasmin, who'd lived for many years in America.

Muhammad's brother gave us a warm welcome and then led us into a room of sorts, which held some purple plastic chairs. The chairs were hot, for the room had no roof, as if someone had forgotten to finish it, or had run out of money or time or inspiration. It overlooked lush grape orchards below, which during Rushdi's time as a fugitive, had housed six or seven tents of soldiers.

The IDF commonly demolished the houses of militants and suicide bombers, but the Rushdi house was still standing. That was because, the brother said, the Israelis had considered Muhammad to be a real soldier—Muhammad had told his soldiers not to kill civilians, only soldiers, so the Israelis had respected him like a real soldier, and had given him the benefits of a real soldier. When he himself had been in prison, the brother said, a Colonel Smith had said to him, "Look, we can blow up your house, but we won't because killing soldiers is not terrorism—killing soldiers is something equal."

Rushdi's mother and father came out to greet us. The mother was eager to talk. She was dressed in a light blue gown embroidered with white daisies, a thin white gauze scarf was wrapped round her head, and on her feet were sandals with little metallic roses—delicate attire that seemed to belie an undeniable impression of a hard fearlessness.

"Muhammad was one of the best," she said. "There wasn't anyone better than him, and he was the smartest. He was studying in Ramallah to be a teacher . . . studying in an institution. He scored the highest on the general exams."

"What did he study?" we asked.

"Mathematics," the mother said. "He was a teacher of mathematics." He was to be placed in an agency, she said, but then the soldiers started coming for him. "We want Muhammad," they said, and when the mother told Muhammad about their visit and suggested that he turn himself in, he said to her, "I don't want to turn myself in to the soldiers. They'll just abuse me. Whenever I'm in prison, they just abuse me." The next time the soldiers came, Muhammad wasn't at home again. Soon, the soldiers began coming every day, day and night, saying they wanted Muhammad.

"When was this?"

"All this that I'm talking about was three years ago—September 15."

"How old was Muhammad?"

"Twenty-five."

"He was twenty-five years old at the time?"

"No, when he was martyred."

"And how old was he when the soldiers started coming for him?"

"He was twenty-five. And for six months, the soldiers searched for him. They broke into the house—they broke everything. They set off a stun-grenade and tied my sons and me up. They took my three sons to prison. And then one night, late at night, at two in the morning, I saw light from those hills over there in Wadi Surir. And then the soldiers came to the house. They surrounded the house, and they took us all outside, and they took my husband, and they took my brother-in-law and my sons, and they took them to Hebron to show them his body. And they took my other son—they took him to prison. Without reason! Without reason, they took him! Because of Muhammad, that's it!"

"The lights were the battle in which Muhammad died, or lights from the soldiers' jeeps?"

"They were small lights near the settlements."

"This was when he was killed or what?"

"I didn't see them," said the mother. "I saw the lights of a plane."

"That was the battle or what?"

"Yes, yes," the brother intervened, "the battle."

"In the mountains over there," the mother said, "there were planes shooting rockets. That was Muhammad there. He was martyred there. And then from the top of the mountain up there, on the day of his martyrdom, they dragged him from up there all the way to the bottom. There were wounds all over him—inside his stomach, wounds in his head. And he was martyred on top of the mountain. Ahh . . . from the top to the bottom. And there were spines in his stomach."

After he died, the brother said, guys from the Battalions came to the *hafal at-ta'bin*, the memorial ceremony held in celebration of the martyr, and chanted, "Tonight is your wedding night," and "O my mother, don't cry, I am with the virgins of Paradise, and they are calling to me, calling to me"—*yunadi ili, yunadi ili*.

The brother put on a video of the hafal for us. The bodyguard, a nationalist, took pride in pointing out that one of the anthems being chanted by the shabab was actually an old nationalist song about 'Izz ad-Din al-Qassam, based on a poem from 1948. No one could dispute the anthem's nationalist origins—you could do dabka to it. The Hamasawis had made it their own, extracting the forbidden music and changing *Filastiyun*, "Palestinian" to *Islamiyyun*, "Islamic."

The brother had not been at the hafal, the mother said, because he had been in prison at the time.

The brother told her to be quiet.

After Muhammad's death, the brother said, the family had been besieged with visitors wanting to offer their condolences—everyone had heard of Muhammad 'Aziz Rushdi—and they printed as many as twenty thousand martyr cards as mementos for the mourners. People came from everywhere—from Nazareth and Jenin, Tulkarem and Qalqilya. There were buses of people—not just one bus but many buses. And not just for one day did they come. They came in droves for days and for weeks. As long as a month after Rushdi's death, they were still coming. From the day of his release, the brother did nothing but sit at home, shaking hands with people who wanted to touch a bit of the glory of the great martyr Muhammad 'Aziz Rushdi.

"Do you think what your brother did will help to liberate Palestine?" we asked.

"History will tell," said the brother.

On the videos, you often hear the mutaradun say the feeling of being hunted is unlike any other. It is the feeling of witnessing miracles. In the video of Shurbaji from Gaza . . ."

"Yes," said the brother.

"He talks about aja'ib, miracles," we said. "He sees miracles while he is hunted. What is meant by this?"

"You know, every occupied nation, whenever anyone struggles and fights, they look to him as an angel. In Islam, we believe that some guys witness miracles—this happened in history, and it happens now. For Muhammad . . . I was with him, and soldiers surrounded us, and we walked right between them. He was carrying a gun, and no one saw him. No one saw him!"

"They should have seen him?"

"Yes, they were two or three meters behind us—all of them saw us, but they didn't know he was wanted or . . . and he was carrying an M-16." What the brother meant was that none of the soldiers recognized Rushdi as a wanted man.

"What about the feeling he talks about—the excitement?"

"You know, the guys who believe that after this life, they will be in Paradise . . ."

"Did Muhammad talk about Paradise?"

"Yes, all the time. He said to me that there is only one shot between him and Paradise."

"What did he think that Paradise was like—did he tell you?"

"No, it is the Paradise that we read about in the Qur'an. You know, in the Qur'an, there are a lot of images—you can hold them in front of your eyes. They tell you what it is like, how it is. I can't describe it to you because there are a lot of differences between the life of the dunya and the life of Paradise."

"But did your brother ever talk of Paradise?"

"Always."

"What did he say?"

"He wanted it. You know, for Muslims, the greatest thing that you can wish for is to be in Paradise. To leave this life and to be in Paradise—this is the greatest wish of all Muslims. He wanted this all the time, and at last maybe, as he wished, he reached it."

"On the video, your brother says, 'We have seen the dunya, and we have found that it doesn't amount to anything.' But as we understand it, in Islam, the world itself isn't bad—it is a good world. So why do people like your brother say the dunya doesn't amount to anything?"

"You look at the world and see it as a beautiful thing, but for Muslims, the dunya is a small step in the journey of any guy to Paradise or to Hell. Bad guys go to Hell—the good go to Paradise. And really there is no difference in how Muslims, Christians, and Jews describe Paradise. All guys want the same thing—Paradise. You know, Christians and Jewish made a lot of mistakes in their holy books . . ."

It was a common charge made by Islamists—that the Jews and the Christians had changed their scriptures in order to hold back the advance of Islam.

Looking at Yasmin, the brother interrupted himself. "Are you a Christian?" he asked.

"Ehh?"

"Are you a Christian?"

Yasmin was slightly insulted by the question, and corrected him. "I am a Muslim," she said testily.

"Mashi, mashi," the brother said, trying to make amends. "Balash, khalas"—Let's go on—it's nothing—forget about it.

"But if all Muslims feel this way," we went on, pushing the thing ad absurdum, "why don't they seek martyrdom? Then they could get to Paradise immediately."

"But it can't be this way," the brother said. "If all the guys want to be fighters, then . . . This is what the Qur'an ordered us—just to fight in groups, not for all the guys to fight. Because you know, we need guys to cook, to grow food, to prepare everything for the soldiers. So the soldiers are a small group in the world."

"But we get the feeling watching the tape that the dunya itself has something bad in it. There is corruption—*fasad*—and the *ifsad* [the spreading of corruption, the undermining of Muslim values] of the dunya is so bad that you must remove yourself from it."

"No, this is wrong," said the brother. "Look, the dunya is not a good place to be in, but at the same time, we have to live in it with good manners, to behave well. It is not the . . ." He stopped himself. "Look," he said, "in the West, all of you think that the Muslims want to be fighters because they hate the dunya—no. All of us like it, to live in it—to buy cars, to have fun. But to do it in a good way, not making mistakes and behaving badly. We like the dunya—to live in it, to have fun, to be tourists. We like it."

49. A Khanjar, Floating

The sun was getting hotter and hotter. The conversation continued.

"We didn't say all Muslims. We're talking about the people on the video. Your brother said . . ."

"Yes, yes, fighters," the brother said. "You know, the life of a fighter is difficult . . . He can't put his gun away and go to jail."

"So what do you make of 'Abdullah 'Azzam when he says, 'There is only one death, so let it be on the path of Allah'?"

"All right," said the brother, taking up the challenge, "in your life, robbers are killed, spies are killed. They are not good guys. But you can see the difference between the robber and the guy who is fighting to free his people. So, if you want to die, there are different ways."

"So, on the famous tape in which 'Abdullah 'Azzam is speaking with his Kalashnikov, to whom is he speaking? All Muslims or only fighters?"

"He is talking to all Muslims," said the brother, "but the ones who make the decision to fight are only a few. You, in this camp . . . if you want to call them to fight, you can get one or two guys at most. The others are Muslims, but they don't want to fight. You know, to be a fighter is a very difficult decision, and not everyone can choose it. Just special guys. Always, the great guys take the difficult decisions. Always in Palestine, if you talk about fighters, you are talking about tens of guys. Maybe one or two hundred among two million. It's a very small percentage."

Another brother entered the room. A few pleasantries were exchanged back and forth, and then he got right to the point.

"Excuse me," he said, "my brother told me you are from America and working at a newspaper there?"

"No," we said, "we're actually working on a book that deals with the decision people like your brother take."

The brother said that there were several reasons that would lead a guy like his brother to take such a decision. He, too, spoke of Muhammad as being "bored" of prison. Perhaps, he said, Muhammad believed that he would have to spend his life in prison, which would be unfair, he said. Another reason was his beliefs—like any good Muslim, he wanted to go to Paradise. And then there was the occupation. People watched their friends being beaten or killed, and they wanted to save them—wanted to do good things for their people.

"Did your brother ever talk about yom ad-din—the Last Day, Judgment Day?" we asked.

"Yes, yes."

"He believed that these are the last days?"

"You know, all Muslims believe in yom ad-din."

"But did he believe it would happen soon?"

"No, he did not believe it would happen soon. But there is a difference between the day of death and yom ad-din. The day of death is the first step of yom ad-din. For good guys, there is the questioning."

"Munkar and Nakir."

"Ah, you know it." He stopped for a second, smiled, reconsidered us.

"For good guys," he continued, "there is no torturing—they only ask him questions politely, and they open a window for him so that he can see Paradise. For bad guys, hahaha, something else, hahaha."

"Do you wish your brother were alive today?"

"Yes."

"Would you have stopped him if you could?"

"You know, at the time you can't imagine it. Maybe I would try, but there are different emotions that move a guy. Maybe if you hear your brother or your son say, 'I will be killed in a minute,' maybe it is not your mind that moves you but your emotions. Maybe it will force me to stop him at that time. Now, he's gone away."

"Did Muhammad watch the videos and listen to the tapes of Hamas—the anashid, the anthems?"

"All the time," replied the brother; "we had a video in the house, and any time he had he would spend watching."

"So they influenced him a lot."

"Oh yeah."

"Did he have a favorite song?"

"Song? No, no songs."

"So he didn't listen to anashid?"

"Anashid yes, but no songs."

"Did he have an anthem that he particularly liked?"

The brother mentioned the name of a tape. "This was his favorite," he said, "because it talks about Paradise—about a guy that was killed, as a message for him to the other guys."

"Do you have this tape?"

"It was with me in the jail. It was his favorite tape, so I got it."

"Did he have a favorite videotape he liked?"

"No, no, he just watched a lot of them."

"You saw the video that your brother was on with Mahir and . . ."

"Yes, I saw it."

"Your brother filmed it?"

"Yeah, at first, then he went and sat with them."

"Did he have training to make films?"

"No, as far as I know, this is the first time he did it."

"Did your brother have any military training?"

"Just here," said the brother, meaning the West Bank. It was a silly question in his mind. As he would later make clear, a person couldn't learn how to kill. It was an ability you either had or didn't have. Many guys, he said, found it easy to kill; others found it horrible—if they tried to do it, perhaps their hand would shake. For other people, it was natural. Not because they'd done it before, but because they were born like that.

The brother seemed intrigued with the idea, and began all over again. "You know," he said, "some guys are afraid to cut the neck of a small bird. Other guys—I know one of them—he did horrible things. He killed somebody here in al-'Arub. A lot of guys saw him. He cut his neck like a sheep and after that cut his hands off. Cut his arm off and threw it away, cut his neck and pulled off his head.

"What did people say?"

"Nothing."

The sun was falling lower and lower. It was time to leave. The brother gave us some of the commemorative cards that the family had printed in honor of Rushdi's martyrdom, and as we piled back into Ramsey's car, he told us that we could perhaps get some more from a photographer on the other side of the village. We thanked him and set off to find the photographer, promising that we would meet again to watch *The Giants*.

The photographer's house was like an extended dark room—there were no lights, only a few beams of sunshine entering through the front door. We chatted a little, as we glanced around the darkness. The room was largely bare but for videos stacked everywhere and a large knife suspended on the wall.

The photographer insisted on showing us a video he'd recently taken of a Palestinian house being demolished by the IDF.

In the darkness, our thoughts turned again and again to the floating knife. Finally, looking at the very thing we'd avoided making eye contact with for some time, one of us said with studied nonchalance, "Uhh . . . Is that thing a sakkina or a khanjar?"

"A khanjar," the photographer replied, eyeing us oddly. "I keep it to kill Jews."

The guy was clearly trying to see if we were scared of him. We pretended that he'd just said something about the weather, and chatted some more. Then he handed us a portfolio of photographs and martyr cards, and we ordered about sixteen of Muhammad Rushdi and a couple of Mahir Abu-Surur. They would be ready in a few days.

Some of the photographs were martyr cards composed after Rushdi's death—crude cut-and-paste jobs that associated the martyr with al-Aqsa Mosque or placed him at the heart of a map of All Palestine. The others could be characterized as "mujahid cards"—they depict Rushdi as a holy warrior. Known as "al-Kanas," the Sharpshooter, Rushdi was renowned for his way with a gun. People said that he could knock over a stone some ninety feet away. Many of these photographs were actually photographs of photographs with the make-do backdrop—ground or table—clearly visible at the edges of the picture, the negatives, one presumes, having been lost.

In the shots, Rushdi is wiry and muscular—very much the black belt in karate, the star athlete with fifty trophy cups and medals for everything from Ping Pong to netball. He wears black jeans of a type popular in the Bank and Strip—baggy through the thighs, tight at the ankles, low-dipping pockets—and a matching black T-shirt, the sleeves of which have been cut off. In some of the photographs, he wears an Islamic green skullcap, thick white headband, or aviator sunglasses. In others, he has covered his face with a purple balaclava, which matches the T-shirt he's wearing and features a white band reading, "The Battalions of al-Qassam." The head covering is so tight you can see the exact shape of his nose and lips through it. He crouches in a shooting position with a grenade dangling from his finger, weapons strewn nonchalantly over his shoulders and waist, or tucked in his belt—M16s, Uzis, daggers. In other of the photos, he stands erect, cartridge belts draped bandolier-style around his neck like so many necklaces. In one shot, he holds three guns. He can barely support the weight of all of them, and is forced to lean preternaturally backward in order to keep himself from toppling over.

A group of three photographs can be distinguished from the rest. They feel as though they might have been his last. Rushdi is no longer weighed down with weapons—he has only his M-16, his pistol, and two grenades. He is dressed in green pleated trousers and a purple T-shirt, covered by a long-sleeved chambray shirt. It could be the photograph, the way it's been developed, but his hair is no longer coal black but a rusty red, as though it's been hennaed. His shoes are brand new. They are powder blue, almost luminous—and you wonder where on earth a guy could get a pair of shoes like that in the West Bank, or anywhere for that matter.

50. A Second Appearance

The video is nearing its end. The Giants are no longer in the olive grove but rather in the comfort of a house, somewhere in the West Bank. A poster of worshippers at al-Aqsa Mosque adorns one wall. Three chairs garlanded with cartridge belts are lined up against another, while laid out on a coffee table for the eye of the viewer are a collection of Qur'ans and weapons—pistols, guns, clips, handcuffs, knives and daggers, bullets arranged so as to spell out "Hamas of al-Qassam." It must have taken someone a fair amount of time to form the round and sinuous Arabic characters, the sun letters and moon letters, with the hard straight bullets. You imagine them feeling something like beads, smooth and reassuring to the hand.

Now and then, the viewer catches a glimpse of Rushdi and the other guys scuttling around the room, making last-minute arrangements. Snatches of their conversation are picked up over the screech of chairs being dragged across the cement floor. A scratchy rendition of *ar-Radd*, "The Reply," plays in the background, vigorous and resolute like a military march. A baby cries. The camera pans over the motley weapons the guys have assembled, back and forth, for close to ten minutes, lingering over them with fetishistic hunger.

Then Abu-Surur appears. He is dressed in the stolen IDF uniform he will wear the next day on the operation. He offers his name as though we've never seen him before. He is hunted "in Palestine, in all of Palestine," he tells us, "from its river to its sea and from its land to its sky. Hunted for Allah. Allah chose me to be hunted by the enemies of Allah." He alludes to his killing of Haim Nachmani, "one of the most prominent [members] of the General Security Service." He says that the two cousins who helped him kill the agent "will be on white pages that will never die, and when I also am martyred, I will always remember them; I will never forget them." The words have a special meaning for him, one feels, but the viewer doesn't know what it is.

He presents jihad as both a duty and as "terrible," a combination that suggests he thinks of it as something like medicine, as though he might rather be doing something else. "For jihad is incumbent upon us," he states, using the religious term *fard*, signifying a duty, "and it is terrible." "And it is possible that we detest something that is good for us, and it is possible that we love something that is detestable to us, and Allah knows, but we do not."

"Through these words," he says, "it is necessary that we cleave our path to Palestine not through hotels or around tables in Madrid, but we will force it by our bullets and our dark-red blood with which we will fill the streams of Palestine and irrigate its soil so that freedom and glory will grow and so that we will remain with our heads raised not lowered, no matter the circumstances, and whoever says that the politics of the existing matter has forced a solution from here and there, these words have come back against them, for it is a collaborative policy."

Rushdi's next question makes one think that Abu-Surur has only recently been made a member of the Battalions. "Brother Mahir," Rushdi asks, calling Abu-Surur by his birth name, "we don't know, what is your association?"

Abu-Surur begins, and then falters before taking off on a lengthy exposition on "the clash of civilizations." His usage of the term *milestones* refers to the major work of the Islamist thinker Said Qutb:

> My association . . . My association and my sole identity are 'Izz ad-Din al-Qassam. Al-Qassam whom the mountains of Jenin witnessed and the battle of Qastel witnessed, who remained with head held high until the last moment, his raised head showing up Arab weakness. And thus, we are those who are known as the Sons of al-Qassam, the sons of this movement that takes upon itself . . . that takes upon itself the drawing of milestones for the umma and drawing a new map for the identity of the struggle—a struggle that has appeared to be a struggle over land or borders or regions, but which, in actuality, is, as we make plain, a struggle of 'aqida, a struggle of one civilization against another, a struggle of truth against falsehood. Such is our road in the Battalions of 'Izz ad-Din al-Qassam, and such is the road I have chosen with them, and thanks be to Allah that he gave me the gift of being one of the soldiers of Islam, a mujahid on the pure soil of Palestine, just like the jihad warriors among the first Companions [of the Prophet]. And, insha'Allah, we, we and all the mujahidun in this land, will be torches; indeed, we will be fuel consumed by fire to light the sky of Palestine.

"Does being hunted make you feel tired?" Rushdi asks Abu-Surur—surely, one of the more personal questions you'll ever find on a martyr video.

"First of all," replies Abu-Surur, "every man moves from one reality to another, to which he adjusts with difficulty, but we, as Muslims, have been forged, and we adjust to any reality and any circumstance because this is planted inside us. It keeps us firm, and fills us with the cargo of faith and patience and mighty jihad." This is, of course, classic Qutb, who argued that it was 'aqida that gave the Muslim stability, the power to persist in the face of change.

"We cling to the book of Allah the Most High," he continues. "Believe me, were it not for the book of Allah, I would not have been able to pursue this journey, and might have chosen another road, whose end [he pauses and gives a knowing little laugh] is not praiseworthy. We thank Allah for this road, which is a sweet road if you live it with Allah, and a bitter road if you live it without Allah." He pauses, and as the pause lengthens to an awkward silence, he says to Rushdi in a low voice, "Go ahead." Ask me another one.

"I notice a weapon in your hands that is striking in its modernity," remarks Rushdi. "We don't know where you got it or where you bought it because this type is unknown on the market now."

Abu-Surur responds with a smile of sheer delight, if not transport. "By Allah," he says, "it is new . . ."

"Mahir," Rushdi interrupts, suddenly addressing Abu-Surur by his birth name.

"It was booty from the mukhabarat officer, Haim Nachmani," Abu-Surur continues, with growing excitement, oblivious of Rushdi's apparent efforts to stop him. "I wanted my friends to have such booty," he says, "so that I would be a partner with them, share with them from the outside, and they were sharing from the inside, but fate decreed that they be inside, as I said . . . that . . . it was booty, difficult booty to acquire."

"Booty for you or for the Muslims?" Rushdi asks, as if trying to bring Abu-Surur down a notch or two.

"By Allah," exclaims Abu-Surur, "it's booty for the Muslims! In Islam, everything—our lives, ourselves, and everything we do—belongs to Allah and to the Muslims, for without Allah and Islam, it would not be possible for us to exist."

Rushdi requests that Abu-Surur address "a last word to the shabab of Palestine," and it is at this point that Abu-Surur begins the curious exercise of clapping his hands at certain points in his speech.

"Is it necessary for the journey for one to be hunted?" Rushdi asks, bringing up the subject yet again.

"It is not a condition," says Abu-Surur. "It is not a condition. In every situation, you can serve Islam. If you wage jihad with your words, with your bullets, with your ideas, with your wealth, then you are a mujahid. It is not a condition that you be hunted or that you not be hunted."

"And for non-Muslims?" asks Rushdi.

Abu-Surur replies that he hasn't finished yet, and claps his hands again, as he begins to talk of the duty of Muslims to continue the journey until victory or martyrdom is theirs. He then turns to the question of the "uncommitted," saying, "I call on them to open their eyes wide and to use their brains in another way and to reprogram the computer system that exists in their minds until the specific change is in place and, insha'Allah, they recognize the truth. And I heard that there was a foreigner who sat twenty years searching for the truth, then he found it in Islam."

Rushdi brings up the martyrs Hatim al-Muhtasib and Ya'qub Mutau'a. Only four days have passed since their martyrdom, he says. Abu-Surur had been a friend of Hatim al-Muhtasib, Rushdi tells us, and he responds to Rushdi's request for "a last word" with a poem:

> ABU-SURUR: First of all, I say, Patience, my brother, through the pain of separation. Since the fire and the longing remain when our skeletons have decayed and fallen to pieces, still my spirit turns to your spirit in an embrace. That's how we were . . . that's how I was . . . I and my brother Hatim . . . We were friends for the sake of Allah. We were mujahidun for the sake of Allah. We had no aim but that of raising the word of Allah. And we had vowed to continue advancing either to victory or martyrdom. And Allah has chosen for him the more blessed life, eternal life, which is the life of martyrdom and Paradise and the virgins of Paradise [hur al-'ain].

> RUSHDI: Is there something he gave to you to remember him—a gift or something or . . . ?

> ABU-SURUR: By Allah, there is a very dear gift—a dagger. And he bequeathed me this gift so that I could cut off the head of a Jew or a collaborator. If, Allah permitting, I remain alive long enough, then I will be able to fulfill the vow.

> RUSHDI: Insha'Allah, Lord of the Worlds.

> ABU-SURUR: Last, a word to all the men. Everyone longs for martyrdom, but if you want to be martyred and die, then it is incumbent upon you to decide on a noble death, either to die thus or no, a thousand no's. Wa-as-salamu 'alaikum warahmat Allah wabarakatuhu. Your brother in Allah, Hamza Abu-Surur.

Another interview with Muhammad al-Hindi also appears in this section of the video and follows the interview with Abu-Surur. Rushdi seems not to know al-Hindi well. He appears to have trouble remembering his name, and his questions often seem forced. One gets the feeling that he is fulfilling a duty expected of him—granting the last boon of the martyr-to-be even though the martyr-to-be has relatively little left to say. Most of the interview is devoted to greetings to various people and groups.

Rushdi asks al-Hindi first to direct a word to his "brethren," and al-Hindi responds by saying that he has "found the blessing of brotherhood and the blessing of friendship":

> They are our family here, and our beloved in Allah—our friends, without whom it would not be possible for us to do anything, and without whom it would not be possible for us to proceed. Through them and with them, we

proceed to realize our goal, which is jihad on the path of Allah. How else, for Allah commanded us in the well-aimed [verses of] His Mighty Book. "O you who believe! What, when it is said to you, 'Go forth on the path of Allah,' you cling to the earth?! Are you so pleased with the life of the dunya as compared with the Hereafter? The pleasures of the dunya are as nothing compared with those of the Hereafter" [Qur'an 9:38, "The Repentance"]. These are the verses that impel us to jihad on the path of Allah; these are the verses that light our road. How could we not strive for one of the two beautiful conditions—either victory or martyrdom?

Rushdi next asks al-Hindi to address his "believing murabitun brothers in Marj az-Zahur" and after al-Hindi has done so, Rushdi asks him whether he would like to remain in the West Bank or return home to Gaza. Under the circumstances, it seems a curious question:

RUSHDI: Do you want to remain in the Bank or return to Gaza?

AL-HINDI: By Allah, every man wants to be martyred in his original homeland, except there . . . there is martyrdom in Gaza, so the brothers here or the brothers there . . .

RUSHDI: Of course, brother Abu-Hamza [the nom de guerre of Salah 'Uthman] is not with you.

AL-HINDI: Yes, Brother Abu-Hamza left us yesterday and went to [his] station. We ask Allah to send him success.

Al-Hindi speaks next of al-Muhtasib and Mutau'a, presenting the suicide operation he's about to carry out as an act of vengeance for them and for six others who had been martyred a few days before in Gaza. He sends greetings to Sheikh Yasin, and then to al-Muhtasib and Mutau'a, and assures those in the Muslim Brothers and the Islamic Movement that they are in the right. He ends the interview by issuing a call to "all the brothers who have abandoned Islam." "Open your minds," he tells them, "and race down the path of al-Qassam and journey with the sons of the Islamic Movement, the sons of the Islamic Resistance Movement, Hamas, and join its rank, for victory, Allah permitting . . ."

The tape ends abruptly, as though something very urgent had called him away.

51. Any Number Compared to Infinity

After Muhammad Rushdi became wanted, it seems he started something of a killing spree. First, his brother says, he killed an Israeli colonel. The soldiers didn't find him because they thought that anyone who did such a thing would never even think of going home afterward. But that's exactly what Rushdi did. He went home, screaming, "I killed him! I killed him!" and jumped up and down. Like this, the brother said, jumping up and down in imitation.

After that, Rushdi set out to ambush an Israeli car—any car would do. A van approached, and when Rushdi looked through the windshield and saw who was inside, he jumped into the middle of the road and began firing away. The driver of the van, it turned out, was a captain in the IDF named Kubi. Muhammad Rushdi knew him. Everybody knew him—all the young guys. He was responsible for what was called "al-Hashabiya" in al-'Amara, the Israeli detention center in Hebron, which the brother described as something like a big tent with iron flats for a floor. Sometimes, Kubi kept seventy or eighty guys in a small room there. People had to take turns to sleep.

It was Kubi's fiefdom, that little room. He kicked people, shouted at them— anything you can imagine, says the brother. He made them stand with their hands raised above their heads till they thought they would drop. Muhammad Rushdi had been in that room not once but five times.

Everybody turned back to the video. "Can you stop it there for one minute?" we asked. "Where is that olive grove? Here, in al-'Arub?"

"You want to visit it?" asked the brother. "It's only three kilometers from here in a village called Murah Rabah. Near Efrat."

"They were running around with guns right by a settlement?"

They often operated right under the nose of the settlers and soldiers, said the brother. "A lot of times," he said, "Muhammad was hidden in places where there were Jews. There were soldiers surrounding the place, and he was in it. Khalid ad-Dazir, the guy who was the driver of the car at the time Muhammad was killed . . . "

We interrupted. "The driver of what car?"

"The last battle in which Muhammad died," answered the brother. "In that time . . . ," he began and then paused. "Do you know how it happened?" he asked. We didn't.

"All right," he said," in a few words."

The story was long and complex, and sounded like a movie script.

Muhammad and a few other Hamas guys—Khalid ad-Dazir, Muhammad ad-Daqaqa, Ibrahim Salama, and 'Abd ar-Rahman Hamdan—had been preparing to shoot a bus in Wadi Surei'a, not far from al-'Arub, when they saw three soldiers approaching them in a jeep. They shot them, and directly after that, a bus approached them, and soldiers on the bus began to shoot at them. They fled in Khalid ad-Dazir's car—a Peugeot—and after three or four kilometers, they hit a roadblock manned by four Israeli soldiers. The soldiers motioned for them to stop. The group approached the soldiers slowly, and when they reached them, they shot and killed them.

Muhammad Rushdi and the other guys soon discovered that there were a lot more than just four soldiers. Other soldiers began to shoot at them, and as they tried to get away, their car flipped over. By the time the guys managed to get out of the wreck, Israeli soldiers had surrounded the area. They went about ten meters, and then Muhammad commanded them all to run—he would stay and fight, cover their backs. One of the guys—Muhammad ad-Daqaqa—insisted on staying with Rushdi, telling him, "You are injured!" for Rushdi had been shot twice in his left hand. But Rushdi said to him, "I am your leader—you must obey me."

In the end, Muhammad Daqaqa gave Muhammad Rushdi six clips and five or six grenades, and left. Rushdi then ascended to the top of the hill and hid under some big rocks. Meanwhile, Ibrahim Salama, another of the group, had climbed up a tree four or five meters away from where Muhammad was hiding. He had broken his leg in the car crash and had also lost his gun, so he could not escape. He remained in the tree until dawn, and saw everything that happened.

Rushdi fired his gun at the soldiers until he found that he had but one clip left, and when he saw that, he stood up. "He was the leader, and he knew a lot of information," the brother says. "If they caught him, they, too, would know a lot. And at that time, no one knew about him and the other guys. So he made the decision to die. He stood up—he's a tall man . . . almost six and a half feet—he stood up and began to shout to the soldiers, and began to use the word *Allahu akbar*! He told them, 'If you didn't know me, know me now. I am Muhammad 'Aziz!'" And they shot him to the ground. Later, they found nine bullet wounds in his body. And as he lay on the ground, two helicopters and two F-16s came and shot him again, this time with a missile.

"They used fighters and not helicopters?!" we exclaimed.

There were two helicopters, the brother said, but they also used jets because they didn't know how many guys there were. The brother said that he later saw Yitzhak Rabin in a documentary saying that the F-16s had been passing by at the time, and had been recruited for the task of killing Muhammad Rushdi.

From somewhere inside the house, the brother brought out a painting of Rushdi's last stand on the mountain. It was large—probably a good six feet tall and four feet wide. The artist had captured Muhammad well—hairline, widow's peak, beard, furrowed forehead, brown eyes. He stands behind the Dome of the Rock, whose elaborate sixteenth-century Iznik tile work has been rendered by the artist in polychromatic detail. The mosque, massive brown tangles of roots extending from its base, has been torn from the ground as if it were a tree. The platform of the mosque is held aloft by four arms covered with so many veins that they resemble the roots of plants. They sit in what resemble exploded pods. The earth is the color of New Mexico turquoise, fissured, and scattered with blood, red roses, and unspent cartridges. Muhammad Rushdi stares into space, firing his M-16 into the unknown, and the firing is so intense that fire spurts from the end of the gun's barrel. Above him appears an intricately rendered Qur'an held aloft by a disembodied hand that juts straight up from his upper arm. The Qur'an is open and reads, "Our army surely must conquer" (Qur'an 37:173, "Those Arrayed in Ranks"), and above the open Qur'an, light streams from a sun almost occluded by blue clouds and the figure of Rushdi, while lightning streaks across the sky. Rushdi is bleeding, but seems oblivious to the thick, glutinous blood seeping from the hole near his heart. The blood drips in globs over the mosque onto the ground.

They were common motifs in Hamas media—mosque, Qur'an, sun, arm, tree, rose, blood—but the way in which Muhammad Rushdi has been depicted is not common at all. He has been drawn as an angel, complete with wings, which are somehow both massive and wispy at once. Their span is huge—almost four feet wide—and the wings are painted an electric blue bordering on green.

We would later meet with the artist who had done the painting, a guy who did work for almost everybody—the Islamists, the nationalists, even Israeli peace groups—and who had a particular fondness for carving disembodied ears out of stone.

"This is like your brother's last moment, when he stood up," we said. "He has wings like an angel."

"The wings . . . ," he began, falteringly, before starting over. "Our belief," he said, "is that any guy who is killed as a martyr goes to Paradise."

"He becomes a bird."

"No, no, but his soul goes quickly," said the brother. "They take their souls in their throats and travel with them as they make their journey to Paradise."

"What is this about their throats?"

"*Al-hausala* . . . you know, the birds . . . when they eat, they put the food here . . ."

"A crop, a crop in English."

"They put the food and the souls there."

"So this is where the souls are?"

"Yes, they carry them there, but with an open mouth."

"So what do those wings represent?"

"Those wings mean that he is an angel."

"And also a green bird."

"And also this . . . it has a double meaning. And you see that green line?"

"A path."

"That means that what happens to him in this place—fighting, killing, injuring—leads on this road to the light. The light means *al-janna*—Paradise—and it also means a light to our people, to get out of the occupation. This is the light."

The room fell silent.

"Shall we turn the video back on?" someone finally said.

"And we have seen this ephemeral world," Rushdi is saying, "and we have found that it doesn't amount to anything."

"What does this mean exactly?"

"We believe in the Qur'an that this life, all this life, will disappear," said the brother. "All the people will die—there will be no animals, no trees . . .

nothing. Something like a volcano will destroy all the earth. We believe that there will be an angel who will use a trumpet, and when he uses it, all will die—no animals, nothing on the ground. Then he will use it again, and all the people from the beginning of the world, all of them, will come back to life, all of them. This is yom ad-din."

"What does this mean?"

"It's not worth anything," the brother said. "You know, Muhammad said that all of life is like a tree that a man passing, a traveler, sits underneath. All of life is like sitting under this tree. He sits under it, gets up, and keeps going. This small moment—this is our life. Another time he said that this life is not worth anything. If it were worth anything, Allah would not permit the unbeliever to have even a drink of water. Another time he said that this life is not worth the wing of a gnat. These are from the hadith and the Qur'an. Several verses of the Qur'an talk about this."

"Do you remember them?"

The brother recites them quickly and without effort.

"Ha ha . . . wow!" we said.

"That means," said the brother, "this life just tricks guys."

"Which sura?"

"Several verses, this is the surat al-Hadid. About verse sixteen or seventeen. (It actually seems to be from "The Family of 'Imran," verse 185.)

"Are you a hafiz?" we asked, using the honorific for one who has memorized the Qur'an.

"Yes . . . no, not all of it."

"Almost a hafiz."

"A lot of it . . . So this life isn't worth anything. This is one meaning. Another meaning is that all of life, from its beginning to its end—if you want to compare it to the life of Paradise, you'll find that this is like a small moment. You know, in mathematics, any number when compared with infinity is zero."

"Muhammad studied mathematics, yeah?"

"Yeah."

"Did he ever say what you just said?"

"Yeah," said the brother, "he liked that."

52. The Paradise Hotel

No one had thought of Abu-Surur as a poet, at least not while he was alive, for he never let anybody read any of his poems. Perhaps no one should have read them after he died either, but that would have been too much to ask of people who, one imagines, had long wondered what secret thoughts the strange young man was keeping to himself.

"I never read his poems until after he was martyred," his aunt told us. "He used to say that they were only for him, and he wouldn't let us see them." Now that Hamza was dead, the poems had become the sign of a gift; his martyrdom, the seal of greatness. "There was something special in him," said the aunt, "but we didn't know what it was"—didn't know, that is, until he became a martyr.

Our tape recorder was being drowned out by calls to prayer from a nearby mosque when Hamza's uncle, Muhammad, suggested that we drive to the Paradise Hotel in downtown Bethlehem to talk some more in quiet and go over Hamza's poetry. Everyone was eager to go. There were five of us—we'd brought Ramsey and Yasmin with us again. We crammed ourselves and our equipment into Ramsey's little Mazda and set out for the hotel.

Yasmin and the uncle were squished close together in the front seat, but they didn't seem to mind. Yasmin extracted a chocolate bar from somewhere in her purse and shared it with everyone, with the uncle particularly, tearing off jagged, half-melted pieces for him. They were, we observed, actively flirting with one another—despite the fact that the uncle may very well have been Hamas, like his famous cousin, and Yasmin wore blue jeans and acted like the American she was. We stopped on the way to the hotel and photocopied Hamza's poems and also a little booklet that the cousin said Hamza had liked to read.

At the Paradise Hotel, Shocking Blue's "Venus" was playing over the sound system. The lobby was grand with orange marbelesque floors and sixties-style décor—striped wooden paneling, half blonde, half brown; shiny floors, walls, and ceilings. Mirrors were positioned in so many places that were someone to flick on all the lights full blast, you might be blinded. The entire space was highly articulated, divided into segments, everything absolutely symmetrical— light-mirror-light, mirror-woodcut-mirror. The entranceway featured two bookcases on either side of the entry. Two round pictures occupied the space directly above the bookcases. In front of the bookcases were two gold standing ashtrays symmetrically aligned with the cases.

Big wooden dividers embellished with carved deer magnified the effect of segmentation, offering semblances of privacy in what otherwise would have been just a huge, echoic chamber. Oversized Ethiopian canes and decorative khanjars adorned the walls; a glass case held some cycladic figurines. Perched in nooks and niches here and there were the olive-wood carvings for which Bethlehem is famous—the Virgin Mary, Jesus' sorrowful face, Jesus as a shepherd, Michelangelo's Moses—all rather out of keeping, one would think, with the red martini glass tipped and oozing a few drops of liquid that adorned the little sign over the bar reading BAR, everything in the lobby of the Paradise Hotel having been labeled as in a supermarket, as though you might get lost in it—BAR, CASH-IER, and so forth. The counter at the bar was a true work of art with gigantic mirrors and arches lit from below, like some cheesy watering hole in Las Vegas.

Muhammad, we suddenly noticed, was wearing a gold belt buckle featur-ing two stallions facing off, and was flirting with Yasmin again. He had obviously forgotten that he was a Muslim Brother, if that's what he indeed was, and really shouldn't be doing that kind of thing. He said that the main idea in all of Abu-Surur's writing was to bring back the land. Hamza, he said, was always telling his mother that she had run away from Beit Natif, a village near Hebron in the West Bank. Whenever his mother would say to him, "Don't make problems," he would reply, "You can't say anything because you ran away from your land . . ." If she hadn't run away in 1948, like the other Arabs, he would have been somebody—that's what he said to her all the time.

"O.K., which one should we start with?" said Yasmin, spreading out the five poems on the coffee table before her. We all sipped our tea, our cups faintly clinking. Yasmin said she wanted two cubes of sugar in her tea, and this remark triggered a lengthy conversation about sugar. The hotel's specimens were examined minutely.

"You have one, and I have one," Muhammad said to Yasmin, offering her yet another cube. They were at it again.

The uncle said that he kept all the ninety-nine Names of God in his pocket. He extracted from his pants a small piece of yellow paper on which a chart of the Names had been drawn.

Finally, it was decided that the first poem we would discuss was the one entitled "And What Next!!"

> She stood
> She hugged a child
> She planted love
> A burning ember rolled down
> Her cheek
> It landed on the ground
> It dug a hole and there a tree grew
> It stood steadfast, crying out, "Where is honor?!"
> Women screamed
> The screams echoed, "O Mu'tasim!"
> The mouths are calling for help from Salah ad-Din
> Where are the leaders? Where is Farouk?
> ['Umar ibn al-Khattab, caliph and leader of Muhammad's army]
> Ah . . . your days, O Hattin!
> Where is the green land? Where is the arid?
> Nay, where is the arid land and where the green?
> They have burnt it, O my son
> The stole the za'tar and uprooted the threshing floor
> They burned the churches, O Virgin
> They burned the mosque and destroyed the minbar
> They have killed my brother
> The body of my father
> Woe unto you, O settler,
> She convicted him with pointed finger
> She accused the arrogant Arab
> She raised her palms calling for the help of Allah

Mightiest of Lords, Greatest of Lords
Calling for the Merciful to unite the broken ranks of the Arabs
She asked Him to guide her away from the evil of arrogant men
She sat
She was quiet
She hugged a child
A smile broke forth, flowing with blessings
She said, "My Lord, with you I am victorious"
This is fate; this is decreed

The end
Hamza Abu-Surur

The poem is dated 3/3/86—it was written about a year before the intifada broke out. Everyone agreed it was about "the sadness of a child," but other than that, there was no consensus about anything. Muhammad insisted that the poem was written in the third person. Yasmin, on the other hand, thought the poem was written in the first person—that is, it was the boy Hamza who was speaking. But you can never tell in Arabic, she said, referring to the fact that the language has no vowels, the reader forced to rely on small diacritic marks inscribed above the consonants to distinguish one word from another; if the marks aren't there, one simply has to guess.

A second disagreement broke out over the word *nakhwa*, which in classical Arabic denotes pride and dignity, something like munificence; while in Palestinian colloquial, it signifies help.

"Nakhwa," Muhammad said, "is like when somebody stands behind you."

"Pride?" we asked.

"Not pride," said Yasmin. It's like when you say, 'I need money.' And I'll tell you, "Don't worry, my neck is for you. I'll give you the money you need."

"Is it fusha or 'amiya?" we asked. Classical or colloquial?

"Fusha," said Yasmin.

"'Amiya," said Ramsey, having made a secret vow to himself never to miss an opportunity to correct Yasmin.

"It has a different meaning in fusha?"

"Usually the Bedouin use it," said the uncle.

"So it has a different meaning. It is 'help.'"

"Here it is . . . " said Ramsey. "Let us say that Muhammad wants some money from me, and I don't have it. And you come over . . ."

"The Bedouin use it," Muhammad interrupted.

"It's like help or aid?" we asked again.

"It's like help," Muhammad said, "but usually it's like if someone needs something, then another comes and says, Don't worry, I have something for you; I will do everything."

"It's like help to the nth degree. Like sticking your neck out for someone?"

"Like . . . where is the Arabic . . . where is the Arabic nakhwa?" said Yasmin, gesticulating with her hands, palms raised upward. "You're not going to help him like you promised?"

"Like *'arub*," we said, referring to Arabitude, the ineffable quality attributed to being Arab.

"It's like if someone were to say something bad about your country . . ."

"It's almost like honor."

"Yeah, like honor," we said, "*sharaf.*"

"Sharaf?" Ramsey repeated. "No, you can't say that."

"No," said Yasmin, "you don't say, "Where is your honor?" You say, "Where is your . . . your offer?""

It went on for some time like this.

53. The Gun Dance

"I take refuge in Allah from cursed Satan," the masked man on *The Giants* is saying.

He identifies himself as *al-Hajj Barakat*, an atypical nom de guerre combining *hajj*, the honorific given one who has made the pilgrimage to Mecca, and *barakat*, a word meaning "blessings." Palestinian war names begin, almost invariably, with "Abu-," as in "Abu-Jihad," "Father of Holy War." "Al-Hajj Barakat," in contrast, is more self-contained even as it suggests an overflowing munificence. It has a baroque, old-fashioned ring to it.

"We ask Allah that there be a blessing for us," the guy says as though he, too, were about to embark on a suicide operation. He has turbaned his face in a kefiyyah, and wears an Army Rangers-style hat, which he has draped with the ends of the keffiyah, the bizarre arrangement towering upward a comical foot or so into space like the Cat in the Hat. A pair of aviator glasses completes the ensemble. The figure's voice is muffled—it takes you a minute to recognize it as Rushdi's. It is unclear why, here at the end of *The Giants*, he has seen fit to shroud himself in such a getup and call himself by another nom de guerre as if speaking of someone else.

"May Allah grant you life," responds Hamza Abu-Surur, now playing the role of interviewer.

Rushdi launches into a sermon of sorts, which he begins by quoting two verses from the Qur'an—8:12, "The Spoils of War," and 8:60, respectively: "Allah, Great and Majestic, says, 'Your Lord told the angels, I am with you; give firmness to the believers. I will inspire terror in the hearts of the unbelievers, so strike their necks and hit their every joint.'" And he also said, "Prepare what you are able from your forces of war so that you may put terror to the enemies of Allah and your enemies and others whom you do not know but who are known to Allah."

He then offers a mini-history of Hamas. The movement's military apparatus, he tells the viewer, was founded by Faraj Shahada and later called "the Wing of the Martyr, the Sheikh 'Izz ad-Din al-Qassam." "And it arose," he says, "for the sake of the welfare of Islam and to raise the banner of 'There is no god but Allah, and Muhammad is the Messenger of Allah.' It does not desire worldly riches nor glory nor a famous name, but rather is working in secret night and day until it meets Allah, Great and Majestic, so that He may be pleased with it in order that it revive the spirit of jihad in this umma, and, by the grace of Allah, it carried out numerous heroic actions that became the talk of the street, and the heroes began to glory in the Battalions of 'Izz ad-Din al-Qassam."

He says that as a result everyone started to want to be a soldier in the Battalions, and he expresses gratitude to the movement for accepting them as members. "And this is an honor and a gift for us," he says; "we will never be able to repay it, what has happened to us, never in all our lives, and we will never be able to satisfy the debt of its kindness."

"Please, my brother Ahmad," Abu-Surur interrupts.

We ask Allah, Mighty and Majestic," Rushdi continues, "that He make us obedient soldiers working for this Islam and that He place not even a seed's weight of hypocrisy in our souls."

"My brother," says Abu-Surur, "it is often said that the time of military actions has ended and that we are in the shadow of overwhelming powers, enormously strong in weaponry and ordnance and that we are not capable of standing up to it, that we are merely a group, or small Palestinian groups, fighting with our weapons, airplanes, and artillery. How do you respond to that? Please."

"Naturally," says Rushdi, "these words could not be mouthed except by men who have completely forgotten the existence of the Supreme Power, and forgotten reliance on the greatest power, which is the power of Allah, Mighty and Majestic. And if we look to our own trivial strength and then compare it to the power of the enemies, then certainly we would remember, or it may be that we would never set out on any action or activity."

The solution, he says, is to rely on "the power of Islam," "applying the verse, 'And it was not you who smote them, but Allah smote them' (Qur'an 8:17, "The Spoils"). "We know that Allah, Mighty and Majestic, is the one who directs the battles, and if Allah, Mighty and Majestic, is with us, 'Is not Allah enough for his servant?'" (Qur'an 39:36, "The Troops"). "Yes, indeed," he says, "for we depend on Allah, Mighty and Majestic, in the beginning and the end; as for putting our reliance on something other than the mightiest power, we say that it will come to nothing very shortly and will be trodden underfoot by the Muslims, Allah, Mighty and Majestic, permitting. This is the promise of Allah, Mighty and Majestic, in His Book, and Allah will never fail to keep His promise."

"Insha'Allah," responds Abu-Surur. "With regard to what we're aspiring to, my brother, a last question puts itself forward. The Madrid negotiations, in fact, are the topic of the moment. It is well known that the Israeli hornet doesn't give honey, but rather death. It is constantly trying to get the world to believe that it wants peace, so what is your reply, in the shadow of an occupation whose right hand is extended in greeting, while in its left hand it carries a knife and a dagger to stab us and end our dream?"

Such negotiations, Rushdi says, "are tantamount to negotiations between Israel and those who obey them—Israel or, rather, those whom Israel nominates for negotiating with them." In contrast, "those who [truly] represent this people," he says, "are those who live among us, whereas those who are talking in the name of this people are those afflicted with woe after woe"—a jab against Yasir Arafat and the nationalist leadership, which had recently returned to the Strip after many years of exile in Tunisia.

Connecting the ninth round of negotiations with an increase in the number of martyrs and demolished houses, Rushdi says, with pride, "In little more than eighteen days, the number of martyrs has reached thirty-five, and this number did not exist in the past, and we have never seen a number like this except under the shadow of negotiations"—a sign, he believes, that Palestinians have finally become their own authority. "And if Allah is with you, he will never let you fail," he continues, quoting from the Qur'anic chapter entitled "Muhammad" (47:35). In the end, he says, the "comedy" of the Madrid negotiations "will result in failure." It is inevitable.

Abu-Surur notes that recent slogans have pointed to the fact that "the solution to the crisis has collapsed." That, Rushdi says, is because such a solution "carried within itself the causes of its collapse, because it is far away from the program of the Lord of the Worlds."

Before closing, Rushdi displays some weapons in the possession of the Battalions, even demonstrating how to use a couple of them, if unsuccessfully. He touches each of them. Among them are an M-16 "of the dangerous advanced type," several clips, the pistol of "the treacherous Haim Nachmani," a rocket that was seized from an Israeli military barrack (it will be stored away, he says, for "a great day, a black day, for them, insha'Allah"), a .22 rifle with no bullets, a grenade, and some older weapons described as of Turkish and Canadian make. In case people get the wrong idea and feel that Rushdi is exhibiting too much pleasure in handling these instruments, he takes pains to add that they "are worthless without Allah, Mighty and Majestic, granting them success because we do not shoot them except that we say, 'O Allah, we take aim!' because it is Allah, Mighty and Majestic, who directs our shooting."

"In your opinion, my brother," Abu-Surur asks Rushdi, "what will be here after these rockets?"

"Insha'Allah, Lord of the Worlds," Rushdi replies, "victory is from Allah, and he will remove the suffering from all the Muslims, insha'Allah."

"And a speedy conquest, insha'Allah," adds Abu-Surur.

"Insha'Allah, Lord of the Worlds," says Rushdi.

"Thank you, my brother," says Abu-Surur, "and may Allah grant you life."
Rushdi responds in kind, despite the fact that Abu-Surur will be dead by the morrow.

"Allah permitting," says Abu-Surur. "Goodbye."

At the end of the interview, Rushdi gets up and begins arranging the room for another presentation. To the accompaniment of Hamas anthems blaring from a pocket tape player, the three Giants choreograph a bizarre dance of weapons as if they were Sufis in trance. At one point, Abu-Surur, in the lead and sporting one of his trademark headbands, even takes the rocket for a round. Intoxicated by their coming glory, they circumambulate the table, their guns held aloft. They gaze at the weapons as though they were ritual objects. They caress them—are one with them. Cold, hard, inanimate, immune to pity, they are everything they will need to be as they head off to kill a whole lot of people.

54. A Few Hours Later;
or, The Trail of a Dagger

On July 1, 1993, around 6:45 in the morning, Abu-Surur, 'Uthman, and al-Hindi board Egged bus #25, on French Hill, a fortresslike Jerusalem neighborhood of white limestone apartments not far from the Mount Scopus campus of the Hebrew University of Jerusalem.[4] Abu-Surur is heavily armed and dressed like an IDF soldier on leave. He wears fatigues and carries a duffel bag. More specifically, he is meant to look like an IDF soldier who is also a new immigrant from Russia, a deception that may have enabled him to get into the capital when the West Bank and Gaza were under military closure. 'Uthman, in the guise of an Israeli student—jeans, sunglasses, close-cropped hair, backpack—seats himself directly behind the bus driver, while Muhammad al-Hindi, dressed as an Israeli businessman, gets on at the back of the bus. Besides their weapons, they carry with them a leaflet demanding the release of Sheikh 'Abdul Karim Obeid, a leader of the Hizbullah in Lebanon, who in July 1989 had been kidnapped by the IDF under the cover of an early morning mock jet attack and was being held in an undisclosed location in Israel.

What happens after the three board the bus is unclear. According to David Yom-Tov, the bus driver, Abu-Surur points his gun at him, and although he is unarmed, Yom-Tov jumps him, but not before Abu-Surur gets off some shots, hitting him in the thigh. Olga Khaikov, a new immigrant from Russia, is killed in the melee. The double bus continues on its way, eventually jackknifing in the middle of the street. People fall out of the doors onto the ground, screaming. Abu-Surur and al-Hindi flee, leaving behind their bombs, which later end up in the police's Department of Lost and Found, both sappers believing that the other had searched the bus. They also leave behind Salah 'Uthman, who has been shot in the head. Along with the other injured passengers, he is rushed to Hadassah Hospital in 'Ein Kerem, where Israeli doctors in the neurosurgery intensive care unit manage to save his life. For days thereafter, he will lie in bed, answering all questions with "Allah be praised" and "Allahu akbar!"

Pretending to be Israeli policemen, Abu-Surur and al-Hindi begin to search for a getaway car. Abu-Surur carries a pistol engraved with the word "Hamas," as well as a bag of grenades and explosives; al-Hindi carries an M-16 assault rifle. Walking the streets around the bus, the two stop to speak to a number of people, including a woman standing outside her apartment, an armed school guard, and worshippers at a nearby synagogue on Mifratz Shlomo Street. "There are terrorists around," Abu-Surur tells them in perfect Hebrew. "Get inside your houses!"

From the hilltop vantage point of the synagogue, they spy a woman getting into a Renault 5 on Midbar Sinai Street in the neighborhood of Givat Hamivtar. Jeanette Kadosh-Dayan, a teacher from Ramot Eskol, has been preparing for the bar mitzvah of one of her sons to be held the following day. Abu-Surur and al-Hindi force her at gunpoint to take them with her. Taking Hebron Road past the Old City, they direct her to drive to the military checkpoint at Gilo Junction on the way to Bethlehem, where she frantically waves her hands at the soldiers. According to some reports, the soldiers believe that she is about to throw a grenade at them and shoot her. According to other reports, Abu-Surur and al-Hindi shoot her in the legs, but she manages to continue to drive until they shoot her again and throw her body out of the car. Still others say that she tries to escape by jumping out of the car.

Abu-Surur and al-Hindi fire at the soldiers and toss hand grenades at them. The grenades fail to explode. The soldiers open fire. The car goes out of control, traveling for some twenty meters or so before colliding with a tree and blowing up. After the fire is extinguished, explosive devices are found, as well as an M-16, a knife, Qur'an, pistol, and the bodies of Abu-Surur and al-Hindi, charred virtually beyond recognition.

Before setting out that morning, Abu-Surur had given Muhammad Rushdi two gifts—Haim Nachmani's pistol and the dagger given him by the martyr Hatim al-Muhtasib on condition that it be used "to slit the throat of a collaborator or a Jew." Rushdi is now the steward of the dagger, and he will be the next to die.

Meanwhile, back in the camps, there is another boy waiting in the wings to take his place, waiting for the dagger, which by now has passed through many hands. He, too, wants to fulfill the script, to become an exploding star on a black night. He, too, is smiling.

■

A Brief Glossary of Terms

Ansar   Israeli military prison in the Negev desert created to house Palestinian detainees during the intifada

'aqida   creed, doctrine, tenets of belief

ard al-Isra'   an Islamist term for Palestine that references Muhammad's ascension to heaven from al-Aqsa Mosque in Jerusalem

'Azzam, 'Abdullah   leader of the Palestinian "Afghans," those Arabs who went to Afghanistan in the late 1970s and 1980s to make jihad against the Soviet Union; former mentor of 'Usama bin Laden; and, according to some, co-founder of al-Qa'ida

basmala   the invocation "In the name of Allah, the Compassionate, the Merciful," used by pious Muslims to initiate any significant act

Battalions of the Martyr 'Izz ad-Din al-Qassam   the military wing of Hamas

bid'a   innovation—the sin of introducing new concepts into Islam that have no basis in the Qur'an or sunna

caliph   a title used by early Islamic rulers to signify the deputy or successor to the Prophet Muhammad

Companions of the Prophet   the early converts to Islam who became the leaders of the Muslim umma during the lifetime of the Prophet and immediately thereafter

dabka (Palestinian colloquial, dabkih)   a folk dance in which men join hands and stamp their feet to the rhythm of a song—a tradition firmly rooted in Palestinian folk culture and, accordingly, eschewed by Islamist groups like Hamas

Dajjal   a figure from Islamic eschatology similar to the Christian Antichrist, whose end-time drama will take place in and around Jerusalem and environs. Also known as "the one-eyed Dajjal" and "the Lying Liar"

da'wa   the call to Islam, evangelism; also the name of the propaganda arm of Hamas

Democratic Front for the Liberation of Palestine (DFLP)   a Marxist-Leninist group that split from the larger Popular Front for the Liberation of Palestine in 1969. The group split again in 1991 with one faction allying itself with Arafat and the other, headed by Naif Hawatma, maintaining a rejectionist stance

dunam   a unit of land measurement equivalent approximately to a quarter of an acre

dunya   the earthly world as opposed to *al-akhira*, the Hereafter

fasad   corruption or depravity, often attributed in Palestinian Islamist discourse to the Jews

Fatah   the dominant subgroup within the Palestine Liberation Organization, founded in 1965, and led since its inception by Yasir Arafat

fatwa   a formal legal opinion or verdict in Islamic law

fida'i (pl., fida'yun)   self-sacrificer, commando

fitna   schism and confusion, with strong religious, sometimes apocalyptic, associations

Gaza Strip   a thin slice of land consisting of 163 square miles, bordered by Egypt, Israel, and the Mediterranean Sea and inhabited by approximately one million Palestinians, most of them refugees from the 1948 war. Previously administered by Egypt, the territory fell to Israel in the 1967 war

Green Line   the cease-fire line of 1949 separating Israel from the West Bank, which was held by Jordan until the war of 1967, and Gaza, which was under the control of Egypt until that same war

guna   the traditional long, black garment worn by women in the Gaza Strip

hadith (pl., ahadith)   the collected sayings and acts of the prophet Muhammad and the first Muslims

hafal at-ta'bin   a memorial ceremony held in celebration of a martyr

hafiz   the honorific awarded one who has memorized the Qur'an

hajj   the annual pilgrimage to Mecca, the fifth pillar of Islam

Hamas   the acronym for the Islamic Resistance Movement, meaning "zeal." Founded shortly after the outbreak of the intifada in 1987, as the armed wing of the Muslim Brotherhood in Palestine, Hamas quickly became second only to Fatah in political power. Its ideology calls for the elimination of Israel and its replacement with an Islamic state

Hashaf   the acronym for the Palestinian People's Party (PPP), formerly the Palestinian Communist Party. A small Marxist faction maintaining a non-violent strategy in its confrontation with Israel

Hattin   a hilltop above the Sea of Galilee where the Muslim army under the Kurdish leader Salah ad-Din defeated the Crusaders in a decisive battle in 1187

hur al-'ain (or houris)   the dark-eyed virgins of Paradise

ifsad   the spreading of corruption, the undermining of Muslim values

insha'Allah   Allah willing

intifada   the Palestinian revolt against Israeli rule that began in December 1987, and ended, arguably, with the signing of the Oslo Accords in 1993. The word is derived from an Arabic root with the connotation of "shuddering" or "shaking off"

Islamic Jihad   A radical Islamist group that rejects any compromise with Israel, demanding the eradication of the state. It split from the Muslim Brothers around 1980. While much smaller than the rival Hamas, the group has carried out numerous suicide bombings in Israel and the Palestinian territories

al-Isra' wa al-Mi'raj   Muhammad's midnight journey from Mecca to Jerusalem, and thence to heaven and back again to Mecca in the course of one night

jihad   holy war

Kauthar   abundance, bounty—a fountain in Paradise

khanjar   a curved dagger with a double-sided blade, a common symbol of masculine pride in parts of the Arab world

al-kifah al-musallah   armed struggle, a nationalist phrase indicating the means by which the nationalist groups believe that Palestine will be liberated

mahr   an obligatory gift of money, property, or possessions made by the groom to the bride, usually at the time of their marriage

mawwal   the chanted introduction to a song or anthem, plaintive in tone

minbar   pulpit

mithaq   covenant, used herein to refer to the founding document of Hamas

mizan   the weighing scale on which the deeds of humans will be measured by God on the Day of Judgment

mulaththamun   masked ones, a term used by Palestinians to refer to members of Palestinian strike forces operating in masks or hoods

mujahid (pl., mujahidun)   holy warrior

mukhabarat   security service—a catch-all term used by Palestinians to denote a number of Israeli (and later, Palestinian) security organizations

musta'ribun   those who pretend to be Arab. Name given by Palestinians to Israeli Special Forces who dress as Arabs in order to catch wanted men

mutaradun   the hunted, a reference to Palestinians wanted by the Israeli security services

al-Mu'tasim   'Abbasid caliph (833–842 CE), said to have heard a Muslim woman cry out, "O al-Mu'tasim!" after her honor was violated in a Byzantine prison a thousand miles away. Al-Mu'tasim mustered up an army and redeemed her honor, announcing upon arrival, "Labaik, Labaik!" "At your service, at your service!"

nashid (pl., anashid) anthem sung by men with minimal instrumental accompaniment, musical instruments being considered un-Islamic by Hamas and other Islamist groups

Palestine Liberation Organization (PLO) organization founded in 1964 and since 1968, headed by Yasir Arafat, with a nominal legislative body of three-hundred members and a powerful fifteen-member Executive Committee. The long-time goal of the organization was the "liberation" of Palestine through armed struggle and the creation of an Arab state of Palestine, but since 1988, its goal has been a two-state solution to the Israeli-Palestinian conflict; following the signing of the Oslo Accords, the organization eliminated the clause in its charter calling for the destruction of Israel

Palestinian Authority (PA) governing authority in the West Bank and Gaza Strip established as part of the Oslo Accords between the PLO and Israel with the understanding that it would become the basis for a future independent Palestinian state

Popular Front for the Liberation of Palestine (PFLP) founded in 1967 by George Habash as a Marxist movement calling for the liberation of all of Palestine and the destruction of Israel as well as many traditional Arab states that it considers reactionary and oppressive. The PFLP split from the PLO in 1993 in opposition to Fatah's decision to open a political track with Israel. The fall of the Soviet Union and the collapse of Marxism as a compelling world system has relegated the PFLP to the status of a minor player in the West Bank and Gaza

Popular Front for the Liberation of Palestine-General Command rejectionist offshoot of the PFLP founded in 1968 by Ahmad Jibril

Qutb, Said seminal Islamist thinker, Muslim Brother, and author of *Milestones* (1965), arguably, the manifesto of modern political Islam. He was executed by the Egyptian government in 1966

Salah ad-Din Kurdish leader who defeated the Crusaders and founded the Ayyubid dynasty that ruled over what is today Syria, Iraq, Egypt, and Yemen, long used in Arab polemics as a symbol of the eventual vanquishment of the Jewish state

shabb (pl., shabab) young guy—a term used by Palestinians to refer to a street activist of the intifada

shahada the testimony of faith, one of the five pillars of Islam—"There is no god but Allah, and Muhammad is the Messenger of Allah." The word also means martyrdom

shahid (pl., shuhada') martyr

shahida a term meaning both tombstone and index finger, and in the media of Hamas, trigger finger as well. In addition, it is the name given to the "one-way sign," the fist with the index finger raised heavenward, used by Islamist activists to signify their allegiance to the ideology of the Islamic Movement

sharia the corpus of Islamic law based on the Qur'an, the sunna, and the work of the Muslim jurists, in that order. Islamists want to replace legal systems based on civil law with sharia

shibariya a knife like the khanjar but whose blade is longer and straighter

Shin Bet the Israeli domestic counterintelligence and internal security agency

shirk the attribution of partners to God, one of the gravest sins in Islam and a capital offense under sharia

shuq a Jewish open-air market

sunna the words and deeds of the prophet Muhammad

suq an Arab open-air market

tafsir commentary on and exegesis of the Qur'an

umma the Islamic community, based neither on ethnicity nor geography but rather on faith. Conceived by Hamas and groups like it as serving as the basis for an Islamic state under the rule of a resurrected Islamic caliphate

Waqf property held in common as an endowment as regulated by Islamic law

West Bank an area of land, consisting of 5,640 square miles, located west of the Jordan River. The territory fell to Israel in the 1967 war, and was previously administered and claimed by the Hashemite Kingdom of Jordan.

yom ad-din Judgment Day

zaghrada   a high-pitched wailing sound made by women upon the entrance of a bride and groom at their wedding and on other joyous occasions

zajal (pl., azjal)   metrical folk verse sung in colloquial Arabic

za'tar   an aromatic mixture of spices containing thyme, sumac, toasted sesame seeds, and salt, often mixed with olive oil and used as a dip for pita

Notes

INTRODUCTION

1. The twice-amended (1977, 1987) military order no. 101 of 1967 prohibits "acts of incitement and hostile propaganda." See also the "Order Concerning Security Instructions (Judea and Samaria)" (no. 378) of 1970 amended in the early 1980s, in which "information" is defined as "including false information and any description, plan, slogan, sign, formula, object or any part thereof containing information or liable to constitute a source of information." Also of relevance is the "Tamir law," a 1980 amendment of the 1948 Prevention of Terrorism Act, according to which one who publishes "in writing or orally, words of praise or sympathy for, or an appeal for aid or support of, a terrorist organization" is guilty of a criminal offense punishable by up to three years in prison, a fine, or both.

2. It is interesting to note here some of the recommendations of the American Association of Suicidology for reducing what it calls "cluster suicides" and "suicide contagion"—"reporting should be concise and factual, minimizing repetitive, ongoing or excessive reporting of suicide; limiting morbid details and sensationalism; and avoiding 'how-to' descriptions of suicide." According to other recommendations of the organization, news stories about suicide should not be printed on the front page, the word *suicide* should not be included in the headline, a picture of the person who committed suicide should not appear in print, details of the method of suicide should not be given, and the suicide should not be presented as

le. See <http://www.afsp.org/education/recommendations/5/
>.

riginally from the village of Silat al-Hartiyeh near Jenin, the West Bank,
'Azzam graduated from Cairo University with a degree in Islamic law and,
like many of the members of Islamist movements, began his political career
in Fatah before becoming disenchanted and joining the Muslim Brotherhood at a young age. He played a key role in the recruitment of young Palestinian and other volunteers throughout the Muslim world to the mujahidin
of Afghanistan, traveling widely in pursuit of members. He lived in the United
States for a while, where he was something of a Muslim celebrity and was
accompanied by four or five bodyguards wherever he went.

4. "Martyrs: The Building Blocks of Nations." <http://www.religioscope.com/
info/doc/jihad/azzam_martyrs.htm>.

5. In *Jihad sha'b Muslim*, 'Azzam describes the Muslim's struggle against the
Russians as an "intifada," thus linking the Afghani war and the Palestinian
revolt. In a chapter entitled "The Seven Historical Intifadas," he attempts
to lend *intifada*, a word rarely used prior to the Palestinian uprising, an
Islamist genealogy by applying it to Muslim battles fought in south Asia
over the centuries.

6. <http://english.aljazeera.net/NR/exeres/8BC5C846-1B3A-424E-BC65-
65CF2917989E.htm>.

PART ONE ■ Saint Yasin

1. For books on Gaza, see also G. F. Hill's translation of Mark the Deacon's
Life of Porphyry, Bishop of Gaza and Downey's *Gaza in the Early Sixth Century*, which attempts to chronicle Greek-Christian thinkers in the Strip
during the Byzantine period.

2. Interview with the authors; Gaza City, 1989.

3. <http://www.religioscope.com/info/doc/jihad/azzam_caravan_6_?
conclusion.htm>.

4. *The Finality of Prophethood* (Lahore: The Islamic Publications, Ltd., 1962).
See <www.usc.edu/dept/MSA/fundamentals/prophet/finalprophet.html>.

5. We rely on 'Adwan's biography of the sheikh throughout this section. The
book was published in 1991 by the Islamic University of Gaza.

6. As Shai Lachman points out in his essay "Arab Rebellions and Terrorism
in Palestine 1929–39: The Case of Sheikh Izz al-Din al-Qassam and His
Movement," al-Qassam's was one of the few mass movements in Palestine
at the time not organized around existing power structures—that is, around
the Husaini and Nashashibi clans and the religious establishment—but
rather on the idea of a purified and militant Islam. See *Zionism and Arabism
in Palestine and Israel*, eds. Elie Kedourie and Sylvia G. Haim (London:
Frank Cass, 1982), pp. 61–78.

In the covenant of Hamas, al-Qassam is cited as the first link in the jihad against "the Zionist aggression": "And Hamas is a link amongst the links of jihad against the Zionist aggression, connected and bound by the uprising of the Martyr 'Izz ad-Din al-Qassam and his brothers amongst the mujahidun [those engaged in jihad] of the Muslim Brethren in 1936 [sic] and continues with other links including the Palestinian struggle and the efforts of the Muslim Brethren in the war of 1948 and the jihad activities of the Muslim Brethren in 1968 and that which followed."

7. Many within the leadership of Hamas insist on the authority of commands rather than commanders. Responding to a question on the leadership of Hamas by a journalist from *Filistin al-Muslima*, Dr. Mahmud Zahar asserted, for example, that Hamas is led only by God and holy text:

> Everybody wants there to be leaders in Hamas; Israel wants there to be leaders [in Hamas]; indeed, many Palestinian tendencies want there to be leaders inside Hamas. I assure you that the likes of these leaders do not exist and, Allah willing, they will never exist. This is because any issue that comes up is settled by referring it to Allah—"And in that which you disagree, refer it to Allah." And so we refer everything to Allah and to the *sunna* [the words and deeds of the prophet Muhammad] of the Messenger.

See "*az-Zahar li-Filistin al-Muslima,*" *Filistin al-Muslima*, November 1994, p. 18.

8. Qur'an 9:14, "Repentance."

9. The name was originally used by Israelis to refer to soldiers of the Palmach—the strike force of the Haganah, the military wing of the Jewish leadership during the British mandate of Palestine, whose members (which included Moshe Dayan and Yitzhak Rabin) often masqueraded as Arabs in order to scout out locations and carry out sabotage operations against Axis forces in Syria and Lebanon.

10. Throughout this section, we have relied on a number of reports, especially, Serge Schmemann, "Release of a Hamas Leader: A Tangle of Mideast Intrigue," *New York Times*, October 2, 1997, and "Israelis Bemoan Failed Attempt on Hamas Official," *NYT*, October 6, 1997; Alan Cowell, "The Daring Attack that Blew Up in Israel's Face," *NYT*, October 15, 1997; and *Jerusalem Post* staff, "Hussein Calls Attack on Mashaal 'Reckless,'" *Jerusalem Post*, October 5, 1997.

PART TWO ■ The Portfolio

1. The traditional symbol of the Evil Eye, which is still used by both the Jewish and Arab inhabitants of Israel and the territories as a talisman against envy, achieved a political transvaluation during the intifada. It was commonly used

by Fatah activists to symbolize vigilance as well as to warn potential wrong-doers, as in their well-known byword, "The eyes of Fatah never sleep," a slogan that Hamas often generalized and applied to itself. Compare the "Verses of the Throne," Qur'an 2:255, in which it is written, "Allah. There is no god but He, the Living the Eternal. He neither slumbers nor sleeps. To Him belongs all that is in the heavens and the earth."

2. The *safina al-khalas*, or "Ship of Salvation," is a traditional Islamic design which has its roots in the Qur'anic story of Nuh (Noah). Arab calligra-phers often transmute the *basmala* and verses from the Qur'an into the shape of the Ship. For Palestinians, the figure has gained the added mean-ing of *safina al-'auda* or "Ship of Return," a reference to the "inalienable right" of all Palestinians to return to their homes lost to Israel in 1948. The symbol was brought to life in dramatic fashion in February 1988, when the PLO chartered the Sol Phryne—dubbed "the Return"—to carry 130 Palestinian deportees to Haifa. The ship was disabled by an explosion, re-portedly set by the Mossad, as it sat in the harbor of Limassol, Cyprus.

3. Song two, side one of *The Call of Jihad*.

4. The Tatars were a Turkic people who conquered the Muslim heartland in the thirteenth century ce. The influential medieval cleric ibn Taymiyya issued fatwas stating that although the Tatars claimed to be Muslims—they converted to Islam—their behavior put them outside the pale of the community. They could be regarded, essentially, as unbelievers, and their attacks could be met with jihad. In like manner, most of the figures in this song are Arab and the incidents listed were carried out by Arabs and Mus-lims rather than Israelis.

Kufur Qassem refers to an event that occurred in 1956, when Israeli Border Guards open fired on a truck carrying forty-seven residents of the village as they returned to their homes after a curfew had been declared during a time of high tension caused by numerous armed incursions by Palestinian fedayeen. Eight of the policemen were later tried and convicted.

Deir Yasin is the name of a village near Jerusalem that was attacked by two right-wing Jewish militias during the fighting that broke out before Israel's creation in 1948. During the battle, over one hundred Arab resi-dents of the village, combatants and noncombatants, were killed. The event has become a major symbol of Jewish infamy in the Arab world. Israelis, on the other hand, point out that the high noncombatant death toll was anoma-lous, carried out by dissident factions, and thoroughly denounced by the mainstream leadership of the time.

The Jordanian towns of Jerash and 'Ajlun were the sites of major battles between Jordanian soldiers and PLO militants during the PLO's failed attempt to overthrow King Husain in 1971, during what Palestinians call "Black September."

Tel az-Za'tar is the site of a Syrian massacre of Palestinians, combatants and noncombatants, in 1979 during the Lebanese civil war.

In 1982, during the Israeli invasion of Lebanon, close to a thousand Palestinians were massacred in the refugee camps of Sabra and Shatilla by Lebanese Phalangist militiamen. Outcry over the event led to Israel's withdrawal from Beirut and the fall from power of Ariel Sharon, then defense minister of Israel and architect of the invasion, who was held indirectly responsible for the massacre by an Israeli court of inquiry.

In May 1991, after being rejected by his girlfriend, Israeli soldier Ami Popper shot dead seven Palestinian workers on the outskirts of the town that Palestinians call 'Ayun Qara and Israelis call Rishon leZion.

5. The references are to King Husain ibn Talal of Jordan, King Fahd ibn 'Abdul-'Aziz of Saudi Arabia, Qabus ibn Sa'id, Sultan of Oman, and Hosni Mubarak, president of Egypt.

6. Palestinian daylight-saving time began a month earlier and ended a month later than Israeli daylight-saving time.

7. A closely related symbol is the octopus. In one painting we recorded in Khan Yunis Refugee Camp, a fighter is depicted encased in the pottery for which Gaza has long been renowned and which in the work of the Palestinian artist Kamal Mughani has come to serve as a major symbol in and of itself. He clutches a rifle with one hand, while stabbing an octopus with the other.

8. For the paragraphs on ibn Yasin, we draw on the work of Ira M. Lapidus, *A History of Islamic Societies* (Cambridge: Cambridge University Press, 1988), reprint, 1991.

   Sharia refers to the corpus of Muslim law. It is based, in order of importance, on the Qur'an, the sunna, and the work of the Muslim jurists. Central to the demands of most Islamist movements is the replacement of a legal system based on civil law with one founded on the shari'a.

9. The writer here employs an exact rhyme to suggest an equation of sorts between the Israeli occupation and internal decay, the literal meaning of *ihtilal*. But one character separates the two words, which are derived from the same root.

10. The *subar* (< *sabara*, "to be patient" and "to endure") often marks the location of Palestinian villages lost or destroyed in 1948, and is used by Palestinians as a symbol of identity. Israelis also make symbolic use of the cactus. In Hebrew, it is known as a *sabra*, and is commonly used to symbolize citizens of the state born in Israel rather than in the diaspora. A prickly exterior protecting a sweet interior, the sabra is also said to signify a particular personality type—tough on the outside, soft on the inside.

11. Vol. IV, Jihad: 48.

12. The Chief Mufti of the Palestinian Police, Sheikh 'Abd as-Salam Skheidm, specified the rewards of the martyr according to Islamic tradition in the Palestinian Authority daily newspaper, *al-Hayat al-Jadida* in 1999 (September 17):

"From the moment his first drop of blood spills, he feels no pain, and he is absolved of all his sins; he sees his seat in heaven; he is spared the tortures of the grave; he is spared the horrors of Judgment Day; he is married to black-eyed virgins; he can vouch for seventy of his family members to enter paradise; he earns the crown of glory whose precious stone is worth all of this world."

13. *Al-Hayat al-Jadida*, the official Palestinian Authority daily, November 30, 2000.

14. All corporeal inscriptions gained during one's sojourn on earth will be erased, including circumcision. In an interview we conducted with a group of professors at Al-Quds University, College of Science and Technology, in Abu-Dis, Jerusalem, in July 1994, this same detail was stressed.

15. 'Abd al-Qahir Abu-Faris, *Shuhada' filistin* (Martyrs of Palestine) ('Amman, 1990/1410), p. 33.

16. The Cubs authorize their message by reminding the public of two of Fatah's military actions, "Dimuna" referring to the first armed action carried out by the group during the intifada in 1988 in which an Israeli bus was attacked in the Negev; "'Ailabun," to the first armed action carried out by al-'Asifa, the military wing of Fatah, in 1965 in which Israel's National Water Carrier was, after several attempts, successfully damaged by explosives.

17. Israeli society saw little valorization of the child in this way, with the notable exception of ultra-nationalist elements in the settlement movement. These groups produced posters in which children were presented as "answers" to the intifada and the means by which a "complete Israel" would be achieved. Settlers brought their children to confrontations and demonstrations, and sent them on politicized "nature hikes" through Palestinian territory. One such outing at the beginning of the intifada resulted in the death and wounding of Israeli youth in the Arab village of Beita, and their subsequent transformation into rallying banners.

18. "Jerusalem syndrome" refers to a condition marked by religious delusions of grandeur and mission brought on by sheer contact with the city. Hundreds come to Jerusalem every year on regular tours and find themselves bitten by the strange bug. Until the moment they landed, they were perfectly normal. Suddenly, with their feet on terra sancta, they realize that they are, in actuality, prophets, missionaries, and saviors.

19. IDF intelligence claims seven to eight hundred; the BBC's figure is eight hundred, while CNN's estimate amounts to more than a thousand.

20. See Lamia Lahoud's "PA Minister: Uprising Planned since July 2000," *Jerusalem Post*, March 4, 2001.

21. The *waqfa* or eve of *'Eid al-adha*, the Feast of the Sacrifice, and 'Eid al-Fitr, the Feast of the Breaking of the Fast, were particularly popular times for the execution of collaborators and attacks against Israel.

22. As in the heavily cut and spliced videotape *Sad* + *'Ain* + *Sin* (the names of three Arabic characters).

23. That is, Christianity and Judaism.

24. This is perhaps an allusion to the popular symbol of "the Islamic knight," commonly depicted as a mounted man-of-arms wearing a helmet, green cape, and uniform bedecked with Palestinian flags, holding in his right hand the Islamic green banner inscribed with the *shahadatain* ("I witness that there is no god but Allah, and Muhammad is the messenger of Allah"); in his left, a rifle.

25. That 'Azzam's intended audience is able-bodied young men capable of jihad is here made expressly clear by the reference to *al-khawalif*, meaning those who remain behind while others wage jihad. In the next line, Azzam validates his poetic plea with an authoritative verse taken from the sura "Repentance" (9:87), which is reiterated with slight variation in verse 93 of the same sura, "The way [to blame] is only against those who ask permission of you though they are rich; they have chosen to be with those who remain behind [*al-khawalif*], and Allah has set a seal upon their hearts so they do not know." Compare verse 83, "Thus, if Allah brings you back to a party of them and they ask your permission to go out [to fight], then say, You will never go out to fight with me, and you will never go out to fight an enemy with me; surely you chose to sit the first time; therefore, sit with those who remain behind [*al-khawalif*]."

26. 'Azzam here evokes several meanings of *shahida*, a word that, like its better known cognate *shahid* or "martyr," is derived from the root *shahada*, "to witness." *Shahida* literally means both "tombstone" and "index finger," but also, as 'Azzam makes clear, the trigger finger. In addition, it is the name given to the "one-way sign," the fist with the index finger raised heavenward, used by Islamist activists to signify their allegiance to the ideology of the Islamic Movement. In intifada graffiti, the fist and finger are often formed calligraphically by the word *Allah*, with the index finger serving as the *alif* and the knuckles of the fist serving as the base of the rolling *lam*s and *ha'*.

27. The letters *QSM* stand for *al-quwa al-islamiya al-mujahida*, "The Islamic Mujahid Force," the military wing of the Islamic Jihad Movement. As a noun, *qasam* possesses the meaning of "oath," a common word in the intifada lexicon, usually denoting steadfastness to a program of action. QSM also, of course, brings to mind *al-Qassam*, the strike-forces of Hamas, named for the famous leader and cleric of the 1930s 'Izz ad-Din al-Qassam.

PART THREE ■ A Death on the Path of God

1. See *Ha'aretz*, Wednesday, January 13, 1992.
2. No date or place of publication listed.

3. P. 26.
4. We have relied here on interviews and news reports, particularly, Bill Hutman, "Bus Driver Shot Struggling for Terrorist's Rifle," *Jerusalem Post*, July 2, 1993; and Bill Hutman, "Second Woman Dies after Capital Bus Attack; Police Identify Terrorists as Hamas Members," *Jerusalem Post*, July 2, 1993.

Index

202

Index